Praise for *The Relatively Public Lij*

'Browde writes a precise, elegant prose, warmed by an appealing candour and understated lyricism. His book is both a tangential biography and an amusing account of the perils and pleasures of learning to be a writer. In counterpoint, the voices of the "young storyteller" and his grandfather show how a life is made in interaction and relationship, among family and friends, in the stories we tell one another and ourselves.'

Ivan Vladislavić,
author of *Portrait with Keys*

'This unusual memoir within a memoir delivers several narratives. It is the story of a top courtroom advocate who, over the apartheid decades, stood on the side of those the system oppressed; the story, too, of a struggling writer, his grandson, reaching across the generations to preserve the most telling memories of a beloved paterfamilias. As a storyteller in these pages, as in life, Jules Browde is always engaging and persuasive; moving too. If this were a novel, critics would hail him as a brilliantly realised character with an unforgettable voice.'

Joseph Lelyveld,
former executive editor of *The New York Times*

'Daniel Browde's account of Jules Browde's life is rich, engaging, intriguing and delightful. Crammed with human and historical interest, it reveals Jules Browde as a large-hearted, generous man, whose expansive spirit encompassed warfare, politics, family and friendship across critical decades of our democracy's history and prehistory – but whose life, pre-eminently, was committed to elementary justice for all in our country.'

Edwin Cameron,
Justice of the Constitutional Court of South Africa

Published in South Africa in 2016 by
JONATHAN BALL PUBLISHERS
A division of Media24 Limited
PO Box 33977
Jeppestown
2043

ISBN 978-1-86842-720-8
eBook ISBN 978-1-86842-721-5

*Every effort has been made to trace the copyright holders and to obtain their
permission for the use of copyright material. The publishers apologise for any errors or
omissions and would be grateful to be notified of any corrections that
should be incorporated in future editions of this book.*

*Unless otherwise stated, all photographs are from the author's private collection
and are used by permission.*

Twitter: www.twitter.com/JonathanBallPub
Facebook: www.facebook.com/JonathanBallPublishers
Blog: http://jonathanball.bookslive.co.za

Cover design by Thenjiwe Niki Nkosi and Marius Roux
Design and typesetting by Martine Barker
Set in Caslon/Optima 11/13.2

Printed by **paarlmedia**, a division of Novus Holdings

DANIEL BROWDE

the relatively public life of jules browde

JONATHAN BALL PUBLISHERS
JOHANNESBURG & CAPE TOWN

For my grandparents

and for Lum,
whoever you are.

contents

[I]

[II]

[III]

[I]

chapter one

In which we meet a young storyteller
who feels the need to lie about the subject of his book

It had rained earlier that evening. The air coming down off the dark slope held the smell of pine needles and wet earth. A few paces from where I stood – on the patio at the rear of the house – I could see the beginning of some stone steps, slick and puddled after the rain. The steps rose quickly and curved into the darkness. I'd been here before, so I knew what I'd find if I climbed them: the heavy palisade fence that marked the edge of the property; the enormous rocks beyond the fence; and the view, back over the house, to the lights on the Brixton ridge. I considered these steps. I knew the climb would probably do me good. But I stayed where I was, held by the faint sounds of the dinner party still going on inside. I looked up at the stars and I tried to enjoy them, to take them in.

I'd been out here less than five minutes when a thickset man in a panama hat appeared in the kitchen doorway and lit a cigarette. With his hat and cigarette he made a neat silhouette against the rectangle of yellow light. This was one of the more well-known guests, a sculptor who had recently returned from mounting a show in the United States.

He must have seen me looking at him.

'Taking a breather?' he asked.

I nodded. 'Yup.'

I was standing in what I imagined to be the beginning of the shadow, at the far end of the bricks.

'It's lovely out here,' he said.

I said, 'Aah, it's great.'

And for a few seconds, that seemed like it was going to be it. I tried to think of something to add, but before I could think of anything he left the doorway, took a few steps towards me and told me his name, as if I didn't already know it.

I'd spoken to him once before, and told him so – not to prove a point so much as to establish a truthful context. He'd given a talk at the Johannesburg Art Gallery and I'd stayed behind afterwards to ask him a question. He nodded neutrally at this information and asked if I often went to the JAG.

'Now and then,' I said. 'When there's something on.'

I told him about my girlfriend, Thenji, and explained that this was how I knew our hosts, Diana and David. Diana was an established painter who for reasons of her own kept a studio in the same run-down building in Fordsburg as Thenji had hers.

He said, 'And you? Are you an artist too?'

I hesitated for an instant. Sometimes I do think of myself as a sort of artist, usually when I'm overtired, but how are you going to *say* you're an artist, especially to some famous sculptor?

I said, 'No, I'm not an artist.'

I said, 'I work at a newspaper, as a subeditor.'

Often people don't know what that is, a subeditor, but I could see he did. He even seemed quite interested to hear this, and nodded again, this time just once, abruptly, as if a fly had landed on the end of his nose. He had finished his cigarette and was half looking around for what to do with it.

I told him the name of the newspaper I worked at.

'That's probably the best paper we have,' he said distractedly.

Watching him, I realised I could still feel the effects of the wine I'd drunk during the first part of the meal.

'Do you want an ashtray?' I asked. There was a square metal ashtray on a heavy wooden bench at the far end of the patio.

He smiled.

'On that thing over there,' I said, nodding towards it.

He walked over and mashed his stompie into the ashtray and came back. I felt a small sense of accomplishment then, to have been of use.

The sculptor put his hands in his pockets and asked me if I enjoyed working at the newspaper.

I told him that I liked the repetitive, meditational aspect of the job, and also the fact that my workday only started at two in the afternoon.

I saw his interest pick up a notch. That always happened when I told people about the two o'clock-start thing.

'So I have my mornings to myself,' I said. Which was what I *always* said at this point. Some conversations have you, instead of the other way around.

'What do you do with your mornings?' he asked.

For a moment I had the uncomfortable sensation that he was humouring me. There was really nothing to give me that impression, though, and I tried to put it out of my mind. I said that in the mornings I usually went for a run, and then worked for a bit on my own stuff before going in to the paper.

'And what's your *own stuff*?' he pressed, rocking slightly on his heels.

This was all surprising to me. I'd always assumed that in a social setting he would be arrogant, or at least aloof, because of his fame and his hat and everything. But he seemed genuinely interested in what I had to say. And maybe it was because of this, or maybe it was the wine, or the fresh air and the trees, or all of it together – whatever it was that encouraged me – I told him that I was working on a biography of my grandfather. This wasn't something I'd said out loud before, and the minute the words were out of my mouth I regretted them. Because then it came: 'Oh really?' he said. 'Who's your grandfather?'

Now if this were a scene in a movie, here would be what is called the *turning point*. That moment, that question right there, which sobered me up in a second, and not because it took me by surprise, but precisely the opposite: the point is just how ready I was to hear it, just how clearly I understood (or thought I understood) what he meant by it. Because even if the sculptor didn't intend it, I heard in his question a challenge, and saw before me – in the space between us – the same thing I saw whenever I considered that I might, in fact, be writing the book I'd told him about: I saw a pantheon.

It was a classical pantheon, Ancient Greek, but vaguely animated like a cartoon. The set designer in my subconscious had given it a floor of white cumulus clouds. Seated in the centre, on high-backed thrones, were the Giants. Your Churchills, your Mandelas. People who shook the world like elephants shake a tree, causing thick hardcover biographies to fall to the ground all around them. To either side of the Giants stood the Famous: artists, athletes and scientists possessed of such searing talent that crowds lined up to read about their lives like villagers gathering around a winter fire. Then on either end stood the Well-Known: judges, academics and community organisers, people who had Made a Contribution, ordinary heroes who, but for the single book written about them by some noble noticer, might have remained unsung.

What I needed to do, I decided (and come to think of it, I must still have been slightly drunk), was to convince the sculptor that my grandfather belonged there, somewhere near the edges of this pantheon. I hadn't rehearsed the argument, which became obvious as soon as I opened my mouth.

I said, 'He was born in 1919 in Johannesburg.' Then, after a moment, 'So his first memory is of the miners' strike. The Rand Revolt? Which was in 1922. He was three years old in 1922! Which I think is kind of amazing. That he remembers that. And he still lives here. He stills *works* here.'

By the light of the kitchen I saw the sculptor lose interest. He hadn't said anything, but I read a whole paragraph of boredom in the angle of his hat.

The hat said, 'Oh, so it's minor league? A family memoir. A tribute to your ancient *zeyde*. Something to ring bind and hand out to family members here and in, I'm guessing, Australia?'

He was leaning to go inside, I could tell. I had to defend my grandfather! I had to defend myself! Charged with insignificance, we were about to be sentenced to summary dismissal from the mind of a famous sculptor.

'He's also had a relatively public life,' I said quickly.

I saw the sculptor's eyeballs turn in their sockets to take me in more squarely. The angle of his hat changed back, it seemed, to mildly interested. This was what he was waiting for: the claim to fame.

'He was a very well-known advocate,' I said. 'He did a lot of human rights work.' Looking through the open door at the little dimples of light in the dark-red kitchen floor, I said, 'He was one of the founders of Lawyers for Human Rights.'

'Okay ... *okay* ...' the sculptor nodded. 'Sure. What's your grandfather's name?'

He was doing some kind of calculation in his head. Had he heard *my* surname earlier?

'Jules Browde.'

I could feel myself straining away from this conversation and into it with all my might. We were weighing my grandfather's human worth. Now I had uttered his name, and I was waiting for the sculptor to pronounce on whether he did have a claim, after all.

'Oh, *Jules Browde,*' he said. 'Yes. His wife is …'

'Selma,' I said. 'That's my grandmother.'

'Of course. The doctor. Yes. A very well-known couple.'

Two other smokers came out of the kitchen. A journalist and a photographer. The photographer was holding a small cup of coffee. The sculptor greeted them. The meal was obviously over. Thenji must have been wondering where I was.

The sculptor took a crumpled pack of cigarettes from his shirt pocket and extracted one with practised efficiency. 'Jules Browde was one of the Rivonia Trial lawyers, wasn't he?'

I almost lied and said that, yes, he was. If the answer to that question is yes, the conversation stops there. Case closed.

'No,' I said. 'He wasn't.'

I hoped I didn't sound crestfallen.

'But he's very good friends with George Bizos and Arthur Chaskalson, all those guys …'

I really did say that, reaching the hard bottom of the barrel right there. And how I wished, at that moment, how desperately I wished that my grandfather had been part of the Rivonia defence team, like his friends, next to whom he suddenly didn't seem to measure up.

'I remember Selma from when she was in politics,' the sculptor said, bringing the flame from his lighter to the tip of his cigarette, illuminating his face for a few seconds.

'Oh, really?' I said.

He'd taken a deep drag, now he blew the smoke out the side of his mouth.

'Yes. A very dynamic woman.'

The rest of the smoke followed out of his nostrils.

So he really *had* heard of them. *Public life!* Maybe I could smuggle them onto the pantheon together.

'They're an amazing couple,' I said, scraping. 'They're one of very few couples to have *both* been awarded honorary doctorates from Wits. Nelson Mandela and Graça Machel are another. To give you an idea.'

'Is that so?'

I nodded, hating myself. I was dealing in goddamn *titles* now, *prizes*, begging this man, this stranger, to accept my grandfather's credentials.

I had to talk about something else before I started stamping my feet, tearing my hair out, spitting on the floor.

'The book isn't going to be a traditional biography,' I offered. 'I want it also to be like a sort of history of Joburg, because he was really there, *here*, I suppose ...' I laughed nervously '... *here* through most of the twentieth century. And he's still going. Still going strong. So I sort of want the book to be ... you know ... something like that, too.'

I realised, as the words fell from my mouth, that this was just another apology: if your subject isn't enough, haul in the dog-eared metropolis. I was dying for a drag of his cigarette. I was dying to go inside. I wanted to fetch my phone from my backpack in the entrance hall and call my grandfather to apologise for feeling disappointed in him, for making excuses for him, for feeling the need to lie about him as if he wasn't good enough to tell the truth about.

And the feeling of shame only became more acute after the sculptor wandered inside and left me there, and a wind picked up, and Thenji came out to look for me in the artist's garden, dark and suddenly creepy at that late hour.

The Encyclopaedia Britannica

Interview 16
Date recorded: 05/04/2006

Let me just tell you. It was a Saturday afternoon near the beginning of
... Well, it must have been about 1958 or '59. Selma and I were out in
the garden when a man poked his head around the side of the house.

The boys – and I'm speaking now about your father and your uncle
Ian – were about eight and ten years old at the time, so when this chap
told us he was selling the *Encyclopaedia Britannica*, we invited him to sit
down. Which he did.

He sat down, took some brochures from his briefcase, and started
to tell us why we should buy the twenty or so volumes in the set. While
he was speaking, I considered the position. The full set cost more than a
hundred pounds, which was quite an outlay, but my practice was doing
better by then, and I thought it would be a good investment for the
family. I looked over at Selma and she must have known what I was
thinking, because she nodded. So in the middle of his pitch I slapped
my knee and said, 'We'll take it!'

This fellow, the salesman, glared at me and said, 'Please. Do *not*
interrupt me.' And he then merely carried on where he'd left off. By
the time he was finished, I had a good mind to tell him I didn't want
the bloody things after all. But we did take them. I signed the requisite
papers right there in the garden and, a week or so later, the encyclopae-
dias were delivered to the house.

Now that's almost by the way. Why I'm telling you this – aside from
the fact of this salesman's rather odd behaviour – is that about a month

later I appeared in the magistrates' court for an insurance company that had insured the owner of an antique furniture shop on Fox Street.

On Fox Street, in those days, there were all *manner* of second-hand furniture people. Upholsterers, repairers, refurbishers, all that sort of thing.

A man – the plaintiff in the case – had left some furniture at this shop for repair, and shortly after he did there was a fire on the premises and his furniture was destroyed. So he was suing the owner for what he said was the value of the furniture. The insurance company was of the view that the man was exaggerating the claim, and the precise value of these pieces became the issue before the magistrate.

The magistrate was a man by the name of Immelman, and I remember that he became very amused at something that transpired during my cross-examination of a witness, a man brought to court by the plaintiff.

The witness's name was Mr Plotkin, and he was alleged to be an expert on the value of furniture. He was an old Jewish man who spoke with a pronounced Lithuanian accent.

My opponent in this case, by the way, was a colleague of mine by the name of Sidley – also, like I was, a relatively young advocate at the Bar.

So Sidley called Plotkin as a witness and tried to establish his expertise. Plotkin said he had been in business for so long that he had become an expert in many different fields. This was relevant because there were a variety of pieces involved. 'I am an expert on furniture, fixtures, fittings, *everything*,' he said.

I noted this.

When Sidley was finished with him, the magistrate said to me, 'Have you any questions for this witness?'

I said, 'Yes I do, your worship.'

And so the magistrate told me to proceed.

'Mr Plotkin,' I said, and I looked down at my notes. 'You said that you are an expert on furniture, fixtures, fittings, everything.'

'That's right,' he said.

So then I said, 'You're an expert on *everything*, sir? How can you be an expert on everything?'

He said, 'I have been for *thirty-four* years in this business. I'm an *expert*.'

And then I asked him, 'Would you say you're an expert on … books, for example?'

He said, 'Books? Sure. I've bought books, sold books …'

'All right, Mr Plotkin,' I said. 'I have just bought a brand new set of

Encyclopaedia Britannica. You've heard of the *Encyclopaedia Britannica*?'

'Oh, yes, this is a very popular name,' he said.

So I asked him, 'How much would you say should I have paid for the set?'

Plotkin looked up at the magistrate and said, 'Your worship? This case, it's about furniture or it's about books?'

The magistrate, who was enjoying Mr Plotkin's performance, said, 'Don't worry what the case is about, Mr Plotkin. You just answer the question.'

So I asked again, 'Now come on Mr Plotkin, what should I have paid for a new set of *Encyclopaedia Britannica*?'

He said, '*Encyclopaedia*, hmm? Well. This is very expensive. I would say this costs about thirty pounds.'

'And what if I told you, Mr Plotkin, that I paid 120 pounds? Not thirty pounds,' I said.

Plotkin thought about this briefly. Undeterred he looked up at the magistrate and said, 'Your worship, this must be with *hard* covers.'

Sidley put his head in his hands, and I remember that the magistrate, Immelman, had to adjourn the court to conceal his amusement.

chapter two

In which the young storyteller is introduced to his task

The idea had been much simpler, once upon a time. It was something I'd heard for as long as I could remember: *These stories should be written down.* His friends said it. People in our family said it. So did those he worked with. Even, now and then, someone who'd known him long enough to hear him tell just *one* of his famous tales would say it. *Jules Browde's stories should be written down.* But it wasn't until April 2003 that anyone suggested how this might happen.

I was twenty-six years old that autumn and had grown increasingly afraid, over the summer, that I was becoming depressed again. It was four years since my last real depressive episode but I still imagined myself to be on the edge of a precipice.

The Buddhist centre where I'd been living then for three years – a beautiful old house on Langermann Kop – had started to seem desolate. The stillness of the place, the permeating quiet, which once I'd found so helpful, now felt alien and forbidding. Convinced, finally, that the centre was adding to my problems, I asked my grandparents if I could live with them for a while. I needed to go some place safe and familiar, I told myself. Some place that was like home, but wasn't home-home; the thought of moving back in with my parents left me feeling soft-centred and regressed.

My grandparents said that they'd be happy for me to stay with them for as long as I wanted. My parents were more circumspect about the idea, and over the course of several long discussions with me they tried to figure out whether to be worried or relieved. It was during one of those conversations that my mother, trying to look on the bright side, said that, apart from anything else, living there would give me a perfect opportunity to sit with my grandfather and finally 'get his stories down'. To me in private she added, 'Remember, he's not going to be around forever.'

18 Orange Road

While the walls of the houses in Orchards are not as thick or high as in the neighbouring suburb of Houghton, still, most have electric fences on top, and on the pavement across the road from my grandparents is a simple wooden structure known as 'the guard's house' – a common sight in the neighbourhood. So I sometimes find it a wonder that Orange Road can still present such a picture of daytime tranquillity, yet it does. After dark, fear falls like a cold mist over all of these suburbs, but under a blue sky the street's pavement lawns and leafy facades can feel almost hopeful. My grandparents' place is one of the leafiest on the street. Their wall is covered with plants: tangles of ground cover and dense bushes that climb to meet the vines of competing creepers and the slender brown limbs of a Johannesburg Gold.

It was on a Saturday afternoon, about a month after the talk with my mother, that I pressed the buzzer on the wall next to the gate, and waited.

The voice that came over was my grandfather's. 'That you, Dan?'

A minute later he was down at the gate to see if I needed his help.

He was wearing a pair of blue jeans and a striped jersey, his usual weekend get-up. My suitcases and boxes were heavy with books, so I told him I'd manage.

It took me a while to get all my things into the house, as he stood by and offered encouragement. 'That's my boy … Oopsie … *There* you go … You've got it …'

I was going to stay in the guest room, which was next to his study in the corner of the house. 'Nana tidied this whole thing up for you,' he said, looking around the room. He was holding a book in one hand, using his index finger to keep his place. 'She's at a meeting at the hospital, but she'll be home in a little while.'

After checking that I wasn't hungry or thirsty, and telling me to shout if I needed anything, he left me to my bags and boxes and took himself back to the lounge.

My new room was at the end of a short broad passage. At least three-quarters of the floor space was taken up by two single beds, pushed together in the middle of the room and draped in white duvets and soft blue pillows. On either side of the bed were little white tables with pull-out drawers that housed left-behind copies of *The New Yorker* and the *London Review of Books*.

In that first week I paged through these things every night after I got into bed. Since primary school I'd occasionally entertained a fantasy of becoming a journalist, but these long, airtight articles filled me with self-doubt. Still, I was falling asleep more easily there, and my days began to unfold with a distinct and comforting suburban pattern.

In the cold early mornings I'd run around the golf course near the house. These runs were often no more than bleary, meandering walks, but I'd promised my father that I would do some exercise, and at least I was getting out of bed and into the world of air and trees and cars.

By the time I got back to the house – usually around seven am – my grandfather would already be sitting at the wooden table in the corner of the kitchen, dressed for work. Sometimes Gladys, their housekeeper (sixtyish, wryly funny), would be in there with him, but mostly I remember him alone – coffee, toast and newspaper set out artfully in front of him. The wood-framed glass door to his right, which gave out onto a small wedge-shaped courtyard, let in the crisp morning light. I would stop in there on my way to the shower.

He'd look up and say, 'Morning, laddie.'

I'd say, 'Hi, Broncs.'

Next he'd say something old-mannish, like, 'You won't believe it, but I was once a fit fellow like you,' and then look back down at the paper.

He was in energy-conserving mode; he had a lot to do. He worked for the provincial legislature as its integrity commissioner – a position he had pioneered. He had an office in the City hall, and from the shower or the bedroom, getting dressed, I'd hear him heading off to town in his white Hyundai.

When my grandmother emerged – usually fifteen minutes or so after he'd left the house – she would often be in her nightgown and slightly out of focus. She is a night owl, and would frequently sit at her computer until well after midnight.

By this time I would have showered and dressed, and I often had breakfast with her. She would stand close to the kettle while she waited for it to boil, exchanging a few blurred sentences with Gladys, who also had to battle herself out of a morning funk.

But it wasn't coffee that my grandmother needed to get going, it was a topic of conversation. And soon after sitting down at the table she'd come up with one herself. She'd raise it and then lean into the discussion, sleep sheeting off her now like water. I would usually have to stop her mid-sentence and pull myself away if I wanted to get to work on time. (I had a job at a small production company in Greenside, doing preliminary edits on music videos and documentaries. I'd ended up here, on the outskirts of the film industry, after finishing my BA at Wits and then working for a year as an actor. Unless you were willing to humiliate yourself, there was little work to be had performing.)

At suppertime we would meet up again at the table in the kitchen, this time all three of us, the morning's newspaper now stacked on a pile on the fourth chair.

In those first weeks I still read all kinds of sadness into those meals, and into my own life. In the block-mounted Monet print that hung on the wall over my grandfather's left shoulder I saw the dreariness of past centuries living on in this one. In the slices of pale-brown bread that lay limply, one over the other, on the narrow silver platter in the middle of the table, and in the dust-grey plates and heavy silver cutlery I'd known since childhood, I could find all the reasons I needed to be glum.

But there was something else that happened on those nights, something that I didn't – that I *couldn't* – find sad, even if I tried. Now and then my grandfather would say, 'Look here, that reminds me of a story,' and he'd gaze off to the right for a moment, as if the story's beginning

15

was out there in the dark. Then he'd turn back, eyes illuminated, and tell us a tale. Some were memories from childhood and some concerned his experiences during the Second World War. Others related to cases in his fifty-year career as an advocate at the Johannesburg Bar. There were so many in his vaults that almost anything could remind him of something else. Some had become as worked-out over time as jokes, with their set-ups and their reveals, but his delight in telling them was so unaffected that they never came over as slick. Their performance happened in the small movements of his head, in the expressions on his face, in his quick eyes. His hands animated quietly, drawing you in.

I had been living at Orange Road for about a month when the cloud over my head, the cloud I'd found so ominous, started to break harmlessly apart. I still worried about myself, but only in patches, and less and less so. The surest sign that I wasn't getting depressed, that I was further inland than I'd thought, was this: I felt myself looking forward to certain things. And one of the things I looked forward to could happen on any given night in the kitchen. It was hearing my grandfather say something like, 'Have I ever told you about the case I had where the fellow ran onto the track at Kyalami?' And if I had heard a story before, I'd say, 'Tell it again.' I could listen for as long as they lasted and never get bored.

Now, I don't know – I can't tell – if my mother thought that the task of recording my grandfather's stories would help *me* in some way. She is a constant reader, and reads lots of books, mostly novels, about the Holocaust: books that return obsessively to themes of loss and memory, testimony and forgetting. So my guess is that she thought about the job mainly from that point of view: preserving his stories for a future in which he would not be here to tell them. But when I look back at my own position at that time – oriented almost entirely inward – and consider the kind of mother she is, I have to believe that she did think the exercise would be useful for me too. Whatever her reasons, she wouldn't let it go, and if she was around when he told a tale, she'd look at me when he was finished, tilt her head slightly, and I'd know what she was thinking. Though my grandfather was still strong and vital, and his mortality as unimaginable as anyone else's, I knew she was right. Despite our resilience, human life is precarious: death can come with no warning.

The seed she'd planted in my imagination must have been taking root, because now, whenever I sat there at the kitchen table on an ordinary night and my grandfather began a story, I could see the words that followed rising from his mouth like white smoke, the plumes of his sentences drifting and curling, waving and intertwining above his head for a few moments before being swallowed by the mouth of the air.

Mevrou Schultz

Interview 19
Date recorded: 13/06/2006

I was appearing for an insurance company that was being sued for damages arising from a motorcar accident in Mossel Bay. The plaintiff, a Mr Green by name, had been injured, and was claiming damages on the basis that he'd had a head injury, and that as a result of this head injury he'd had a change of personality. Which is not an uncommon thing. But for some reason my clients had serious doubts about the authenticity of his story. And while Mr Green was asking for many hundreds of thousands of rands, the insurance company instructed me that the claim was exaggerated and it was prepared to pay him only a much smaller sum.

The night before the case was to be heard in Cape Town, I consulted with two policemen in the instructing attorney's office there. One was a sergeant, a fairly senior man, and the other was a young constable. They had come from Mossel Bay with a plan of the scene of the accident, which they had prepared for the purposes of the case.

They went through the plan with us a few times, showed us very carefully how the accident had happened, and I remember it was fairly late by the time we'd finished. I thanked the policemen for coming and we all left the office together.

While we were waiting for the lift to arrive, and merely to pass the time, I turned to the sergeant and said, *'Ken jy vir die Green gesin?'* Do you know the Green family?

To which he replied, *'Mosselbaai is 'n dorp, jy weet.'* Mossel Bay is a small town, you know. As if to say: Well, of course. Everybody knows everybody there.

I said, 'Well? *Do* you know them?'

'Look, *Advokaat*,' he said to me. 'We came here to show you the plan, and we have shown you the plan. Now if you don't mind, we don't want to get involved in this case any further.'

At which point the young constable piped up; to the sergeant he said, '*Moet ek hom vertel van Mevrou Schultz?*' Should I tell him about Mrs Schultz?

The sergeant, becoming quite angry, shouted, '*Nee, los dit man!*' Leave it alone!

Then the lift arrived, and I decided not to ask any more questions.

The next morning I arrived early at the High Court, which is in the city centre. On the way to the advocate's robing room, I noticed a sign announcing a memorial service that was just about to be held in one of the courts. A prominent judge had died in Cape Town a few days before. So, after putting on my robes, I wandered into the court to hear what was going on in this ceremony. It didn't take very long.

As I was leaving a man came up to me. I recognised him as a friend of Selma's from her younger days in Cape Town. He was now an attorney in Cape Town. Pinsky, his name was. He said to me, 'What are you doing here?'

I told him. I said, 'I'm here for an accident case in another court.'

To which he replied, 'Oh, well I haven't got much to do this morning. I think I'll come and listen to the Great Cross-Examiner from Johannesburg.' There was a bit of sarcasm in his voice. So I just shrugged. I mean, what do you say to something like that? And off he went.

My opponent that day was a man by the name of Sextus de Wet. A huge fellow – very tall – from the Port Elizabeth Bar. He came in to court, greeted me, and sat down. I looked around the court. I noticed that Pinsky had taken a seat in the corner of the public gallery and was waiting for the matter to start.

De Wet had stage-managed the whole thing very well. Once we were all ready, the usher left to call the judge. Soon afterwards, the judge (Michael Corbett, who would later become the chief justice) entered. Everybody stood up. Then the judge took his seat on the bench and we all sat down.

Corbett was a slight chap. He peered out across the court. 'Yes, Mr de Wet?' he asked. It was the prerogative of the claimant to open proceedings. So De Wet stood up again and told the judge what his supporting evidence would be. It would include, he said, not only the details of the accident, but also expert medical evidence regarding the nature of Mr Green's injuries. He told the court that he had a number of expert witnesses lined up.

None of us had yet seen Mr Green, of course.

When De Wet was finished with his opening address, the judge asked him if he would like to call his first witness. De Wet said yes, he would; he said he would like to call the plaintiff's wife. And with that he went to the back of the court, opened the door and stepped outside. I really didn't know what this fellow was up to.

When he came back he was walking very slowly beside a woman who was, in turn, pushing a man in a wheelchair. The Greens. Mrs Green wheeled her husband into position beside De Wet's chair, and then went to take her place in the witness box. Mr Green just sat there in his wheelchair, looking very sorry for himself and a bit dull.

Led carefully through her testimony by Sextus de Wet, she told the story of what a wonderful husband he, Mr Green, had been. How he was marvellous to her, wonderful to the children. But then, she said, suddenly after the accident he had started being awful to her. Treated her *shockingly*. Didn't stay at home at night. (So much for the wheelchair, I thought.) Became nasty to the children. And generally speaking, had a complete change of personality. Attributed, as she put it, to the accident.

Well, it was a sad story. And the atmosphere in court was clearly sympathetic towards her. The room was completely silent. No one spoke or moved. Even the judge sat very still for a minute. Then he turned to me and said, 'Have you any questions for this witness, Mr Browde?' He made it clear by his tone that it was absolutely his obligation to ask this. As if to say: You know, I don't know what you can possibly say to her.

I said, 'Yes I do, my lord.' And I then stood up.

I was thinking of what she'd said about him being a model husband and that sort of thing, and I remembered the strange end to the conversation from the night before. I thought it might be an interesting point at which to start my cross-examination. I looked at Mrs Green, who blinked a few times. Then I looked at Mr Green, sitting in his wheelchair. And after another moment or two I said to her, '*Mrs Green*' – all in Afrikaans – '*Ken jy miskien vir Mevrou Schultz?*' Do you perhaps know Mrs Schultz?

Well, she looked at me as if she'd seen a ghost.

20

She said, *'Me–Me–Mevrou Schultz?!'* – and then she leaned forward sharply and tried to support herself on the edge of the stand, but her knees buckled and she fainted right there in the witness box. The clerk and the usher rushed forward to see if she was all right, and the judge peered down over the edge of his bench.

Of course I was more surprised than anyone, but I couldn't show it. What I did was – I couldn't resist it – I turned around and I looked at Pinsky, who had come to listen to the Great Cross-Examiner. His eyes were popping out of his head. I raised one eyebrow.

The judge said, 'The court will adjourn until the witness has composed herself.' And then he left the court. De Wet took his clients out. Mrs Green was helped from the courtroom by the usher, who walked out step by step at her side. Mr Green was wheeled out after them.

After a minute or so, De Wet came back in and said to me – because I knew him well; I knew him from cases I'd fought in Port Elizabeth – he said to me, 'Jules, tell me, who is Mrs Schultz?'

Now, in the ordinary course of events, I would have told him, but having no idea who she was, I said, 'Sextus, I don't know.'

He said, 'Come on, man. Tell me who she is.' He said, 'If there's something I should know tell me, and I'll see what I can do about it.'

So I said, 'Sextus. Believe me. I have *no idea* who Mrs Schultz is.' And I was just about to tell him what had happened the night before, when he said, very angrily, 'Oh you Joburg chaps are all the same,' and then stormed off.

About ten minutes went by, and they all came back. De Wet came in first. Mrs Green tiptoed in after him, looking pale, and then her husband was wheeled back into position by the usher. De Wet helped Mrs Green back onto the stand, supporting her by one elbow. The judge came back into court, and there was silence once more.

The judge then turned to me and said, 'Yes, Mr Browde. Carry on, please.'

'Thank you, my lord,' I said, rising.

And then I said to Mrs Green, confidently now, *'Kom nou, Mevrou Green. Sê vir sy edele* – tell his lordship – *wie is Mevrou Schultz?'*

'Edelagbare,' she said, *'Mevrou Schultz is ...'* She turned to look up at the judge; she said, *'Mevrou Schul ... Schultz ...'* but before she could get another word out she fainted again. And this time the usher actually had to carry her out of the courtroom. Judge Corbett left again, now

21

muttering and shaking his head. And I can only imagine what Pinsky thought of *me*. The Great Cross-Examiner indeed!

Shortly after that, the case was settled. The attorneys of both sides met to discuss the matter and Mr Green accepted a very small amount in settlement of the case. I flew home to Johannesburg that afternoon. Which goes to show, I suppose, that sometimes you have to have some luck in these things.

chapter three

In which the young storyteller toys with the idea
of getting the stories down

His place at the kitchen table was a good spot: safely in the corner of the room, with the glass door to the right offering a view of trees and sky. Often I'd sit there and read, or just watch the tiny birds jostling for space on the feeder he'd strung up in the smooth-barked tree that stood in the centre of the courtyard. It was a sanctuary and a lookout, a place to go to resolve matters or just let them resolve. That's what I was doing one afternoon – sitting there, letting my thoughts go more or less where they pleased – when I found my attention drawn to the newspaper he'd left on the table earlier in the day. He'd been doing the crossword puzzle; his thin silver pen was still lying on the table.

I stared at the paper: the antlike columns of words; the grainy pictures with their tiny captions; the skeleton of the crossword, half filled-in. I picked it up and lifted it to my nose. Since I was a kid, the smell of newsprint has filled me with a cool fascination, and that afternoon – I remember it as an overcast Saturday afternoon – I found myself wondering where along the line I'd given up on my dream of being a journalist. The realisation that I hadn't really ever given up on it, but rather that I just had not thought about it in a long time, left me feeling oddly off balance. I could see no good reason for the way things were.

This feeling of groundlessness persisted and, as that winter dragged on, I began to spend time in my grandfather's study reading through newspapers and magazines and my own notebooks, wondering whether

I could be a journalist and what sort of journalist I could be.

When spring came, my grandfather would spend his weekend mornings in the garden, removing weeds and planting flowers. When summer arrived, he'd take brief wading swims in their small pool and then spend forever drying himself in the sun, looking up towards it, his eyes crinkling. Weekend afternoons he would read his book or files in his favourite chair in the corner of the lounge, or watch games of cricket on the TV in the living room.

My grandmother would spend the same weekend hours in her study, staring deeply into her computer screen, lost in thought. After retiring as Professor of Radiation Oncology at Wits University, she had started two organisations: one a hospital palliative care team and the other an NGO fighting HIV through education. She spent hours and days writing guidelines, proposals, reports. Because she cared about each word, she typed slowly – sometimes so slowly it was as if she wasn't typing at all.

Occasionally they had friends over for supper, and on these nights they would often invite me to sit with them at the table. Some of their guests I'd known my whole life and only as I got older learned that they were *known*: scholars and surgeons, artists and ambassadors – powerful, highly specialised. These people would often appear fascinated by the young house guest, and their fascination made me feel like I was mysterious, which I liked. I hardly ever joined them at the table. I preferred to sit in my grandfather's study and read, listening with half an ear to what was going on in the dining room.

The conversations were most often bright and lively, flowing easily from one topic to another. Sometimes, though, they'd be tense and stilted, and it was then, particularly, on those unobliging evenings, that I noticed the effect my grandfather can have on a group.

When, on such a night, he started a story ('Now look here, that reminds me …') a different sort of silence would fall, a peaceful stillness, and I'd sit at his desk and imagine him in there, telling his tale: his luminous eyes, his measured delivery. When he was done, a warm and joyful laughter would usually fill the rooms of the house.

On one such strained evening, he came into his study to fetch a bottle of wine. (He keeps a ragtag collection in a cupboard in the corner.) When he saw me sitting at his desk, his eyes lit up with happy surprise.

'Hello, laddie! How are you getting on?'

His shirt collar was open and he looked relaxed.

'Fine,' I told him. 'I'm just reading. How's it going in there?'

He lifted his eyebrows and tipped his head a few times from side to side, making a face that said 'so-so'.

While he looked in the cupboard for a suitable bottle, he explained that one of their friends was telling 'all the old stories'. He said it with massive disappointment; he was purposefully overacting, but under this aped disapproval there was, unmistakably, the real thing. No one likes the old stories more than he does; this other guy was butchering them – and on *his* turf. I cracked up. He shut the cupboard and with a bottle of wine in one hand, turned to face me, smiling. He squeezed his eyes shut tight, opened them again, and left me laughing by myself in an empty room.

The next day – Sunday afternoon – he called me to help him find something he'd misplaced in the study. Though I don't remember what we were looking for, I remember clearly what happened next. He was sitting on the edge of the old brown swivel chair in the corner, going through a cardboard box resting between his feet. I was standing on the other side of the room, his desk between us. While he was digging around we were chatting, and he started to tell me about something that had happened to him during the war. It was a story I hadn't heard before. It took place in 1941 in Eritrea, and involved a panel van, two mechanics, and a soft-hearted Italian bartender. His words were coming in one ear and my mother's quiet, enormous warning was playing in the other. I saw the delicate white smoke curling, disappearing. That was the first time I tried to hold on to the words.

Once he'd finished – we'd given up looking for whatever he'd lost – he went off to another room, and I grabbed a piece of paper and a pen and wrote down all I could remember of the story. An account of life on the outskirts of the war, it had a few twists and turns and ended on an unexpected note. I wrote it down right to the end. Later, when the coast was clear, I took the scribbled notes to my grandmother's study and typed out the story on her desktop, adding a few things, here and there, that came back to me while I was typing.

I gave it a heading – 'U636' – which was the number plate of the hexed van. Then I printed it out, stapled the pages together, and put the document into one of the translucent plastic envelopes I used in those days to store odds and ends.

Over the next few days I took it out several times and I read it through from beginning to end. I knew I hadn't captured it exactly as he'd spoken it, which frustrated me, but I'd been able to remember much more than I'd thought possible, and it pleased me to think of what I'd done.

But I didn't tell my mother, or anybody else. It felt like a secret, a piece of childish espionage. And I decided to do it again when next I saw the chance.

Less than a week later we were in his study again. I was sitting at the desk and he was in his swivel chair, scanning through some pages. Once we got to chatting, it was not difficult to get him to tell me a few more brief stories. I flicked the switch in my head on again and this time tried to note the precise word choices he made and how he phrased things. On this day he told me about a particular judge he remembered from the early days of his career. I'd never listened like this before. Beneath the placid surface of my listening face, my mental cogs were working furiously.

As soon as he was finished, I hurried to my bedroom and wrote down all three of the stories, awkwardly lying on my stomach with my feet over the edge of the bed.

Again I was surprised by how much I remembered, but this just made me more keenly aware of the holes, moments where I knew he'd used a certain word, or turn of phrase, that I couldn't remember. I was painfully conscious of how many of the words I'd forgotten and had to replace with something similar: similar, but entirely wrong. This gnawed at me, because the actual words – the phrasing, the vocabulary – seemed important.

Reading through these new stories in the days after I wrote them down, it struck me that this spying game might have something to it beyond the words and the order of the sentences. The protagonist of one of the tales was Joe Slovo, who practised as an advocate in Johannesburg before he went into exile. To preface this story, my grandfather told me how Joe had reminded him of the events in 1985 in Zambia, where my grandfather had travelled as chairman of the National Convention Movement.

Frederick van Zyl Slabbert, who was then leader of the official opposition, had started the NCM, through which, my grandfather explained, he hoped to bring interested parties together to negotiate an end to apartheid. He asked my grandfather to chair the organisation, and one of his first responsibilities as chairman was to travel to Lusaka to meet the ANC leadership in exile. On the Saturday night of his stay there, he said, 'the whole crew' – which included, among others, Joe, Mac Maharaj, and a young Thabo Mbeki – ended up in his hotel room, drinking beer and telling stories …

Mbeki, Slovo, Van Zyl Slabbert – these were names that had become vessels, word-shaped containers into which people poured their hopes or scorn. But in this story – I considered – through my grandfather's eyes, they were turned back into people, characters from one raucous night in a hotel room. Stories like this shone a torch beam on the underside of History with its concrete, capital H.

Jules Browde and Oliver Tambo in Lusaka, Zambia, 1985

I had often seen a recording device, about the size of a small cellphone, gunmetal grey, lying around in his study, either on the desk or on one of the bookshelves. It was the dictaphone he'd used when he worked as an advocate, dictating heads of argument for his secretary to type. He still used it sometimes to record his findings at the legislature. It had sat there silently all this time, but now it refused to stay quiet. Every time I went into that room it called to me, and I'd think: I should just use *that*; I should just sit down with him and get him to tell me all his stories, no matter how long it takes, record them and then type them out.

But the pressures of duty felt overwhelming and I kicked against them. I knew I *should* get these stories down, that it would be good to do it, but something in me, some instinct for self-preservation, prevented it.

There was no story in my life – no dramatic tension, no momentum, no suspense – just days that turned, each seamlessly into the next. Sitting down to hear stories from this life that spanned nearly a century – the battlefields of war, a celebrated legal career, a marriage and a family – carried a vague but certain threat. Somehow I'd worked out that if I wasn't to be pinned down by the weight of his stories, I'd have to start living my own.

When my employer told me in October, as I knew he would eventually, that he was going to close up shop at the end of the year, I went home and looked up the contact number of the journalism department at Rhodes University. I found out that I could still apply, and what it would cost, and then I phoned my father to speak to him about it. I didn't have nearly enough money to afford this. My father told me he liked the idea. About the cost he said, 'We'll make a plan.'

And when I left my grandparents' house, and Johannesburg, and an assortment of personal ghosts, in the middle of January of the following year, I left those few scant sheets in the translucent envelope jammed inside a cardboard box among other cardboard boxes in the storeroom at the end of the passage.

U636

Written from memory
Story told approx. 15/09/2003

We were in a long army convoy in mountains north of Addis Ababa when we received the news that the Italians in East Africa had surrendered. The men in my regiment were overjoyed. Beside themselves. All but a handful of us were Afrikaans-speaking, so *'Ons gaan huis toe!'* was the big cry among the men. 'We're going home!'

They thought this was the end of the war for them. We'd been sent to kick the Italians out of East Africa and we'd done that. Secretly, I had my doubts that matters would be solved so easily. And I was right in my suspicions of course. This was not the plan for us whatsoever. It was May of 1941. As it turned out, for most of us the war had only just started.

Our colonel explained to us that until we heard otherwise, we would continue north on the road to Asmara in Eritrea. And we pushed on through those mountains. I was a gunner, the equivalent of a private in the infantry, and had been assigned to drive the vehicle of the gun position officer, Lieutenant Jan Pieters. About three or four assistants to the officer travelled in the back of the van, which had the registration plate U636.

A day or so after we heard the news of the capitulation – we were now in the far north of Abyssinia, near a town called Korem – U636 seemed to be overheating, so I pulled over to the side of the road. We were stopped on a steep incline. To the one side of us was the rock of the mountainside; and to the other side, a sheer drop. The gun position officer got out on the passenger's side, I got out on my side, and we met at the front of the vehicle. I opened the bonnet to take a look at the engine. It looked all right, but very hot and dry.

Just as I started to loosen the radiator cap, slowly so that it wouldn't boil over, I felt U636 starting to roll away from us. Getting a *terrible* shock, I shouted and ran to the side of the vehicle, banging on the side and shouting to the fellows in the back to jump out. They had to open the back doors from the inside, but they all managed to get out with no problem – all except one. The last one out, Ivan Booyens, tripped and fell as he hit the ground, and I can still see it – it's something I will *never* forget – both sets of wheels, the front wheels and the back wheels, went over his legs, before the van veered to the right and went clear off the side of the mountain.

For a minute I struggled to breathe. I was so upset. I kneeled over Ivan. He was in a great deal of pain. I held him and spoke to him until the ambulance personnel arrived on the scene.

As they took him away, I played the scene over in my mind. Could I have done something different? I knew I had pulled up the handbrake, but I wasn't sure if I had put it in gear. Which I was supposed to do. I *thought* I had, but I couldn't remember now. I could still see the wheels going over Ivan, but the rest I battled to recall.

The two men in charge of the vehicles in the battery were Joe Brough and Koos Reyneke, both trained mechanics. They knew everything there was to know about engines. More than that, they loved these vehicles like they were their children. The two of them stood side by side on the edge of the precipice, with their hands on their hips, looking down at their van, which fortunately had been stopped in its fall by some trees that were growing on the side of the mountain. The expletives that fell from their lips I will not repeat.

Ivan Booyens was taken to hospital. (Probably in Nairobi.) He was not as badly hurt as I'd feared, but nevertheless, as a result of his injuries he was sent back to South Africa for treatment and took no further part in the war.

A couple of months later I received a letter from him with a photograph of himself in uniform, smiling. He had written on the back of the picture, 'Please don't worry about it.' Which was such a great relief to me that I almost cried.

The engineers pulled U636 up with a winch, and the badly damaged vehicle was then towed into the nearby village of Dekemhare, over the border near Asmara. The rest of us followed. We were now told that in Dekemhare we were going to regroup, clean our guns, and far from going home, we were going to be sent to the western desert, where the British Eighth Army, under General Wavell, was facing the powerful and well-equipped German army.

Dekemhare was a small town about twenty miles from Asmara, which was the capital of Eritrea. It had only a few simple buildings in it, but it had an airstrip with a very large hangar. In the hangar there was a deep pit, over which they had positioned U636 to enable them to work on the underside of the vehicle. And here Joe Brough and Koos Reyneke, together with some other men (some gunners of the regiment who were called in to help), started on the job of repair. They started with some panel beating, and re-ducoing, and generally replacing all the parts that had been destroyed near Korem.

While Joe and company were busy on U636, the rest of us were involved with cleaning the 18-pounder guns which were to be sent back home to be used at the Artillery School in Potchefstroom. By the way, just as an aside, when we dismantled the guns we were astounded to see, stamped on the inside of the jackets that protected the bore of the guns, the words: *1918. For drill purposes only*. Such were the guns that helped to defeat the Italian army in East Africa!

Now there were two things I wanted to do: I wanted to find a pub and I wanted to have a shave. The other chaps thought I was crazy to even *think* of allowing an Italian with a cut-throat razor near my neck, but I've always trusted Italians. And I met this fellow, a barber, and spoke to him – I knew a little Italian by then – and he agreed to shave me. He gave me a proper shave, and I paid him. We had some Italian currency by that time. And I also gave him a tin of bully beef, which he was especially happy about.

I also found a pub. A little corner place about halfway up the main road of the town. Some of us used to walk there in the evening after we had completed our tasks for the day. I got to know the pub owner. He was an Italian who did not look like a typical Italian at all. He was a tall fair-haired man with blue eyes, whose name was Luigi Coperchini. He had been in Eritrea for five or six years. I got on with him rather well. For some reason he took a liking to me, I remember he called me Giulio. And I had long talks with him. He told me about his life in Italy, and I told him about mine in South Africa.

Meanwhile, in the hangar, they continued to work on U636. The front suspension had been badly broken and they had to put in a new one. We were in Dekemhare for three weeks and they worked on it the whole time.

One day Joe Brough came to my tent and said to me, 'Come and have a look at U636.'

Joe was a sergeant, much older than I was. He must have been in his mid-thirties. He was married with children back in South Africa. I was twenty-two years old.

I went in there and couldn't believe it. It looked new. They had made a brand new vehicle out of it. Panel-beaten, ducoed and mechanically perfect.

So Joe said to me, 'Get in. I want to take you for a ride, show you how it goes.'

I got in next to him, and we drove out of the hangar and onto the road. Of course they were all dirt roads; none of the roads there were tarred. Oh, *man*, U636 went like a bird. It was absolutely amazing. The engine sang! We went for a long drive down the road and back. He was so excited about it he was actually singing as we came back and drove into the airstrip, into the hangar, and crashed headlong into the pit.

It was unbelievable. Koos Reyneke, who had stood watching the whole thing, really could *not believe* what he'd seen. It looked as if Joe had done it on purpose. (Which of course he had not.) The front part of the van was completely buckled – almost as badly as it was before – and there was white steam hissing out from under the bonnet.

Fortunately neither of us was hurt. But the same could not be said for the van. Huge damage was done to U636. The front axle and suspension – the brand new suspension – were again so badly damaged that they needed to be replaced. Well, once more the expletives flowed. From both of them. Twice a write-off! This time at least I wasn't to blame.

Before we pulled out of there, I went to say goodbye to Luigi Coperchini at the pub. And I want to tell you about that, because Luigi looked at me with tears in his eyes. He said to me, 'Giulio. Giulio. Please listen to me, my friend. You have been fighting Italians in Abyssinia. We are not fighters. You will see this, one day, when you go to Italy. You'll see.'

Neither of us knew then that I would be going there as part of this war, by the way.

He said, 'You'll see in Italy, Giulio. We are a nation of artists. We are interested in opera, music, ballet.' He said, 'You're going now to the western desert. You are going to fight the Germans. Giulio, they will *keel* you all!'

Which, incidentally, represented the feeling of just about everyone at that time: that the Germans were going to win the war. There was no reason why they shouldn't. They had occupied virtually all of Europe by that time. Dunkirk had already taken place, when the British expeditionary force was forced out of France. It looked like nothing could stop them, like they were going to *keel* everybody.

He said to me, 'Giulio, please, go home!'

I smiled and said, 'That's not really for me to decide, you know.'

He said, '*Please go home*. Do it as a favour to *me*.'

Hell, I laughed, man. It was both funny and sad for me. And I said, 'All right, Luigi. For you, I'll see what I can do about it.'

chapter four

In which the young storyteller finds a place of his own

Halfway through my first semester at Rhodes I built a bookshelf from some planks I bought at a timber merchant on the edge of Grahamstown. I dusted the shelf and my books once a week for the rest of the year. I also hand-washed my clothes in the bath and sometimes ironed them late at night after I'd finished my assignments. Every morning I ran. And riding the deep boost of esteem that even such a small amount of self-sufficiency can provide, I returned to Johannesburg in mid-December determined to find a place of my own.

A large news media company had offered me a position on the internship programme it ran out of its headquarters in Rosebank. This was a relatively prestigious course, which people said would give me a good start in journalism. It also promised a small monthly income, due to begin at the end of February. I decided that I'd spend the couple of months until then looking around to see what was available in terms of accommodation, and I took myself back to Orange Road to renew my career as a sort of toothless Harry Haller.

The internship was to be one year long and divided into two parts. In the first part we were going to receive tutoring from a well-known Kenyan journalist and journalism teacher. In the second we would move to our own small newsroom in the building and – at first under our tutor's guidance, then on our own – produce work for various publications in the company's stable.

Our classes were held in one of the windowless training rooms on the ground floor, near the canteen. There were nine of us on the intern-ship, all ambitious in different ways, all wanting to break something open, to write the story that hadn't been written.

Professor Kariithi, our tutor, was a wide, barrel-chested man with a mania for clarity. Our first practice exercise happened like this. He strode into the class and said, 'Okay. I want you to take your notebooks and pens and I want you to go to Gandhi Square. You know where that is? Good. I want you to spend an hour there. Take notes. Tell me what you see and hear. And, listen, I want you to speak to someone while you're there. Tell them what you're doing there. Ask them what *they're* doing there. And then I want you to come back and write me a piece titled 'Who I Met in Gandhi Square'. Okay? Have you all got that? Okay. *Go.*'

Exercises like this, and the searching discussions we had every day in class, gave me the sense, a lot of the time, that I was inhabiting some happy and long-dreamed-of vision of myself. There were days, though, when I didn't feel like that, days when I felt a sense of generalised dis-satisfaction, coupled with a familiar physical hollowness that I hadn't *once* felt during my year away. On those days the enthusiasm the other interns felt for journalism seemed stupid.

These sorts of days became more frequent as the weeks passed. Scared, defensive – but feeling powerless to stop it happening – I watched as I gradually closed down to the other interns, to Prof. Kariithi, to the idea of myself as a journalist. Depression's precipice, which in Grahamstown had receded to an invisible distance, quietly returned as a feature of my landscape. Two or three nights a week I was waking up in the middle of the night, twisted with thought, the guest room at my grandparents' house feeling as alien to me as my room at the Buddhist centre had felt before I left.

The only person I trusted to talk to when I got like this was my father. My dad has had more than his fair share of the precipice, has spent much of his adult life developing ways of thinking and being to keep from going over the edge. I know this to be true not just because his were the only words that made any sense to me when I was in those dumps, but also because of a story my grandfather had once told me.

The story starts with him, my grandfather, making some money on the stock exchange ('for the first and last time') and deciding to use the unexpected windfall to take his family to England to watch the moon landing on television. It is 1969. South Africa has no television yet.

The boy who will one day be my father is eighteen years old and in a bad state. He travels to England with his parents and younger brother, but wherever they go he just sits in the corner and takes no interest in anything, not even 'Mr Armstrong on the moon'.

'I didn't know what to do about it,' my grandfather told me. 'It was awful. I didn't know how to help this young fellow. Then I had the idea that I'd take him to Leeds. A Test match was being played there, at Headingley, between England and the West Indies.

'I'm sure you know that from when he was a little boy your father was mad about cricket. At school it was his *life*. And he was an extremely talented player. So I thought that a Test match at Headingley would be just the thing to snap him out of it. So off we went on the train, bought our tickets, and took our place amid the cheering crowds. And I tell you, Alan took no interest in the game whatsoever. He just sat there like an absolute *zombie*.'

This story had no happy ending – not then, anyway. No happy ending and no twist.

'After the day's play,' my grandfather said, 'I took him to meet Clyde Walcott, who was then the West Indies manager. In his day Walcott had been one of the leading West Indian batsmen. A legend of the game. Even then Alan was barely able to force a smile.'

My father worked with my mother in a small house in Norwood that had been converted into offices, with blue wall-to-wall carpeting and an enormous photocopier in the passage. It took me about ten minutes to walk there from Orange Road.

It was a public relations outfit of which they were half-owners. He met with the clients and wrote the press releases and she sent the press releases to the clients and chased them for approvals.

My dad's office was in the back corner of the house. He had pushed together two desks to create an L-shaped work zone for himself, and sat facing his computer against the wall. When I came inside, he swivelled round and faced me head-on. My father is a big man, with large hands and a full deep voice.

I sat down, thinking about how to put it. I stared out of the glass sliding door into the courtyard that separated his office from the kitchen. Then I told him I was thinking that maybe I should have stayed in the Eastern Cape. I said Joburg felt like it was full of landmines, emotionally speaking. I looked away again; I looked back at him.

He took a long moment, during which he visibly steadied himself, while looking into my eyes the whole time. He was suddenly dead serious.

At last he said, 'But Dan, this is normal stuff.'

I nodded, looking out at the dark slate tiles and white grouting. 'I know,' I said. 'I know.'

'But look at you, boy. Look at your *face*. It's like you've stopped in here on your way to be hanged.'

At this I couldn't help grinning. He smiled too. It lit his eyes and made me feel a few degrees lighter.

'We're human beings, Dan. This is how it is. No one ever promised us any different. Or they shouldn't have, at least. So okay, now you're in a situation where you don't know what to do, or where you should be. That is very normal. It's not easy to know what to do at the best of times. But you have to do *something*. Sitting and angsting about it is just going to make it worse.'

He waited for me.

I knew what he was talking about. I nodded.

He carried on, 'You make a decision, and you do the best you can from there. By all means, go back to Grahamstown. But make a plan and stick to your guns.'

I went to see him a few times that month, and each time I did I left feeling more able to face the future, more determined to be *in* the world and not alongside it.

One afternoon, coming out of my parents' office, I saw an opportunity to take the sort of bold step he was always talking about. In the ground-floor window of the apartment building next door I noticed a sign announcing a flat for rent on the second of the two floors. I studied the laminated photocopy behind the glass: a few light-streaked images. It looked like the perfect-sized flat for one person. I had just received my second cheque from the company and I realised I could probably afford it.

It was the end of March, the end of summer, when I moved my clothes and cardboard boxes from my grandparents' house to the flat up the road. It had an entry area, two square rooms, and a narrow balcony that looked out over my parents' office to the treetops of Norwood. For furniture I had a wooden desk and chair, and my mother lent me the greyish-blue La-Z-Boy she'd bought for herself when she embarked on her short-lived career as a reflexologist.

My grandparents were sad to see me leave, and each separately told me they hoped I didn't feel like I *had* to leave. They were more than happy for me to go on staying there, they said, for as long as I needed to. But I think they also recognised that this was a good thing for me to do.

The bare rooms of my new flat gave me a sense of clarity and potential. On my first night there I stood on the balcony, looking out over the trees, feeling lonely and free. I don't smoke, but that night I could have.

Soon I started hatching all sorts of plans. The internship, which until then had seemed like something I was only incidentally connected to, came to feel like a direct personal opportunity. I set up my laptop on the desk in the other room and in the evenings and on weekends wrote practice articles about things I'd done or seen during my year in the Eastern Cape.

One night – about two weeks after I moved in – I took the cardboard boxes out of the cupboard and emptied their contents onto the parquet floor near my bed. Although it was already late, I started going through it all, paying special attention to things I'd written myself. I found a few bits and pieces I could still bear to read: some poems and a couple of sketches for short stories I'd never got round to writing. I hadn't seen this stuff for more than a year. And it was long after midnight when I pulled a translucent envelope out of the pile and through the gelatinous plastic saw the word 'U636', underlined.

Sitting back against the base of the bed, I read my grandfather's story from beginning to end. After I'd finished 'U636', I took out another story from the same folder – the one Joe Slovo had told him, about the judge. That's pretty good, I thought.

I put the sheets down on the floor beside me and feeling my heart getting lighter I read the second courtroom story. It was just a few lines. Then I read the third one. When I was finished, I picked up all the pages again – four stories in total – and held them together under the light. And after I put all the notebooks and files and envelopes back into the boxes, I left those pieces of paper out, and put them on my desk in the other room. I wanted them around.

When the leaves fell, teams of men in orange vests used leaf blowers to drive them into piles on the side of the road. And as the days grew cooler I felt more and more comfortable and content in this flat I was paying for with my own money. Whatever life was made of felt more pliable. And it was then that I asked my grandfather, one Friday evening at his house, what he thought about the idea of recording some of his stories.

Nine years have passed since that night, but I remember that I arrived early, long before the others. It was just the two of us sitting in the entrance room, him on the short couch and me on the long one. I said I'd been thinking about it. I said we could use his dictaphone to record the stories and I'd type them out myself.

He seemed quietly happy about this. There was no gush of emotion or anything like that, just the calm approval of a sensible plan. It was as if I'd asked him whether he wanted to share a sandwich. He said something like, 'All right. Good. Let's do that.'

But he must have been more pleased than he'd made out, or than I'd understood. Because later, after the others had arrived – my father looking relaxed and tired; my mother keeping an eye on us and on her own mother (my grandmother, Ma); and my sisters, each of them – after they'd all arrived, and we'd all gone through to the dining room and were standing around the table, the two tall candles in the centre still unlit, he said to my father, in a voice loud enough for everyone to hear, 'Do you know what Dan wants to do?'

THE EMPTY CHAIR

Interview 13
Date recorded: 01/03/2006

My mother had a small income from an investment my father had made, but it was just enough to keep her and my younger brother in the flat in Killarney. It was obvious to me that I had to face the real world and get down to doing something. I could no longer expect to be given a dog biscuit and a can of meat and vegetables three times a day as I had been for the past five-and-a-half years.

I told you last time how we landed at the airstrip near Pretoria. Well, a few days after that, I went to speak to the professor of law at Wits, a man by the name of Hahlo, and I told him that I wished to continue with my LLB. Remember, I had started doing the LLB a few months before I enlisted, which was in April of 1940. It was now September of 1945.

I asked him if it would be possible for me to write the first-year examinations in November. Which meant I would have just two months to cover the year's syllabus.

Professor Hahlo, by the way, had immigrated to this country from Germany before the war, and although he spoke English with a very pronounced German accent, he did not like his German origins mentioned. I heard the story that one day one of the students, a young man by the name of Hermann – also a German immigrant – went to see him and addressed him in German, and Hahlo actually threw him out of his office and told him not to come back until he could speak *ze Kink's Englisch*.

But that's just by the way.

The professor said it would be a very big undertaking, but if I wanted to do it he wouldn't stop me. This was a compromise that was being reached with returning servicemen. So it was that just a week after I got back from the war, I started studying for these exams.

I saw little point in going to any of the lectures, though. The thing to do was to read all the material. Because I had none of the books at home, I went to the university library with a friend of mine called Rein, Steve Rein, who had also been in the army. Together Steve and I went through the syllabus in all the subjects. We swotted day and night for the months of September and October of 1945.

Now I think I should also tell you this: in the Great Hall of the university at that time they were showing Laurence Olivier's film of *Henry V*, which Olivier had made in the last year of the war. Several groups at the university were studying the play and to help the students they put the film on every night.

So after our evening session in the library the two of us would wander over to the Great Hall and sit at the back and watch the end of the film. I got to know the St Crispin's Day speech off by heart because we watched the Battle of Agincourt about thirty times in thirty nights. And I have never forgotten it.

> *Old men forget – it goes – yet all shall be forgot,*
> *But he'll remember, with advantages,*
> *What feats he did that day. Then shall our names,*
> *Familiar in his mouth as household words –*
> *Harry the King, Bedford and Exeter,*
> *Warwick and Talbot, Salisbury and Gloucester –*
> *Be in their flowing cups freshly remembered.*
> *This story shall the good man teach his son;*
> *And Crispin Crispian shall ne'er go by,*
> *From this day to the ending of the world,*
> *But we in it shall be remembered.*

Well, we wrote the examinations, and I'm quite sure that because of a rather charitable approach to ex-servicemen, I passed all the subjects – both Steve and I passed – and I started my second year with the rest of the class in 1946.

Now the law library was a small library in those days, with a large rectangular table in the middle with chairs arranged around it. Students sat in the chairs and were lectured to by the professor, who sat at the head of the table.

And I still remember walking in there on my first morning, February 1946. The class was small; there were about twenty of us, perhaps. And as far as I could see, we were all of us white and, apart from one woman, all males.

I sat down. Next to me was an empty chair. On the other side of that sat a fellow renowned for his support of the National Party. The United Party was still in power at that stage, but the Nats were gaining a lot of popularity among the white community, and this was the sort of chap who looked as if he would be one of the guiding lights when they took over. A large, powerfully built man with cauliflower ears. His name was De Klerk. Not *the* De Klerk. Another one.

While we were waiting for the professor, and the last few students were taking their seats, in walked an African man, about my age, carrying his books under his arm. Wits allowed a limited number of black students at that time, although with various restrictions. They were not allowed to stay in the residences, for example, or use the sports facilities.

He was a strapping man; very tall, handsome. He stopped and looked around for a seat. Everybody was looking at him – some secretly, some not trying to hide it at all – but if he noticed this, it didn't seem to trouble him. He saw the empty chair between De Klerk and me, and he came over and took his seat.

The moment he sat down De Klerk made a big show of standing up, and he went to find a seat on the other side of the table. He wouldn't sit next to a black man, you see.

Well, I'm sorry to say, nothing was said about this at the time. And soon afterwards the professor arrived and the lecture began.

After the class, this fellow introduced himself to me. He told me his name was Nelson Mandela. As a result of that coincidence of seating, we became fairly good friends, Mandela and I, and it was a friendship that lasted many years.

When I was just starting out at the Bar, one of the few firms of attorneys that briefed me was the firm he started in partnership with his friend Oliver Tambo. They called themselves simply Mandela and Tambo. They worked out of offices in a building called Chancellor House, on Fox Street, and built up quite a good practice. Tambo, when he qualified as an attorney, asked me to move his admission. In those days, before an attorney was admitted, he had to go to court with an advocate who would motivate for his admission before a judge. Obviously, Mandela had told him I was somebody to be trusted.

And when the Nats tried to have them ejected from those offices, Mandela came to see me about it in my chambers in His Majesty's Building on Commissioner Street. I remember that he showed me a document he had just received from the government, stating that Chancellor House was in a so-called white area and that they had to quit the building immediately or be prosecuted. It was the early 1950s. The government was still fine-tuning the Group Areas Act. At that time there was an organ of government called the Land Tenure Advisory Board. It sat in Pretoria, and a judge by the name of De Vos Hugo presided over it. This board was very powerful: it could rule over whether people had a right to live or work in certain areas. I told Mandela that the only hope we had was to go to Pretoria.

He said, 'All right,' and he briefed me. He was both the client and the attorney, and he gave me a brief and told me to mark my fees on it. I mean, imagine me charging him!

One morning soon after our discussion he arrived at our house in George Avenue, and we set off for Pretoria in my little Vauxhall. There we appeared before Mr de Vos Hugo, who, I recall, bore more than a passing resemblance to Hitler – but that's just by the way. I had prepared something to say, and I said it in a very impassioned way. I pointed out that Mandela and Tambo were leaders of their community. Which they were already, politically, and certainly as lawyers; they were one of the few firms of black attorneys at that time.

When I was finished, De Vos Hugo said he would consider it, and off we went. And as it turned out, he allowed them to continue practising in Chancellor House, and neither Mandela nor Tambo ever forgot this.

But what I wanted to tell you is the following story. When he became the president of the country, almost fifty years after he sat down in our class, Mandela hosted a luncheon near Midrand for people loosely referred to as *veterans of the struggle*.

During the course of this lunch – it was a very large affair, a few hundred people – Nelson caught my eye and called me over to him like this, with his finger, as he used to do, and said, 'Listen to me. I have been looking at you and you have reminded me of something. I want you please to arrange a reunion of our law class. I would like to see what has happened to all those people.'

I said, 'Of course. I'll contact the university for a list of the names.'

'And Jules,' he said. 'Do you remember, when I came into the class on the first day, and sat down, the man next to me got up and went and sat on the other side of the table?'

I told him that chap's name was De Klerk.

He said, 'That's right. *That's* the man. Please see that you ask him to come.'

So I said, 'I'll do my best. I'll see what I can do. But tell me, while I'm about it, why do you want him particularly?'

'Because I want to talk to him,' he said. 'I want to say to him, "Do you remember when I came into the class, you got up and crossed to the other side of the table? Making a statement that you didn't want to sit next to me?" And Jules,' he said, 'I don't mind whether he says he remembers or he doesn't remember. Because I want to take his hand,' and he took *my* hands, and he held them in his. And he said, 'And I want to say, *I* remember. But I forgive you. Now let's see what we can do together for the good of this country.'

When I phoned Mandela after a few weeks, to tell him that the reunion had been arranged, he was very pleased. And he didn't forget what he'd asked me. He said, 'Did you get hold of that fellow De Klerk?'

I said to him, 'For that, I'm afraid, you're going to have to wait for a higher jurisdiction.'

chapter five

In which the young storyteller and the old storyteller
set out on a journey

Something that my fellow intern Sabelo said one day made an impression on me. We were sitting outside the training room talking about what we'd done before turning to journalism. He was already thirty, the only intern older than I was. He told me he'd been a primary school teacher for ten years in Alexandra, which was where he was born and still lived. He said that when he'd started teaching he'd promised himself he would do it for only five years, but that after ten years as a teacher he woke up one day and thought, This isn't like you. So he left and went to study journalism.

I asked him why he'd set himself that limit.

He thought about it for a few moments, before replying, 'You know, in life, some things that you do, you know you're going to do them for the rest of your days, and some things you know you're going to do them just for a limited period.'

It struck me then that not being able to tell the difference could be one of the greatest sources of our unhappiness.

The Saturday morning we had set aside for the first recording session was bright and cold – one of the first properly cold days of that year.

He was standing in the doorway in his jeans and a knitted cardigan. He put a hand on my shoulder and kissed me on the cheek.

'Good to see you, boy. Come on in.'

He turned around and I followed him inside. They had the gas heater on.

'Sorry, I won't be a sec,' he said.

I followed him into the kitchen where he carried on doing what he had obviously been busy with when I rang the bell. The phone book was open on the counter and he started paging through it. 'Hell, man,' he said, 'I'm looking for the number of this chap up the road. The hardware chap. I bought some screws from him to hang a picture, but they're the wrong kind.' A packet of copper screws lay on the counter next to the phone. 'I want to know if he has the longer kind, you see. I should know the name of his shop. I go there often.'

He put his hands on his hips and turned around and looked out of the window, as if trying to summon the name of the hardware shop from the wider world. It was one of those quivering winter mornings when their kitchen seemed to be full of light.

'Really marvellous place. He's got absolutely everything in that shop.'

I told him I knew the place well, but not the name. The old man and his wife had been there for as long as I could remember. I said I wasn't even sure it *had* a name. I wandered over to the other end of the kitchen and opened the fridge for no reason.

'It'll come to me,' he said. Then: 'Right, laddie, haven't we got work to do?'

'Here, let me show you something,' I said. I closed the fridge and walked past him into the entrance room, where I'd left my backpack on the floor next to the couch. I pulled out the pack of batteries I'd bought and handed them to him. 'Double A, right?'

He nodded. 'These should do the trick. Let me get the machine. Have you said good morning to your grandmother?'

He disappeared through the door, on the way to his study. Though he was already eighty-five, there was something still youthful about him. Not something Peter Pan-ish, not boyish like that, but a sense of wonder that lived in his eyes and at the corners of his mouth.

My grandmother was sitting in her paper-strewn study. She is also youthful; she reminds me of a serious first-year university student, constantly grappling with new material. Though she spends a lot of her time sitting right there, there always seems something precarious about her perch, as if either the chair or the desk had been made for someone of slightly different dimensions.

She looked up from the screen, with dark-brown eyes, and her face softened. 'Oh, *hi* Dan.'

'Hi, Nan.'

I smiled, noticing that she wanted to destroy her computer again. She never has any luck with it.

'How's it going?' I said, though I thought I knew.

She made a face like *Don't even ask*. And then smiled, bashful but still frustrated, and turned back to the screen.

I had already thought about where we should sit. There was a chair in the corner of the lounge that he liked to sit in when he read or did crosswords. It was one of a few chairs and couches that surrounded the low glass table in the middle of the room. I said I thought it would feel natural if he sat there.

'I think that's a jolly good idea,' he said. 'Absolutely right.'

It was a beautiful old wooden chair, with maroon cotton cushioning on the seat, backrest and along the arms. He looked very comfortable in it. The light from the big window behind him glinted off his broad, bare scalp.

I sat down at the far end of a long pearl-grey couch, close to him in his chair, and put the dictaphone down on a tall-legged table between us.

'I thought we could put it here,' I said. This table was what he put things on when he sat in that chair: a cup of tea, pens, highlighters.

But it didn't look like it was close enough to his mouth. I frowned.

'No good?'

'I'm just worried that it's too far away from you,' I said. 'What do you think?'

'Should we do a test?' he offered.

I pushed the switch on the side to REC, and then we both spoke: 'Okay. Hello, hello. Testing one, two, three …'

When we played it back, it seemed a little faint to me. I looked around for something to put the machine on, to lift it closer to his mouth.

'Hang on a sec,' I said.

I went to his study and fetched three or four thick books from the lowest shelf of his main bookcase – art books, travel books, cookery books, that sort of thing. I piled these on the table and set the dictaphone on top of the pile. It still didn't look high enough, so I went back and fetched more books.

He was holding with both hands a piece of paper on which he'd written a series of notes in his jagged cursive. I had asked him to start with stories from as far back as he could remember, and he'd made a list of those he didn't want to forget. While I fetched the books he patiently referred to his list.

The pile looked high enough now and I positioned the dictaphone on top of it in such a way that the microphone was peeking over the edge closest to him. We did another test and this time both our voices played back clearly.

I hadn't expected to be nervous but now that we were ready to go I felt underprepared. I hadn't come up with any questions. I hadn't done anything. I'd just bought batteries. But I could see he trusted me absolutely.

'Okay, ready?' I asked him.

'Yebo.'

I leaned across and pushed the switch to REC again. Watching the wheels in motion, I said, 'Okay. Twenty-third of April, two thousand and … five. Jules Browde. Interview one.' And then I looked up and smiled at him. The dictaphone made only a very muffled sound of turning. He nodded, conspiratorially, looked into the middle of the room and started to speak.

'Just let me tell you,' he said. 'When my dad arrived here from Lithuania, I doubt whether he could speak English at all. But he worked hard at it, because he was very keen on freemasonry. In fact, he rose to be the master of his lodge, in what was called the Scottish Chapter. And as the master of his lodge, he often had to make speeches in English. Which he did.

'I don't know if there were any other Jews in his lodge, but he was apparently very popular because I remember that when he died in 1938, at the age of fifty-nine, the Freemasons had a special ceremony for him at the graveside. And they all threw petals, rose petals, into his grave.'

I leaned over and peered through the dictaphone's small see-through window.

'Problem?' he asked.

'Just checking that this thing is working.'

'And?'

'It's okay. Sorry.'

I knew only a few scraps about his father. Came on his own from

Lithuania, ran a shop in town selling sugar and flour. I certainly hadn't heard anything about Freemasons.

'So had your dad been involved with freemasonry in Lithuania?'

'Oh, no, no,' he said, shaking his head. 'He came here as a youngster. He came here at the age of eighteen or nineteen.'

That seemed to be enough of an explanation for him, and so I let him go on. He sat with his legs close to each other, his feet, in black suede takkies, set flat on the floor. With his hands he caressed the list in his lap; he looked down at it every time he came to the end of a story.

That morning he told me stories about his parents, his grand-parents and his aunts, all of them immigrants from the Old Country, and stories about his three siblings who were all, as he was, born here in Johannesburg. He told me stories from the house in Bertrams where he was born, and where his family lived before they moved to Yeoville when he was six.

He told some stories I'd heard before, like the one about how his father sent the children into the country because of the violent miners' strike in 1922, and the one about the pair of horses that ran away with a carriage he'd climbed onto as a curious five-year-old. But he also told several I'd never heard, like the one about his father's mystery sisters, and the one about going to a rugby match with his older brother and being astonished when the little referee sent the giant All Black forward off the field for dangerous play.

The more he spoke, the closer his heart's sound seemed to come to the gravelled surface of his voice. Around his voice a silence spread in which the objects in the room appeared to merge into a dumb, mono-chromatic mass. The only things I saw in sharp colour were his face and the dictaphone, which I obsessively leaned forward to check, to make sure the wheels were still turning.

As he talked I looked at his white hair, thin as spider silk, which he'd combed neatly behind his ears, and I felt an extreme sort of happiness – something like vertigo.

After half an hour, the machine let out a thin, wheedling screech, made some clicking and grinding noises, and came to a dead stop. It took me several panicked seconds to realise that the noise was just the dictaphone's way of telling you that one side of the tape was up.

As I took out the tape and flipped it over, I said, 'This is *incredible*, Broncs.'

'You think it's going well?'

49

I said it was going so well I couldn't even tell him.

'All right, let's carry on,' he said.

He spoke for one and a half more sides, forty-five minutes, ten sto-ries or more, and then, looking up from his list, asked me if we could stop. I found it strange and sad that he had had to ask me that. But I said of course we could and I leaned forward and pulled the switch back.

In this new silence, the room rushed back into focus. Objects re-gained their clear-edged presence. The voice had lost its dominion.

'Amazing,' I said. 'I can't even … How did you find that, Broncs? How do you feel?'

He raised his eyebrows and shook his head slowly. I was not – I am still not – sure what exactly he meant. But he had spoken all the words he had for now. I could see he was tired. The diagonal lines descending from the sides of his mouth looked deep and heavy.

I said, 'We must do this again. Soon.'

He nodded without comment and looked down at his list. I didn't know if he had covered everything he'd wanted to, but I thought I wouldn't ask. Whatever he hadn't got to we could cover the next time. I rewound the tape, counting a few beats, and then anxiously pushed the switch to PLAY. I was relieved to hear his voice coming out of the device, a little soft but clearly audible: *'The Yeoville cinema was owned by a man called Seferis, who used to let us in for sixpence …'*

I put the tape we'd finished, plus the dictaphone – which had a second tape still in it – into a dark-blue pouch with a zip, and buried it in my backpack. Because we didn't know what else to do, we sat there for ten more minutes, chatting about this and that. We spoke about the Test series being played between South Africa and the West Indies. He asked me about the internship and I told him about the exercise we'd done in Gandhi Square. We paid attention, we nodded, we did all the things we always did when we spoke to each other, but it felt peculiar. Now that the dictaphone was gone, I had the brief but uncomfortable sensation that we were putting on a show for no audience. After I'd said goodbye to him and my grandmother, I drove with the backpack on my lap, hurrying home.

A Tongue Like a Whiplash

Written from memory
Story told approx. 20/09/2003

One night in Lusaka the whole crew ended up back at my hotel room. Joe was there, Jack Alexander was there, and Mac Maharaj, I remember. So was Penuell Meduna, who later became the Minister of Justice. And Thabo Mbeki, who was still a young man then. A lot of drinking took place, I recall, and at some point Joe reminded me of the following story: it concerned his first day in court.

It was a housebreaking and theft case, and Joe was appearing for the defence before Judge Malan. Malan J, as we knew him. A very intimidating character. The *corpus delicti*, or physical evidence – in this case the loot that had been discovered at the house of the accused – had been placed in bags and was on display in the well of the court. A policeman stood in the well and, now and then, while the prosecutor led his evidence, took the objects out of their bags and held them up for the court's attention.

Now Joe thought it would be a good idea to go and have a closer look at the evidence. So he did that; he got up from behind counsel's table and went over to stand next to the policeman.

His first clue that something was wrong, he said, was this policeman's face. He said the man looked at him as if he were mad. Then he realised that the prosecutor had stopped speaking. In fact, he said there was complete silence in the court. Suspecting that this might have something to do with him, he looked slowly up at the judge.

Malan was staring at him impassively. He said nothing for a

51

moment or two. Then, in his imperious tone, he said, '*Mister Slovo*. This is a *courtroom*, not a *circus* in which any clown may jump in and out of the arena at will!'

Malan was an Afrikaner, but in court, like many Afrikaans judges in those days, he spoke only in English.

Oh man, Joe laughed like hell to remember it. He said he went back to his seat, flushed with embarrassment, having learned a lesson he would never forget.

On another occasion, an advocate from Johannesburg by the name of Attie van der Spuy was trying to explain the intricacies of a road accident to the same Judge Malan, by pushing two toy cars around on counsel's table.

During his demonstration, Attie noticed that Malan was staring out of the window. So he stopped what he was doing and politely asked if his lordship would mind having a look at him and what he was trying to show the court.

Whereupon Malan, very reluctantly it seemed, turned to him and said, 'Mister van der Spuy, it is bad enough for me to have to listen to you. You don't honestly expect me to *look* at you as well?'

This became a well-known story, told by Attie himself. Malan J had a tongue like a *whiplash*.

Now of course there is another story involving Judge Malan. This one concerns a case in which I was supposed to appear. In about 1965 or thereabouts. A public violence case in which I had been briefed to appear for the defence. It had first been heard in the magistrates' court, where a preparatory examination had been held.

They don't have them any more, but the PE – as it was called – used to be an important part of the criminal justice system. At the PE, every witness who was to be called at the trial gave evidence. Which, among other things, enabled the defence to prepare for the trial before it reached the court. The proceedings were recorded and the record placed before the judge.

This particular case was to be heard in the Supreme Court. What today is called the High Court. In Pritchard Street. Malan J had read the record of the PE and he was going to sit in the trial.

But on the day the case was to be heard, the prosecutor hurried over to me in the morning and told me that since the PE, their chief witness, the man on whom the entire prosecution relied, had been murdered. So the case could not proceed. The prosecutor asked me if I wouldn't mind coming with him to break this news to Judge Malan. He was nervous of him, you see.

I said I wouldn't mind, and the two of us went off to the judge's chambers.

We knocked at Judge Malan's door, and were called in.

The judge was sitting behind his desk. He was a very tall man with a weather-beaten face and an extremely upright carriage.

'Yes …?' he said.

When we told him what had happened, that the witness had been murdered, he nodded slowly and said, 'A very good idea.' Then a smile crept across his lips, something not often seen, and he turned to me and said, 'Was that *your* idea, Browde?'

chapter six

*In which we follow the young storyteller and the old storyteller
on the early part of their journey, and see some exciting things
(and one or two unsettling ones)*

I needed about eight hours to transcribe the seventy-five-odd minutes
of recording. With each sentence I typed, and every time I pressed SAVE,
I felt an almost unprecedented sense of accomplishment: something
like *duty done*. The anxiety of the interview found an exact counter-
weight in the relief of typing it out. When at last I printed it – dated and
titled 'Transcript 1' – the twenty-two pages seemed to hum and whirr in
my hands. I slotted the document into a new translucent envelope with
the four stories I'd typed out, under very different circumstances, more
than a year before. And I set my sights on doing it again.

My grandfather appeared to have learned a few things from the first
interview. When I arrived at the house a week later, on the Saturday
afternoon, he had made a new list on a fresh piece of paper, which he
studied intently while I fetched the same set of large books from his
study. We then spent a few minutes chatting about the stories he wanted to tell, and, after shutting the door of the lounge to forestall any
interruptions, I pushed the switch to REC.

I'd learned a few things too. This time I interrupted him far less often.
Mostly I just let him talk, which he did: one story leading to another
until, after about an hour (a few minutes into the second tape), his voice
grew tired and we called it a day. I now had a thick grey sock to hold
and protect the dictaphone in its pouch. The living weight of the tapes
in my backpack again felt unsettling. I knew I wouldn't be able to relax

until the interview was typed and printed and I held it in my hands.

Something had happened that week that was going to make the job of transcribing much easier. My grandfather had phoned Mrs Magid, who had been his secretary for the last twenty years of his career, to ask her about a machine he'd often seen her use: 'an ingenious device with a pedal that she worked with her foot under the desk'. Mrs Magid said she still had it, this transcribing machine, and insisted on giving rather than lending it to us. 'Everything's digital now. I have no use for it,' she told him when he protested. Her son dropped it round at the house.

We established something close to a routine. I'd go over there, usually on the weekend, and he and I would gravitate towards our places in the lounge. We'd close the door behind us and there usually wouldn't be any interruptions. Sometimes, a minute after the phone rang and stopped, my grandmother would open the door slightly, put her head in, and say that even though she was sorry to interrupt she thought my grandfather should probably take this call. She would linger in the doorway a little after he walked past her into the kitchen. Though I noticed this, it wasn't until much later that I gave it any thought. At the time I could think only about what was happening inside that room, how the words were turning into something else as sentence after sentence was delivered into the magnetic mind of the machine.

Story by story a world was slowly unfolding. The stage was Yeoville now and the period was 1925 to 1938 – one year before the Second World War broke out. The core of the ensemble cast was his family. The two main characters were his father and his older brother, who acted almost as foils for one other. Where his father was warm and hopeful, his brother Len was a mercurial figure, capable of both kindness and cruelty. Lily, his older sister, was a sensitive child, and many of the early stories about her concerned her childhood phobias. Later, as they got older, she figured more in her absence – a remote kindness who found safety with her friends behind a closed door. Only later would his mother move to centre stage.

To transcribe the interviews I carved out time usually at night, once I'd finished Prof. Kariithi's readings or writing exercises. With my foot on the pedal of Mrs Magid's ingenious contraption, my grandfather's voice crawling from the latticed speaker, and my fingers punching the keys, I felt like I was driving a memory machine.

I remember I was transcribing late one night when a detail from that long-ago world caused my own memory to make an unexpected discovery. It was the first time this happened; it would happen again and again as I grew to understand the particularly contagious quality of remembering.

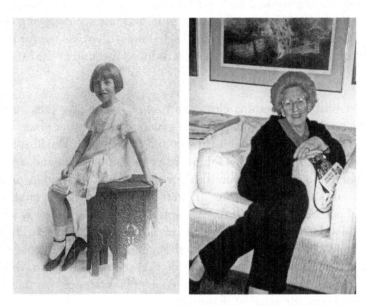

Jules Browde's older sister, Lily, circa 1923 and circa 1980

The story was about Lily and it took place at a Pesach Seder at their house on Page Street in Yeoville. The family had its Seders in the dining room: the front room of the house, the side closest to the street. The beautiful dining-room table, with its six ornately carved legs, was on that night extended to its full length. His grandparents were there, and so were his aunts, to hear again the story of the Exodus from Egypt. The long table was covered with a white cloth and laid immaculately, with one setting, as usual, left empty for Elijah the Prophet. Elijah, tradition has it, will one day arrive as an unknown guest to announce the coming of the Messiah.

It is customary for a child to open the front door of the house to welcome Elijah in, and their father, Isaac, sometimes asked Lily to do it, precisely because she was afraid to. He believed it was important for her to face her fears. It was for the same reason that he sometimes made her take a chicken to be slaughtered by Reverend Taylor, the *schochet*, down the road, even though she would cry and say she didn't want to go.

'Now comes Elijah,' his father would say, when the time came. 'Lily, open please for Elijah the door.'

'She'd look at my dad in fear,' my grandfather remembered.

'Why me?' she'd say. 'Why can't Lenny open for Elijah?'

'I want *you* to, Lily.'

'But I'm scared to!'

'Why are you scared?'

'What if he's there?'

'Go, my girl. He won't do you any ...'

I stopped typing and looked up into the haze of the white wall in front of me. Something had come loose in my brain and now I felt as if I was falling, slowly, forward. Now comes Elijah. Now comes ...

'... Elijah,' my grandfather says. 'Dan, why don't you go and open the door for him?'

We are at their house in Houghton, in the dining room. The long table (which I know is really a few tables put together) has pieces of vine from the garden snaking down the middle of it, nuts and raisins hidden among the glossy heart-shaped leaves.

I slip off my chair and stand on the carpet next to it. It is the first night of Pesach. I am seven years old, not much taller than the chair.

Of all the strange and wonderful elements of the Seder, which each year fills me with wonder and reverence and almost uncontainable joy, this is the one I look forward to the most: opening the door for Elijah the Prophet.

I push my chair back in, take a breath.

'That's my boy,' my grandfather says.

As I turn my back on the faces at the table, I feel the glow of special attention, of being singled out. But outside the room the glow is a curse. I wish someone else had been chosen. In the lounge now, all alone, I tell myself that maybe I should just go back. Apologise. Tell them that this year I don't think I can.

Past the double doors now, and into the long passage, which extends in both directions into ominous pools of darkness. I feel every inch of every step, my body alert with fear. Across the passage is the entry hall, lit by an old lamp on a wooden table against the wall. Time seems to have stopped. I alone move through air the colour of honey towards the heavy wooden door. Stepping over the Persian carpet I am convinced, I *know*, that when I open the door there *will be* somebody standing there, that it really *will* be a man from the Olden Days, and that although he will not mean me any harm I will *die of fright* because he is there at all. I reach up breathlessly for the brass knob and close my fingers around it.

I pressed save and went out onto the balcony. I looked out over the empty streets and the half-lit trees. I hadn't thought of any of this for years. His sister Lily was already very old by the time I knew her, a fragile but poised and graceful woman with heavy eyelids. I saw her sitting in a light-green armchair with her forearms resting Sphinx-like on the armrests, her hands folded over the ends. I remembered in my bones the atmosphere of her house on the day she died. I was nine years old, and it was the first time I'd ever been in a house that felt like that – touched by the edge of some boundless, creeping shadow. I didn't go into the room where she was lying, but my father did. And when he came out, he took my hand and we went home.

The only character from that world, aside from my grandfather, still alive then was his younger brother, Bernard. He lived in a frail-care facility called Our Parents' Home, which was just a few streets from their house. He, too, was an old man by the time I got to know him.

In my grandfather's stories, Bernard was a child who struggled at school and found it difficult to make friends, and I realised he had never stopped being that child. As a kid I didn't know how to think about this old person who seemed to be more like me than he was like the other grown-ups. I was scared to talk to him, scared to be alone with him, and it makes me sad to write this now. Because he always took an interest in me and asked me questions about my life, nodding and adjusting his glasses as he tried to make sense of the answers I gave him. Always such short answers, leaning away.

In the corner of the lounge in Orange Road, stories from the secret mists of early childhood morphed into boyish capers involving snowballs and drainpipes, and then into more sober dispatches from his teenage years, when his participation in the Jewish youth movement Habonim over-shadowed high school and everything else. It was the 1930s. Hitler and anti-Semitism and the desire for a homeland in Palestine dominated the conversations at home and among his friends. Europe was sliding into the obliterating abyss.

The abyss was here, too. The character of Death enters the stories in 1936. He was seventeen years old that year, the year his grandfather died – his mother's father, Louis Meyers.

Like my grandfather's father, Louis had also fled the Pale of Settlement to seek a better life abroad – first in the north of England, where the cotton mills offered abundant work, and then in South Africa. Yet unlike my grandfather's father, Louis made the journey with his wife Annie and their four teenage children – my grandfather's mother being one of them. He opened a photographic studio in Ferreira's Town and took individual and family portraits.

The story in question took place in the Yeoville Shul on Yom Kippur. His father, his grandfather and he were all sitting that afternoon, as they always used to, right in the corner. His father favoured this spot because he liked to feel the breeze from the open window. 'I was sitting next to my grandfather, as usual, and he was pointing out to me the place in the *machzor* – I can still remember his gnarled finger, pointing – when suddenly his hand slipped forward and he collapsed onto the front of the table, where the book was.

'People came with a scurry and a flurry and we all carried him out. He had had a stroke. And he died a few days later.'

His eyes seemed unsure of what to settle on. In the end they settled on me. 'I remember being very upset about it,' he told me. 'I'm actually upset even talking about it now.'

I sat there divided. Though my grandfather was visibly shaken by the force of this memory and I knew, painfully, that in that moment I was seeing him more vulnerable than I had ever seen him, simultaneously I felt a bubbly thrill because this was such *good stuff*, and I remember turning my eyes away from his distressed face to make sure the wheels of the dictaphone were still turning.

Something had gone wrong. I wasn't listening to him any more: I was *listening out*. I was listening out for things, including (though not only) this sort of raw emotion. The cellar under the house in Bertrams, where the chickens went at night; Beit Street in Doornfontein when it was packed on both sides with kosher shops and delicatessens: Fehler and Flax, The Crystal; the old shul near the Alhambra Theatre with the two white stone lions on the outside steps. Anything redolent of that other world made my heart beat faster and my eyes dart across to the recorder on its throne of books. Tram tracks, spats and the sprigs from peppercorn trees. Cheese cutters, cats' whiskers and chizza sticks … it was something like the experience of travelling to a new country and becoming so obsessed with taking pictures that your first thought when you see anything – *anything at all* – has to do with the camera.

Something similar had crept into the transcribing, too. When we'd started, a few months before, I had typed out the stories joyfully with no thought as to how they sounded. I felt happy simply because I was doing something that felt valuable – and it felt valuable then, because words of the air were becoming words on a page. Just that. As my mother had dreamed, I was getting his stories *down*. But now, when I transcribed, I was watching out: for the deft turn of phrase, for the expression of deep feeling, for anything that seemed *literary*. It had to be earnest and old school and elegant, yet at the same time fully fresh. And when I saw it I'd think, Okay, I'm glad I got that. Now that's *really something*.

A Well-Known Hat

Interview 3
Date recorded: 07/05/2005

When I was sixteen it snowed in Johannesburg. This was in May of 1935, and it was the first time that I, or any of my friends, had experienced snow. We thought it was *marvellous*.

It had fallen in the night – quite a heavy snowfall – so when we woke up it seemed as if the whole world had been magically blanketed in white. Walking to school with my friend Dov, I saw that everyone else was just as excited as we were. I don't know when it had last snowed here, but not for *many* years, and people were quite beside themselves, laughing and holding each other and pointing as if perhaps someone might not yet have noticed. Snow covered the streets and the tops of motorcars that had been parked overnight on the side of the road.

We spent the school day mostly looking out of the window as the snow continued to sift down. The masters did not seem to mind. As I recall many of them stood gazing out of the window too. Many of the masters at King Edwards came from Britain – England and Scotland, mainly – so they knew something about snow, but the sight of it falling here on the highveld was so unusual that it turned the world on its head, and we were able to get away with behaviour that ordinarily would not have been tolerated.

Anyway, when the last bell rang Dov and I ran through the snow to the yard of the Yeoville shul. This is where a crowd of us often met after school to play soccer or attend Hebrew lessons. Some of the chaps were there already. And those who weren't soon came half-running, half-skidding through the gate on Kenmere Road. Which brings me to the story I wanted to tell you ...

We were making a snowman and throwing snowballs at each other, and so on – shouting and having fun – when I saw what I recognised as the dark-grey hat of Sharpie Shapiro, the shammas, on the other side of the hedge that separated the yard from Kenmere Road. I could just see this hat travelling along.

And I don't know what possessed me, but I quickly made a snowball and threw it from, I don't know, maybe thirty yards or so, at the hat. Well, lo and behold (I was quite a crack shot in those days), I got a direct hit, and the hat disappeared.

Some of my friends – the ones who'd seen what I'd done – stopped in their tracks and turned to look at me with their mouths open. Those who hadn't been looking just stood there with their unthrown snowballs in their hands, wondering what had happened.

You must understand that this was a very well-known hat. Which belonged to a very feared individual. As you may know, a shammas, or beadle, is the man in charge of the day-to-day running of the syna-gogue. He will often be a shy or retiring sort, but Sharpie was not that sort of shammas. Not at all. Even on Purim he would shush us when we responded with the traditional racket to the mention of Haman's name in the Book of Esther. My dad used to say, 'Sharpie, leave them make a noise!' Sharpie wanted to eject us from the shul. He was a tyrant who thought it his job to make sure that we had as little fun as possible.

And so now Sharpie Shapiro came charging through the gate, wav-ing his fist and bellowing: *'Who did zis? Who did zis?!'*

He had a very pronounced Lithuanian accent. He was a short stout chap with grey hair that was now flaked with snow.

We had formed a semi-circle facing him. All the others – Dov, Lolly Lazar, the Balkind brothers, Nibby Penn, Jake Jacobson – just stood there looking at their feet. There was no way I was going let anybody else take the rap for this, so I stepped forward and told him I had done it. Still clutching his hat in one hand, Sharpie cried, 'You are a naughty boy! You will appear before the committee!'

The committee of the Yeoville Shul consisted of some well-known Jews who lived in the neighbourhood. One was Mr Bradlow, who had a big furniture shop in town. Another was Mr Sive, of Sive Bros and Karnofsky, the wholesalers. These were reputed to be wealthy people. I remember that the Sives lived in one of the very few double-storeys in Yeoville, on the corner of Page Street and Cavendish Road. But that's just by the way. Point is I knew who these men were, the committee members. They came to shul on the High Holidays wearing top hats, and sat in the front row. I used to look at them in their top hats from where I sat with my father and grandfather in the corner near the window.

In due course the day arrived that I was to appear before the committee. This was about a week or so after the incident. The shul had some offices round the side, close to where we had Hebrew lessons. I waited in the corridor, looking around. I wouldn't say that I was *afraid*. I knew I had not done the most terrible thing. But I was a little apprehensive. I had never before been called to face the committee. At last the door cracked open a little and one of them asked me to step inside. I went in.

There they sat, three or four of them, at one end of a large wooden table. Sharpie was sitting with them on the one side, still looking rather displeased. One of the committee members asked me to take a seat at the other end of the table, which I did.

They said they wanted to deal with my, *er*, my attack on Mr Shapiro. They asked if I had anything to say.

I admitted it candidly and apologised to Mr Shapiro for knocking his hat off.

Sharpie just scowled; he said nothing.

The committee members said it was a very bad thing that I'd done. And, they said, they had discussed it, and they were sentencing me to the following punishment: they were going to tell my father.

I said, 'All right, that's fine.' I wasn't scared of my father the way some boys were.

The committee asked me if I had anything else to say. I said I couldn't think of anything else. I didn't know what more they wanted from me.

One of them said, 'You must promise that you will never do it again.'

I said I would never do anything like that again. And I remember wondering when next it might snow to give me the opportunity to do it again. But I didn't say anything about that.

And that was the end of that. The committee members said I could go, Sharpie gave me one last glare, and I walked the five blocks home to Page Street.

About a week later, there came a knock at the front door. It must have been at about six in the evening. It was getting dark. My father had only just arrived home from work. My mother answered the door.

It was one of the committee members, who said he wanted to speak to Mr Browde. My dad came into the hall and shook hands with this fellow. They exchanged a few words and then went through to sit at the table in the dining room, closing the double doors behind them. I stood near the door. I remember that Len came into the hall and asked me what was going on. I told him and he nodded and went back to our room. The three of us boys shared a room in those days.

I pressed my eye to the narrow gap between the doors. While the man was telling my father the story of Sharpie and the snowball, my father sat and nodded. After the story was finished, he thanked the gentleman for having come to tell him. He said he would take care of it. And when presently they established that there was no more business to discuss, he saw the man to the door. Once this fellow had gone, my dad closed the door. And then he laughed, man. He had a deep and rather raucous laugh. He leaned his head back and laughed. I don't think my dad believed that an *attack on Mr Shapiro* was the proper description of what had taken place.

Isaac Browde
'He had a deep and rather raucous laugh.'

chapter seven

In which the young storyteller and the old storyteller
come to a trench of great sadness

The internship coordinator, Paddi, led us to a room at the far end of the building's underground parking garage: a hot, cramped, semi-industrial space with rows of fluorescent lights running the length of a low, perforated ceiling. She told us this was our newsroom. It was a letdown, but we made the most of it. On that first day someone called it the Cave, and the name stuck. My desk partner was Busisiwe, a long wistful girl who spoke softly and listened with her head cocked to one side.

The shortage of oxygen tempered our enthusiasm only a little. We were all keen for the day, only two months from now, when we'd be able to start doing some real reporting. Prof. Kariithi would stay with us until then and after that we'd be on our own. The Cave had all the things we saw in the professional newsrooms upstairs (computers, phones, a combination photocopier–printer), and it felt exciting to have all this at our disposal.

I think it is important, in light of what happened later, to record here that at the time of taping and typing out my grandfather's stories I never once made a connection between that exercise and what I was doing on the journalism internship. If anything, the two projects seemed to have opposing orientations. The internship was about the future, about becoming something I wasn't yet, while the job of collecting his stories seemed to be about salvaging items of weight and shape and colour from the ruins of the past.

It must have been soon after this that he told me the story that marked the end of his childhood. I say this because I remember typing it out over two days in the Cave. I had known the story was coming; he had mentioned a few times that he didn't want to leave it out. Of course I knew he wouldn't leave it out. He had started this story, the story of his father, at the beginning of the very first interview.

There were a few things I'd learned about his dad, whose name was Isaac. I knew he'd come from Lithuania, and though I wasn't sure of the name of the shtetl, I knew it was in the vicinity of Kovno (modern-day Kaunas). I knew he'd sailed to South Africa, aged eighteen or nineteen, mysteriously alone. His siblings – two brothers and two sisters – had all gone to the United States and he never saw them, nor his parents, again. All that I knew.

I also knew that he was a scholar of the Talmud, and that people used to come to their house to ask him questions about commentary and interpretation. I knew he liked to 'pull your leg' and got great pleasure if you took him seriously. That he had a booming voice, like my own father, and had no time for movies, holidays, or doctors. That he simply didn't believe in these things. The things he did believe in were his family and his shop.

His shop was on Commissioner Street, right down at the eastern end, in Ferreira's Town. Every weekday morning he left for work from Yeoville on the earliest tram. I knew that too. And that his business was buying bulk quantities of sugar and flour from mills in Natal and selling it on to retailers in the vicinity of Ferreira's Town, but even as far west as Braamfontein. I knew he had a partner called Greenberg, also a Lithuanian Jew, who was a tall and strange man with a leathery face. And two employees, Jantjie and Ephraim, who helped load the bags of flour and sugar on and off the delivery cart, which they drove with two horses.

Together these bits of information, gleaned from earlier stories, created a suggestive shape, like the numbered points in a dot-to-dot puzzle. The story he told me that day was like the nib of a pen joining the points; but unlike the cartoon shapes that emerge in children's activity books, this one was knotted and troublesome.

'My dad believed Ferreira's Town would become the commercial centre of Johannesburg,' he said, 'and that one day he would make a lot of money out of the stand, which he'd bought for a relatively small amount as a young man, soon after he arrived in the city.

'He told us he had it on good authority that one day a new

magistrates' court would be built just up the road from where his shop was. And when that happened, he used to say, he'd make a *fortzen*. At one time he even opened a little garage next door, with two pumps, in anticipation of the crowds the court would bring.

'But the court was not built in his lifetime. And Ferreira's Town in fact became a rather seedy part of town, and though there was income – he worked hard and built good relationships with his customers – most of what he earned he had to use to pay the rates and taxes on the stand.

'It was in 1938 that my dad realised he could no longer afford to pay these rates and taxes, and that whether or not the magistrates' court was built, he would eventually have to sell the stand, and the business. And I think this realisation made him ill. For the first time in his life, my father was too ill to go to work.'

In 1938 my grandfather was in the second year of his BA at Wits, which he was doing with the intention of carrying on to study law. It was a brave new world after his strict boys-only high school. He had stimulating lecturers. He had his first proper girlfriend. He was a leading member of the dramatic society. He was deep in this exciting new chapter of his life when his father called him to his bedside and asked if he would look after the shop, just until his own health improved.

'And what could I say? There was no one else to do it. Len was already working as an attorney. Lily was married, she couldn't do it. So I had to. I switched to doing my BA part time, and I started to spend the better part of my day in Ferreira's Town, dispatching sacks of flour and sugar. I went to lectures either very early in the morning or else after work in the late afternoon.

'Although I had taken great interest in my father's work when I was a little boy, it now felt like a great drag. Sometimes, if I forgot to bring food from home, I would have to eat lunch with Mr Greenberg and his wife in their place behind the shop. I have vivid memories of both the smell and the dankness.

'Despite his misgivings about the medical profession, my dad saw a doctor, who visited the house with his black bag and did the usual checks and things, and said he had high blood pressure, that he needed to relax, to take a holiday. Holidays, of course, being something else he didn't believe in. Which I suppose confirmed what he'd thought about doctors anyway.

'Still, ultimately we prevailed upon him to do what the doctor had suggested, and get away, and he and my mother and grandmother went to Durban for two weeks.

'When they returned from holiday, he was still not well enough to work. What he liked to do was to spend time playing with his first grandchild. The year before, my sister had had a son, Michael. I've told you the story of the night Michael was born. Even though my dad wasn't feeling well, he still liked to crawl around on the floor with this little chap.

'A few months later, at the beginning of October, a man made him an offer for the stand. It was a decent offer, though nothing like what he'd dreamed he would get. But he knew he had to accept it. And he was heartbroken about it. Because that was, really, the sole way that he could ever see of helping us to live an easy life.

'All that was left was for him to sign the deed of sale. Len did a lot of property work, and a short while later the three of us went off to Loveday Street, and Len's office, so that he could sign the deed. I went with them. I don't know why I did, but I did.

'By the time we arrived there, my dad was feeling faint. He sat down while Len took the deed papers out and put them on the table. Len showed him where to sign his name, gave him the pen. Then my dad leaned over the table and signed. And once he had signed it, he collapsed onto the floor.

'We called an ambulance, and my brother said to me, "Go straight to the hospital, and I'll be there in a minute." And I sat with my dad in the ambulance while Len followed in his car. He had had a stroke. A bad stroke. And he died three days later. Of high blood pressure and a broken heart.'

Slowly turning his head to the left now, away from me, my grandfather appeared to be looking impatiently through the glass sliding door, as if he were waiting for someone who should have arrived by now.

When I played this tape back later I could hear, during these long moments, a very faint sound of scraping, like someone dragging a spade along tar. I didn't hear it at the time; all I was aware of then was the sound of our breathing.

At last he looked back at me and said, 'You know, one thing I will tell you is this. That my personal philosophy is one in which I don't have much room for regret. I'm not a person who has regrets about things. I don't, for example, say oh, if I'd done *this* everything would have been better. Had I bought this share when I was told to buy it, we would have had a lot of money. If I'd done this, or done that … Those kinds of thoughts are completely fruitless and a waste of time. They don't for me have any profit whatsoever. But you know, I do have one feeling of real, serious regret.'

He was still looking at me.

'It was just before I wrote the final exams at Wits in 1938. My dad had come back from Durban, and he had gone back to bed. He hadn't been feeling well at all. I went into the bedroom to see him, and we spoke about one thing and another. I asked him about his holiday and so forth. And then he said to me, "Well, how is it going with your studies?"

'Now, instead of saying to him, "No, it's fine Dad, don't worry about it" – instead of saying that – I said, "Well Dad, how do you expect me to do my work when I have to look after the shop?"'

The hurt in my grandfather's eyes was fresh. He was looking right at me. Did he want me to say something? Did he want me to tell him that, yes, that was a terrible thing to say? If so, I didn't know how to do that.

'Now that is a very distressing thing to say, you know,' he added. All of a sudden he looked his age, sitting there, old and small in the chair. In his lap was the piece of paper, his list, which he hadn't looked at once.

'That must have been a very distressing thing for him to hear,' he said. 'And I've often had deep regrets about that.'

Something had returned to his voice now: some distance, some veneer of retrospect. Whatever that thing is we need to survive our own lives.

There followed a postscript. How they'd had to sell the house in Yeoville because his mother wouldn't live in it without his father. How they'd sold the piano, and the dining-room table with its heavily carved legs, and the chairs. And how they had moved, the three of them – his mother and his younger brother Bernard and him – to a block of flats called Daventry Court in the neighbourhood of Killarney.

That afternoon, a Saturday, was the first time I'd been in the Cave by myself. My laptop was broken so I thought I'd do the transcribing there. It was pitch dark when I arrived, and spooky, until I turned the lights on and it became bright and spooky.

With no breaks I typed for about four hours. There had been other stories that day: the story of Guy Fawkes in Yeoville; the story of Mrs Mendelowitz, his mother's friend, and her great fear of his dog, Spotty; of the night his sister gave birth to her first child, Michael. I got about two-thirds of the way through, and was approaching the story of his father's death, when I realised it was getting late, and decided to come back to finish it off the next day.

I drove home as evening fell, feeling a twilight in me, too. A person's one real regret; I didn't know what to do with that. Was his regret part of the main story, or was it a story on its own?

From my balcony I looked down at my parents' office, empty in the gathering darkness. I thought about how, unless I needed his help, I never went to see my father there. I didn't like seeing him like that: bent over his laptop, his broad back straining against the fabric of his work shirt. I had it in my head that his destiny was to be a farmer, a man of the land, and I'd imagine his mind rumbling in distant fields as he typed out his press releases.

The next day, after running some errands, I went back to the Cave to type out the last few stories, including the one about my great-grandfather's death. While the pain of yesterday's recording session still sat in my chest and made my legs feel hollow, today on the screen, chasing the cursor, the words seemed inert and dry as dust. The story wasn't there. I didn't know what this was. I wanted the words to communicate the feeling of those moments, but they didn't, and I didn't know who or what to blame. I just wanted to be finished now. I was bored with typing: hitting the same keys over and over, going back all the time to correct mistakes. When I'd typed out the last word, pressed the last full stop, I was only too pleased to be done with it. I hit SAVE and then PRINT. It was about four pm, still time to get in a run. I needed to move my body after all this sitting. With the pages of the document still warm in my backpack, I quickly locked up, and I was relieved to drive out of the underground garage into the pale winter sunshine.

Isaac and Ida Browde with Annie Meyers (centre), Durban, 1938

chapter eight
an interlude

*In which we meet three grandparents
through the eyes of a child*

The waters of time have covered the land of the past. Beneath the surface, like iridescent strips of cloth, suspended, are memories, swayed when you put your hand in the water. To look without touching is a practised skill. Too tempting, in the long afternoon, to reach in, stir, and watch from above as the luminous strips move lazily in their suspension, the spiral and the wave, releasing elemental images – an old man by a window, a tall grey tree, a narrow passage that runs through the middle of a house.

Near one end of the passage is my bedroom. My parents' bedroom is close by (though not close enough). Emma, my little sister, sleeps in a cot in their room. We have moved from Cape Town to this city, which is called Johannesburg. Ma still lives in Cape Town in her flat made of orange bricks. When I talk to Ma on the phone I feel like crying. This is called *missing someone.*

Johannesburg is where Nana and Bronco live. Nana is my dad's mother and Bronco is his father. Bronco is called *Bronco* because Emma called him that when she tried to say *Grandpa.* And Nana didn't want to be called Granny. Sometimes we go over to their house for Friday night supper, though mostly they come to us. Usually the time we go to their house is on one of the days of the weekend, which is two days in a row when I don't go to school and my dad doesn't go to work and we can all do whatever we like.

Nana and Bronco are still to me like characters in a book. Bronco, with his thin silver moustache and silver hair, is a good-hearted pirate, broad-souled, experienced in adventure. Nana is harder to see in one go. She is a layered and complicated character, capable of deep magic. Even when she talks in the day it sounds as if she is talking at night.

Their house is a different type of house from ours. It has more zones and each zone has its own peculiar atmosphere. The best is the lounge. This is not a room for children to play in and maybe that's why I like it most: it makes me feel serious and intrepid. I enjoy the scratchy knitted texture of the couches and the low glass table with books on it and the interesting objects that are all around. One object in particular delights me: a small flat square of tough glass with oils of different colours trapped inside – brown oil, golden oil and clear oil like the white of an egg. The oils never mix, even if you hold it upside down or on its side. They just swirl with satisfying slowness in their peculiar two-dimensional world.

The other zone that entices me is the garden: it is expansive, acutely beautiful and rotten, an alternate dimension where fairies dance with hobgoblins all sharp-toothed and green-skin scary in the powerful flowerbeds of colour.

I know it is *their* house – as in, it belongs to both Bronco and Nana – but while my grandmother seems part of its unending mystery, my grandfather stands to one side of it, administrating casually with his tongue in his cheek.

I see him as crisply distinct from his surroundings, wherever he is. He seems to step lightly through the world, like one of those long-legged insects that can walk on the surface of the water. I see him stand at the edges of the pockets of grown-up conversation. I hear him comment on conversations rather than get lost in them. But when I think about Nana, I see her deep in a conversation, deep in the mystery of a dappled tree shadow.

Something I know about her is that she is a special kind of doctor, a doctor for people with cancer. Cancer kills you; she uses beams of radiation to save your life. This information, and the sense I make of it, must have something to do with the spells she seems capable of.

It takes me backwards along a thin black thread to Cape Town, to Ma's flat, where my mother would leave me when she went to university and also, sometimes, in the night, when, for reasons I didn't even try to understand, my parents went out without me.

In the afternoons Ma would take me downstairs to see the squirrels on the lawn, and at night she would sit me in her soft lap and read to me in her low sing-song voice.

Ma was safety in the boundless day and in the duplicitous night, but there was a room in her flat I deeply feared. The room where the photograph albums were, and where the squirrel-shaped nutcracker perched on a shelf beside a framed picture of a man's smiling face. I knew him, or they said I did, but this black-and-white photograph was already more real to me than any pictures I could find of him in my mind. This man was Oups, who was my mother's father. He was already dead from cancer and that is why Ma lived alone.

The route from our house to Nana and Bronco's house takes us along the edge of the golf course, down the giant slope of Osborne Road and then up and around the enormous block that is like a park with its trees and birds – until we get to their road: Third Avenue.

Sometimes my grandfather comes out to greet us. He stands outside the front door with his hands behind his back and a big smile on his face. If he doesn't do that, it means he is working. I know where to find him then.

This is the only place where he seems to melt into the world around him. Where there is no difference between the outside air and the breath in his soul. Where the strange, soft underwater light that touches objects is the same as that streaming from his eyes. It is the last room off the passage before you get to the kitchen. It is a room engulfed by books. It is Bronco's study, and this is where I often find him working when we go there, even on weekends when we go there to swim.

From the doorway I watch him. He sits at his desk, looking down at a neat stack of papers, reading and occasionally writing something with a pen.

When he senses that I am there, he looks up, turns his face to me, and smiles. Never once in all the years does he make me feel as if I'm disturbing him. By then he must have been more to me than a silver-haired pirate or the disinterested administrator of some remote district. I have come to find a real person in here, someone I know will be happy to see me.

'Hello, laddie,' he says.

Then he either asks me to come sit down in one of the other cane-and-metal chairs and talk to him, or else he uses my arrival as a cue to take a break from his work.

I like it when he takes a break, but I also like sitting with him, talking to him in that solemn room. He asks me questions: *How is school going? Am I reading any books?* Sometimes I look past his head at the rows of books behind him. I know these books are not ordinary. They have to do with his work, which is the Law. The light in the room tickles their beetle-black spines.

If he gets up and comes with me to find the others we'll usually stop off at a tiny, dark cube of a room just across the passage from his study. This room has a small fridge in it and he'll fetch me a ginger ale and say, 'There we go, my lad' – and then we'll go to find the rest of them, down at the pool.

The swimming pool is at the bottom of a little slope of lawn, which is always in shade under the branches of the enormous tree. It is a long rectangular pool with a border of copper-red bricks, about three-quarters of a metre wide, around its perimeter. Swimming is one of my favourite activities. I especially like it when one or more of the grown-ups swims with me. Each has a different style of swimming, which I study for clues to the mystery of adulthood. My mother does a careful breast-stroke with her face out of the water to protect her contact lenses. When my father swims, I ask him to pick me up and throw me, which he does; and I break the surface with a breathless splash. He also teaches me what to do if someone should ever try to drown me. I take these lessons very seriously, and swim *down and away* from the drowner's hand. Nana hardly ever swims, because she has a *phobia* – which means a fear – of putting her face in water. But she likes to sit near the pool, and read and watch us swim. When Bronco eases himself into the pool at the shallow end he says, '*Oops, oops, aaah* ...' and then he glides around with lots of concentration for a brief time, opening his eyes wide and blowing bubbles just beneath the water's surface.

On his chest are a few little purple-red spots, raised slightly from his skin. When I ask my mother about these she explains that they are natural things that you get on your body when you get to Bronco's age. She says they are *age spots*. I notice she has some discoloration on her forearms too, but little pale patches, not red dots.

After he has dried himself with his towel, Bronco often walks back up to the house, back to his study. But there are also lots of times when he stays with us late into the fading afternoon. I can see he enjoys being there with us. He says things to my father about me, and I pretend I don't hear them, but I do. I like what he says: things like, 'Isn't he a lovely little chap?'

It makes me happy to hear these words. I am not only welcome as a full citizen of this many-dimensioned district, I am esteemed and celebrated here. This house extends my personal world.

Close to the pool is a simple structure with a thatched roof and a brick floor – a pool house, I suppose – open on one side, the pool side. On the far side of this structure is an area with no grass, only some dapple-shadowed dirt, moist with a natural sheen and strewn with leaves and petals, and behind it the low woven-wire fence that separates their property from their neighbour's.

Sitting in my one-person flat, twenty-five years later, all I see when I think of that fence is a wall of light, white light, catching in the leaves and flowers just beyond it. My childhood world is extended, but not infinitely so. There is an end to it, and that fence is the end. Beyond that fence, even my mysteriously powerful grandfather no longer has any jurisdiction. Beyond that fence are unimaginable creatures and things – maybe even Death itself. I can give no thought to it then, to what lies beyond the fence, because I do not know how to think about it. It intrigues and frightens me. Beyond that fence are total strangers.

THE STREET

Interview 2
Date recorded: 30/04/2005

One side of Page Street, our side, was almost entirely Jewish – apart from the Creewels, who lived next door to us, and another family that lived just up the road from us. The Egans. The Egans were known as 'Boots', because for some reason they all wore knee-high boots.

On the other side of the street were quite a few Christian families. I remember the Taylors, the Sims, the Ogilvys and the Luckins. Doug Taylor played the saxophone and WH Ogilvy was the South African amateur golf champion. He had two daughters whose names I can still recall.

Now there's a story I'd like to tell you about Mr Ogilvy. One day he came down the road and stopped at our gate. Some of my friends and I were playing on the little lawn in front of our house. He was carrying a golf club and a golf ball. He'd obviously been practising somewhere and was stopping in to see my parents on his way home.

We asked him about golf and he started talking to us about it. He said that you had to have an absolutely *automatic* swing. We asked him what that meant. He said, 'Here, I'll show you,' and he came through the gate.

Now you might find this difficult to believe, but he told me to lie down on the ground, which I did: I lay down on my back. He then pulled a matchbox out of his trouser pocket and placed it on my forehead, and on top of the matchbox he balanced the golf ball. I watched as he took his stance above me and did a little waggle of the wrists. I held my breath as he lifted the club high above his head and took a *full swing* at the ball, sending it sailing into oblivion. Which ... well, thank heavens he didn't take a divot, because if he *had*, I wouldn't be here telling you this story.

But now, *as* he did that, my mother happened to come out of the front door and, seeing me lying flat on my back on the ground and this man standing over me with a golf club, she fainted. She thought I was dead.

There was ultimately a big to-do between Mr Ogilvy and my mother over this, because she said that what he had done was highly irresponsible, which of course it was. But Ogilvy was a very charming man, and he said, 'No, no. There was no danger at all.' He would never have done it, he said, if there was any chance that I might have been hurt. So ultimately it was smoothed over. But I remember that my mother had to be resuscitated with smelling salts.

Next door to the Ogilvys lived the Luckins. MJ Luckin had come to this country from Scotland and could best be described as looking like a rather large bear. He had a lot of hair and a big bushy moustache. And Luckin was interested in two things. The first was cricket. He wrote two books about cricket in South Africa in the decade after the First World War, which are viewed by experts as the definitive accounts of the sport in that era. The other thing he was interested in was chess, and he would play whenever he could find somebody to play with him.

One day my father went over to his house and asked him if he would teach *me* to play. Luckin said of course he would. So I'd often go over to his house after school and he would teach me chess. He had a marvellous set of chessmen. The standard shapes, but of a tall and heavy sort, with green felt underneath each piece. He also had a large wooden board. I spent a lot of time with Mr Luckin as a result. Not his sons, who were around my age, but with him. And he was such a fine teacher that I have loved chess ever since. Mr Luckin taught me not only to love *playing* chess, but also to respect it as a game that requires, among other things, the ability to concentrate for long periods and to think laterally.

So, you see, we had quite a neighbourhood there. As I've mentioned, our next-door neighbour was a man by the name of Creewel. Old Man Creewel was an engineer, a captain on the mines, and he went to work on a motorcycle. My memory of waking up every morning is the sound of Creewel's motorcycle. He would start it up next door, in the lane, and wake us all as he left for work.

There were also one or two Jewish families who lived on the other side of the street, the Christian side. One of these was the Mendelowitz family, who lived on the corner of Page Street and Kenmere Road. I remember Mrs Mendelowitz was very keen on my mother, and used to seek her out for company. Mrs Mendelowitz was a large woman who always wore a hat with a pin in it. I remember her phoning up our house and asking to speak to me.

I would say, 'Hello, Mrs Mendelowitz.'

And she would say, 'Please Julian, I want to come and visit your mother. Please hold Spotty.'

Spotty was our dog, a little black-and-white fox terrier. A terrific animal, but very excitable. So I would hold Spotty while Mrs Mendelowitz came to visit my mother.

On Sunday mornings we often had a visitor. How this fellow became friendly with my folks, I don't know, but his name was Lipiansky, an unmarried man who played the violin. He was a dapper chap: he wore spats and was always well dressed. He came to our house every Sunday morning with his violin and a sprig of peppercorn in one hand.

Page Street was not tarred, by the way. It was still a dirt road in those days, with a few of these peppercorn trees planted here and there. The municipality had planted these trees in various parts of town, and Yeoville was one. So Lipiansky would always arrive at our house with a peppercorn sprig.

And my father would say to him, *'Nu, Lippy?'* So, Lippy? He called him Lippy. My dad also referred to him as Lipianer. That's the way some people used to address each other in those days – *Italianer, Lipianer.* And Lipianer used to come along to our house and play the violin, and my mother would play the piano, and we all used to sing. We had sheet music of the times and we used to sing the words of the songs. My mother played the piano very well to the end of her days.

Something that is interesting to me now is that there were two people who worked for our family at that time. One I knew as Bessie Nagel. Bessie Nagel was a young Afrikaans woman who worked as a sort of a general factotum: cooking, looking after the children, making sandwiches for school and cleaning the house. She had a small bedroom of her own at the back of the house.

Also working for us then was a man by the name of Solomon. Quite an elderly African man, with a wizened face. He did the cleaning of the kitchen and the polishing of the floors. Things of that nature.

I remember that on occasion my mother would ask me, 'Where's your father?'

And I would say, 'He's in the room with Solomon.' Solomon's room was in an outbuilding to our house.

My mom would say, 'What's he doing in the room?'

And I'd say, 'He's having tea with Solomon.'

My father would sit and talk to Solomon for hours. I remember that Solomon had a brother, and that my father would ask after his brother. He also learned a lot of Solomon's language from him, and as a result my father could speak it quite well. I believe, although I am not sure, that it was Sotho. I remember he used to speak to Jantjie, an employee at his work, in the language he learned from Solomon.

My father would sometimes say to me, 'Write a special for Solomon. He's going into town.'

A 'special' meant a special *pass*, a pass to the police, which read as follows: 'Please pass' – and these are the precise words – 'Please pass boy Solomon from six am to seven pm on such and such a date. He is going to town and coming back.' That's it: 'Please pass boy Solomon.' Either for a period during the day, or for a few days: whenever he was going and coming back.

I'd ask him, 'When will you be coming back?'

And he'd say, 'I'll be back tonight.'

And then I would write him a pass for a period from the morning till the night. If he said no, he wants to go stay with his brother tonight, then I'd write it for him from seven pm to seven am the following morning.

Please pass boy Solomon. I remember it so well.

It is a commentary on our history that I would write that, when I think about it now. As a twelve-year-old boy I would write that. When my dad said, 'Write a special for Solomon,' I would write, 'Please pass boy Solomon,' and not think much about it, and Solomon would thank me for writing it. He would then put it in his pocket and go off. He'd be stopped by police now and then, and he would pull out his special pass and hand it over, and the police would let him go because he was in possession of a note written by a twelve-year-old boy. And you know, I didn't have a conscience about this. I was brought up in it and I never, not until much later, felt anything serious about it.

Isaac and Len Browde in Page Street, circa 1926
'It was still a dirt road in those days, with a few of these
peppercorn trees planted here and there.'

chapter nine

In which the young storyteller tries his hand at telling other people's stories, and finds it a very complicated business

Between the day we recorded the story of his father's death and our next session, two months passed. I told myself, at first, that this was because we were both busy. Prof. Kariithi was determined to cram as much as he could into our heads before giving us over to the company, so I was working all day, and late every night, finishing his assigned readings, writing essays and doing newsgathering exercises all over the city. My grandfather was busy too, going in to his office at the City hall three or four days a week. I also knew he was using his spare time to read about the war. That was what we were supposed to do next, record his war stories. He said he still had a good idea of it, but wanted to be sure, and so was checking his memories against dates and maps in various books he had.

There was another reason for the break though, one that was difficult to admit to myself. Something about this exercise was not sitting right. It felt contaminated with murky ambitions. I was not sure what I was implicating him in. So I tried to concentrate on the internship and forget for a time about this complicated journey we'd begun.

Then one Saturday afternoon it could no longer be avoided. I was over at their house and sitting, for a change, with my grandmother. We were talking about nothing in particular, just *catching up* – an expression she likes to use, and something she likes to set aside special time for.

Talking to my grandmother can be a disarming experience: unlike most people, she doesn't switch between two different parts of her brain in a conversation depending on whether it's her turn to talk or to listen. All the time she is only trying to *make sense* – *with* her words and *of* yours. She considers words, spoken or heard, carefully. She takes them for things to point and show, not hide and deceive. So, if you're up for it, she is an easy person to talk to, even if you risk being taken at your word.

When the subject of the recordings came up, she said, 'You know, I've been meaning to tell you ...' Her dark eyes shone; she was excited to share something with me. 'I've thought of a name for the book! You ought to call it *War Stories and Law Stories.*'

'What book?' I said, suddenly feeling as if the interviews were some sacred ground that I had to protect. She looked slightly confused. 'Who said anything about a book?' I asked her.

I could feel myself trying to make her recognise how crazy, how *wrong*, her assumption was, and as soon as I closed my mouth I regretted the way I'd spoken to her. But before I could apologise I noticed that she had retreated into a shell, and was regarding me carefully from a private recess where she does her most sensitive calculations. Then she closed her eyes and nodded, slowly. Once, and then again. She was letting me know that she *got it*. And when she opened her eyes it was plain that she was looking at me from a brand new perspective.

This exchange stayed with me for days. Needless to say, I felt like a brat and a charlatan. What was I listening out for if not material for a book? What except guilt had charged the shrill indignity of my response? Whatever she'd *got* I clearly still needed to get.

But the more I considered what had happened, the less I worried about that and the more I thought about her, about her quest to assimilate new information, to build her life from the flow and the changes. I thought about her in a way I seldom did: as a professor of medicine, a world-renowned oncologist. She was – she *is* – a scientist. Through and through. This in turn caused me to worry about something else. I pictured her face in the doorway: apart from its childlike expression of curiosity there was also something else, something I hadn't wanted to see. She as much as anyone else had wanted me to do these interviews, but here she was, forced to crack open a door that had shut her out. Was *this* what I saw mixed into the child's curiosity, the pain at being left out? The small tectonic inconsistency these thoughts stirred turned into a violent shudder in my heart. *Why I was getting his stories down and not hers?*

Aftershocks followed over the next few days and nights as the question came back to me from different and increasingly uncomfortable angles. Eventually I managed, by some bogus arithmetic, to settle the disturbance. She was seven years younger than he was, so I told myself that, as long as I didn't take more than seven years to get down his stories, I would have enough time to get hers down afterwards.

One of the reasons, I reckoned, no one had ever said, 'You should get your grandmother's stories down,' is that, as far as anybody was concerned, she didn't *have* stories – she just had a life. It was a life packed with incident and achievement, a life as rich and varied and instructive as any you can imagine, but in her *telling* of it it remained as raw and ragged as a half-chewed bone. My grandmother tells stories according to the way she is: continuously trying to understand. So, as she recounts an incident, she can't help trying to make sense of the original experience, and it can sometimes sound as if she herself is hearing the story for the first time.

I came to recognise this in my own clumsy way of telling. I am more of a dog's-bone type of storyteller than your smooth-pebble man. Of course I could see how this wasn't *all* bad. I saw that it could stop a person from arriving at conclusions too soon. But I did wonder – as Prof. Kariithi said his reluctant goodbyes, and we were despatched to do our first rotations – if it would get in the way of my day-to-day work as a reporter.

In a news article you are supposed to use the Inverted Pyramid method: start with the Main Point, clearly expressed – what happened, where, when, et cetera – and then elaborate, tapering down from there (as if creating an upside-down pyramid of meaning) to the non-essential elements. But I was often not sure what the Main Point was, especially if something had only just happened, and so I was seldom sure where a story began, or ended.

Our first 'live' story was an investigative piece for the *Sunday Times*. (I was on a roving team with three of the other interns.) A doctor in a hospital on the East Rand had allegedly botched an operation on a little boy, and the kid had died. A few days later, the surgeon, a man from the Democratic Republic of Congo, had disappeared, and it subsequently turned out that he didn't have the necessary papers to practise in South Africa. The headline seemed to write itself, some combination of ALIEN, BUTCHERS, CHILD, MISSING. But the more we looked into it, the muddier it all seemed, and by the end of the week I knew that the story the paper wanted us to tell – the story a part of me wanted to tell – was the wrong story. The *real* story, as far as I could see, needed time: time to research, time to understand and time to tell. But time was what nobody had. Besides, a knotty piece about bureaucracy in the health department was not going to win us the front page. In the toxic heat of the Saturday newsroom our discussions with Prof. Kariithi seemed a world away. It was a tiring and confusing experience, and I was relieved when our hedged article was relegated to a sidebar on Page 3.

The rest of that month was no less tiring or confusing. Even when I was more convinced of a story's merits, I found it difficult to research and write anything so quickly. No matter what the assignment was, I felt rushed and anxious and invariably disappointed with the result. So when Paddi sent round a group email at the end of July to say that *Business Day* was short of subeditors, I wrote back almost immediately to say I'd be happy to spend a rotation helping out. (Paddi told me later that I was the only intern who replied.)

The following Monday she took me to meet the chief subeditor at *Business Day*, an athletic-looking woman with wraparound glasses and a forceful stride. After we had all smiled and shaken hands, Paddi left and the chief led me to a chair at the long bank of desks in the middle of the newsroom. It was about ten in the morning and only two or three of the others subs were there. She pointed to what for the next two months would be my computer, my landline and my set of drawers.

Only having to arrive at work once the reporters had started to file stories – at about two in the afternoon – meant a fertile swathe of time opened up in front of me: the mornings of my week. After a few days of subbing I realised that this was going to be a good time to do some of the things I'd been putting off. One of these – I finally admitted to myself – was setting up another recording session with my grandfather.

Though he and I had spoken several times in the past few weeks about getting started with the war stories, I had not yet suggested a date. But I was restless rather than unwilling. So, still not sure what to do with everything on my mind, I phoned him and proposed that we meet the following Wednesday morning.

It was 10 August 2005. A cold overcast day in late winter. He met me at the front door with a big kiss on my cheek. 'How are you, my lad?'

'Good, Broncs. And you?'

'All right, I think. Come on in.'

I walked past him, out of the chill. He closed the door behind us and followed me into the house. The heater was on and the entrance lounge was warm and smelled slightly of gas. The TV was on too, tuned to BBC World News, but the sound was down.

I swung my backpack off my shoulder and put it down next to the longer couch, deciding that the smell of gas was not too potent.

He sat down on the right-hand side of the shorter one. 'So?' he said. 'What can you tell me?'

I told him about subediting. I explained it using the janitorial terms I'd come to like: mopping, sweeping, polishing. I told him about the unusual hours, that I actually didn't mind them.

'Oh, that sounds marvellous,' he said. 'You're really learning how the whole thing operates.'

I nodded. I liked that; I hadn't thought about it in that way.

The glow from the open doorway to the lounge told me where he'd been sitting before I arrived. The sight filled me with an unexpected sense of anticipation.

Before we went through, I went to see my grandmother in her study. She was standing next to a wooden trunk under the window, looking through some papers from the accumulated piles on the trunk.

'Hi, Nan.'

'Oh, hi Dan.'

When I asked her how she was, she raised her eyebrows and held them there. It's another running joke: her other battle, this room with its endless piles of paper.

'I've made *huge* progress here,' she said, teasingly triumphant. 'I've managed to clear most of it away.'

I cast my eyes around and smiled. It looked more or less the same to me, maybe a little bit better. That was the joke.

'So?' she said. 'What's up?'

I told her a little about the subbing: the polishing, the odd hours. Said I had taken well to the whole thing. She stood as if frozen, papers aloft, all ears. She asked about the people I was working with. I told her about Claire and Phil, the subs who sat on either side of me, the ones who were showing me the ropes. I told her they seemed really intelligent and interesting although I hadn't got to know them well yet. There was no time – there never will be time – to tell her everything she wanted to know.

I said, 'I'll tell you more about it later.'

'Yes, you must. You're coming to us on Friday night, aren't you?'

'I'm not sure.'

'I'll speak to your mom,' she said.

She hadn't turned the light on and the room was dim; a diffuse radiance lit the square window behind her. 'You're going to record some more of Bronco's stories?' she asked.

'Yes,' I said.

I thought of telling her about my plan to record her stories, but it felt flimsy to say it just then. So I just said, 'Yes,' and I found bold encouragement in the smile she gave me.

'Okay, Nan,' I said.

'See you, Dan.'

'Okay,' I said again, but this time I just mouthed the word to myself. She had already returned, her whole mind, to the papers in her hand, to her task and to her vigil.

On my way to his study to fetch the big books, I put my head into the lounge. He was in his chair already, head bent over a thick book open in his lap. On the thin-legged table beside him was another book, this one shut, its pages marked with scraps of yellow paper. I felt a swell of wellbeing. The sad rush of newspaper reporting had made me appreciate something that could unfurl according to its own weight and in its own time.

A few minutes later I had the dictaphone back on its stack of books. The two war volumes he'd been looking at, feverish with placemarks, lay side by side on the low glass table in the middle of the room. He steepled his fingers and gathered his thoughts. He'd made a new list (not of stories, as it turned out, but of places), which he'd folded up and put in his lap. It took me months to put my finger on the relief I felt then. To realise the pure physics of it, the magnetism of a story under way. I leaned forward and pushed the switch to REC. The dictaphone came to life, its tiny wheels revolving, cogs turning bigger wheels inside me. Settling back into the couch, I felt myself being pulled in, carried across into a parallel world, a secret plot, a Once Upon a Time.

DENTON'S UNIFORM

Interview 7
Date recorded: 10/08/2005

By that time – and I'm talking now about the beginning of 1940 – Smuts's government had created in Johannesburg, in common with many other large cities throughout the Commonwealth, an infrastructure dedicated to recruiting young men into the armed forces. The City hall was the headquarters of this infrastructure. They had a whole setup outside there: flags and banners and bunting strung from the pillars, great loudspeakers playing *There Will Always Be an England* and other songs of that nature, and at the top of the steps a table where young men were signing up to join the army in increasingly large numbers.

Now you must understand: I had written the final exams of my BA in November the year before. The war broke out in September of 1939, and those last few months of 1939 were what Churchill would later call The Phoney War – a tentative time of waiting and watching on either side. Like many others, I thought it would all be over quickly. Guided by hope more than anything else, I suppose, we thought that Hitler would soon capitulate and things would return to normal. Especially as one country after the next, including our own, joined the alliance against him.

But, by now, certain things had to be faced. First, Hitler wasn't going to give back the territories he had annexed. In fact he would take *more* if he could. Second, he was going to be more than a match for the Allies. If the war against Germany was to be won, and even that did not seem certain, it was going to be a long war with many sacrifices.

So when I started my LLB in February of 1940, aged twenty, I did so with a sense that I might not finish it. It is difficult to describe to you how things felt at that time. Nothing seemed certain; everything felt temporary, up in the air.

In those days you could do your LLB part time, and that was what I did. I attended lectures in the morning and evening, and for the rest – because I needed to earn a bit of cash and thinking it the right thing to do – I worked as an articled clerk at my brother's firm of attorneys in town.

As a clerk I did a lot of filing, errands, things of that nature. Len did a lot of property work (transfer deeds and that sort of thing), and so every day I would walk up from Winchester House on Loveday Street, where their offices were, to the High Court on President Street, where the deeds office was. I would walk down Loveday Street to Market Street, and then across the front of the City hall.

So it happened that every day I passed the recruiting station, and every day I asked myself what I was waiting for. The longer the war went on, the more the filing of papers for the transfer of property seemed a meaningless and inappropriate thing for me to be doing.

My friend Dov and I used to talk about joining the army. (By the way, the story of Dov Judelowitz and his family is one I haven't mentioned yet, and you must remind me to do so. Dov and I had been brought up like brothers in Yeoville. His father was a Hebrew teacher, and I got to know them very well. There were about seven kids and they lived on the smell of an oil rag. There was perpetual fighting between father and mother in that house. And it was really a very sad home. So Dov used to spend most of his life at our house, which was a comparatively happy place.)

Dov and I used to say that when we joined it would be in the Transvaal Scottish. The Transvaal Scottish was a very famous infantry battalion that had a wonderful record from the First World War. Moreover, our high school, King Edward VII, had close ties with this battalion, so it made sense for us to join. But, while we often spoke about it between ourselves and with some of our other friends, we hadn't joined, and we were not quite able to say what was preventing us from doing so. Which brings me to the story I wanted to tell you.

In April of that year, 1940, I went to a farewell party for Harry Greenberg. Harry was one of the younger brothers of Phil Greenberg, who had married my sister, Lily. Harry had joined the Transvaal Scottish, and was being sent to a military base in East Africa. These, by the way, were some of the first troops Smuts sent out of the country. They were going up to help the British drive the Italians out of East Africa. Remember: Mussolini had signed the Pact of Steel with Hitler in 1939.

I felt very uncomfortable that night. Harry was just a year older than I was, and I couldn't help wondering what he and others at the party thought of me. Here was Harry, dressed in the uniform of the regiment – a beret and a sporran and spats, all of that – going off to fight. And here I was. I had come to his farewell party with my mother. Harry was very nice to me about it. He didn't ask me about my own plans, as some other fellows might have. We simply had a drink together and I wished him well. But once I got home that night I lay in bed unable to sleep, feeling awful.

The next day, when I passed the recruiting station, I spent a longer time there than usual, observing what was happening. And day after day I continued to pass there, until I just couldn't do it any more. It couldn't have been more than about a week, maybe ten days, after the party; I was passing by there and I finally admitted it: I had become ashamed of myself. And when I got back to the office I phoned Dov. Dov was doing the same thing I was, by the way, just at another firm of attorneys. I said I thought the time had come. I remember how my heart was racing. I said something to the effect that it was now or never. Dov agreed. There were two other guys we'd been talking to, friends of ours – Boris Margau and Jock Isacowitz – and in the next few days we put the position to them. And finally we all decided we were going to join.

Of course when I told my mother about our plans, she was terribly upset. She didn't want me to do this. I suppose I'd known she would feel that way, but we had never spoken about it. I think she had been too scared to broach the subject. Now she pleaded with me, crying. She said, 'What do you know about fighting in a war?' She'd lost my dad eighteen months before and she didn't want to lose me.

I told her that this was just something I had to do. It was difficult for me to explain to her how much it now meant to me to be part of the war effort – but I tried. News had filtered through on the radio of the tremendous threat that now existed that the Germans would conquer the world.

This of course also meant something for the future of the Jews, in Europe and beyond. We had some idea of Hitler's feelings towards the Jews. I've told you how my mother was so concerned by what she'd heard, that in 1936 she had travelled from England through Nazi-controlled Germany to see her family in Poland. And I've told you about Norman Lourie, who started the Habonim youth movement, and how he had sensed even earlier – in the early 1930s – that Europe was no longer a safe place for Jews. Of course we didn't know the full extent of it until much later. My mother was still not happy about it, but in some way I think she understood.

Funnily enough, I never discussed it with my brother, Len, nor he with me. I never questioned his decision not to go himself. He was already married by then and in a different stage of his life. But I felt that he understood my attitude and quietly admired it.

A day or so later I went to the university to deregister – a lot of us were doing this – and to tell one of my law professors, Professor McKerron. I recall how McKerron came out from behind his desk and took my hand and said, 'You are doing the right thing, my boy.'

That was just one of the responses, by the way, from people staying behind. There were people, like McKerron, who encouraged us. (He, by the way, later joined the army himself.) There were others who thought we were bloody stupid, doing something unnecessarily dangerous. But we who were going believed we could make a contribution, even if it was a small one.

That same week, when I was still tying up some other loose ends, I was walking, as usual, past the recruiting station at the City hall, when I heard someone call my name.

I looked back and saw a fellow dressed in a smart barathea uniform (a well-tailored tunic and long trousers, which had obviously been made to measure for him), a Sam Browne belt, and a peaked cap. It was Denton. Phillip Denton. He had been at King Edward's at the same time I was there, though a few years ahead of me. I remembered him well: a handsome chap, about my height. Well, he looked very dapper. He shook my hand and said, 'Jules! Good to see you. How are you doing?'

I said, 'I'm doing fine.'

Then we stood talking there at the bottom of the steps. He said, 'Well? When are you going to join?'

He had been in the army before the war, in the Active Citizen Force. He was interested in being a soldier, you see, which I had never been.

I said to him, 'Well, we're actually talking about it right now.'

He said, 'Good. So what are you joining?'

I told him about our plans to join the Transvaal Scottish.

He said, 'Jules, don't be crazy. The infantry is not for you.' And I remember his words: he said to me, 'A man with your ability and intelligence, you've got to join us in the artillery. It's a very interesting study. It requires mathematical knowledge, which you have. And you don't have to walk for miles like the infantry people do. You travel on *wheels,* man!'

When I got back to my brother's office that afternoon, I phoned Dov again. I said to him, 'Dov, listen. I've just been in touch with Phillip Denton,' and I reported what Denton had told me. And I said to Dov, 'There's one thing that I really think we ought to take into account. The uniform they give you in the artillery is really outstanding!'

Which shows you what I knew about the army. I knew exactly nothing.

But Dov, who knew about as much as I did, said, 'Is that so? All right, so let's join the artillery.' He said it nonchalantly, as if to say: Look, as long as we join *something.*

A week or so later we went down to the City hall to join the artillery, accompanied by Boris and Jock, both of whom were, I think, persuaded by my description of the uniform. We were greeted there by a sergeant who welcomed us all very warmly, and then sent us over to see the doctor.

The doctor said to me, 'Say, *Aah.*'

I opened my mouth, he looked, and he said, 'Oh my goodness me!' He said, 'Your tonsils. They'll have to come out.'

I said, 'Are you serious about it?'

'Absolutely,' he said.

They were desperate for soldiers at that stage, and there weren't many things that could disqualify you, but apparently having tonsils was one of them. So I went home and told my mother I was going to have my tonsils out. She was so upset about this, I can't tell you. Not only was I going off to fight in a war, I was going to have my tonsils out too. My mother suffered a lot more than I did during the war, I can tell you.

That afternoon I drove out to the Joubert Park nursing home. I had a little Vauxhall 10 that I went around with in those days. And I saw a doctor by the name of Popper. He said he could take my tonsils out the following morning. Which he did – under general anaesthetic.

And a few days later I went back, by myself this time, to see the doctor at the City hall.

He said, 'Say, *Aah*.'

I said, '*Aah*.' And he looked.

Then he looked in my ears. And he said, 'You're fine.'

I went over to the sergeant, who was sitting at his table, and I signed a piece of paper that said that I wanted to join the army, that I had permission from my parents, that sort of thing. This sergeant was very nice to me, you know, very friendly. With a big smile he said, 'You'll be fine. Everything will be fine.' And then once I'd signed everything, he told me that we should report to the Potchefstroom artillery school the following Monday morning.'

Oh, man, I remember this so clearly. I said to him, 'Sergeant, listen. Monday morning is difficult for me. Could we not make it later in the week?'

He looked at me as if I were completely mad. He wasn't smiling any more. Very slowly, very deliberately – to make sure I understood – he repeated himself: 'You will be there. Monday morning. Nine o'clock.'

That was the first bit of army discipline I had.

Very early on the Monday morning I picked Dov up and we went out to Potchefstroom, which is about seventy kilometres east of Johannesburg. We entered the grounds through a gate with a large arch, across which were emblazoned the words ARTILLERY SCHOOL. We then saw many bungalows and other buildings, some of which gave the impression of residential quarters for students like myself. There were large areas of open ground and a separate section as an ablution block. I parked my car alongside other cars on the one side of a field. It was now winter and very cold. The grass – what little grass there was – was a sort of pale-yellow stubble.

We immediately reported to a sergeant major who appeared to be in charge of the new recruits. This man welcomed us and told us which bungalow we should now regard as our home. He then referred us to a sergeant who was in charge of uniforms.

And what a letdown that was. The fact that Denton had two pips on his shoulder hadn't meant anything to me; I didn't know it meant he was an officer and was wearing an officer's uniform. Instead of the tailored barathea suit and Sam Browne belt that had so impressed me, we were given a rough khaki uniform: a khaki shirt with long sleeves, long khaki pants, a heavy khaki jacket and roughly-fitting brown boots. We put them on: clothes that made one look – and feel – like a convict. They had two sizes in the army: Too Big and Too Small. They gave me a uniform that was Too Big, and Dov got one that was Too Small. I will never forget the way Dov looked at me: puzzled, obviously recalling what I'd told him about the uniform. I shrugged. We knew as much about all this as the Man in the Moon.

From left to right:
Jules Browde, Ralph 'Jake' Jacobson and Dov Judelowitz, circa 1937
'All right, so let's join the artillery.'

chapter ten

*In which the young storyteller realises that the journey
is not quite what he thought it was*

One of the things I'd never *got* was how little the soldiers knew. I mean
the ordinary troops, they knew nothing – not until they had to. They
sailed east after they were told they'd be sailing north, and when they
asked why and where they were going, no one would tell them. So, to
distract themselves, they played chess and drank – in darkness and igno-
rance. They accidently blew each other up in practice drills. They turned
their trucks over in the desert. Because boys is all they were – teenagers,
or kids in their early twenties – terrified that the other side had a secret
weapon.

My grandfather painted a picture of war still not seen enough, a
picture of a 'children's crusade': of boys in ill-fitting uniforms, uncertain
and afraid; of terrible rumours rippling through the ranks; of opaque
authority issuing random instructions.

Many of the war stories he told concerned things that had happened
off the battlefield, stories set in the hours and days and weeks of waiting:
six soldiers grab a new recruit accused of having crabs, and force him
under a cold shower in the dead of winter; Aap Nel, so called 'either
because he looked like a monkey or could climb like one', discovers
the bloated carcass of a jackal at the bottom of their drinking well in
Kenya; their playing cards are so well worn by the time they reach the
Sahara that only Piet Potlood, whose deck it is, can tell what each card
is. ('Which led, as you can well imagine, to all *sorts* of arguments.') So
it was easy to forget sometimes what he was doing in the desert, or on

the open sea, or in a tent on the side of a frozen mountain in the Italian Alps. But always, before long, there it was: that moment of insane violence. A bullet pierces the forehead of the eighteen-year-old on the gun beside him. A kid is torn apart by shrapnel in a rain-soaked field. Harry Greenberg. Jake Jacobson. Bun Hopley. AM 'Ham' Lazarus. Phillip Denton. So many stories of friends and others ended with the words *He was killed* ... a few weeks later, a few months later, at sea or in the desert or wherever it was these young people died.

The more abrasive accusations I'd levelled at myself had made me a more self-conscious listener. At the same time they had scrubbed away some of the obsessive interest I'd developed in the stories' physical details. I listened (and watched myself listening) with more tenderness, increasingly occupied with the *people* in the stories and what was happening to them. I looked less at the dictaphone and more at my grandfather's face as he spoke: his strong, wide forehead; his tall ears. And I smiled as I realised that the main character in these tales had remained unchanged: the little boy, at once headstrong and respectful, both confident and thin-skinned, had grown into a young man with the same delicately balanced set of qualities.

The story of how he joined the artillery (after planning to join the infantry) took one session to record. Tales from his first assignment, as a gunner with the Fourth Field Artillery Regiment fighting the Italian army in East Africa, took another two.

With a disbelieving shake of his head he told me how 'green' he'd been, what an 'absolute rookie' – and he related a few stories to illustrate. Tales of close shaves and narrow escapes – totalled trucks, a badly strained neck, his eyebrow grazed by a fellow private's bullet.

But he then related a different sort of story, a story that spoke of something else – a story I knew was coming. The one about how, in October of 1941, while sharing a dugout on the Libyan coast with his friend Dov Judelowitz, he was summoned to appear before a board of senior army officers. A few days after the nerve-racking interview he was one of just four gunners (from among hundreds in his brigade) to be chosen to return to South Africa to train to become an officer.

With the pleasurable sense that comes from returning to build on foundations already laid, I slipped the war transcripts, dated and stapled, under the pile of childhood stories in the cardboard box in the cupboard.

A broad warmness entered the days, one by one, and before you knew it none was cold. The day before what was supposed to be my last at *Business Day*, the chief came and stood alongside my chair. With a serious expression she asked me if I'd come get a coffee with her. Walking behind her to the kitchen, where the coffeepot was, I thought back over the last few days for something I'd done wrong. I had enjoyed working there. I didn't want it to end on a sour note.

As it turned out, I needn't have worried. After we'd filled our polystyrene cups – during which we made small talk – we sat down at one of the round tables in the atrium and she asked me if I wanted to come and work full time at the newspaper. She said she'd discussed it with Paddi, and that Paddi was happy for me to leave the internship early if I wanted to. She said I should take a day or so to think it over and I said I would, though I already had no doubt what my answer would be. Aside from the actual work, which I took pleasure in, and the hours, which I felt suited to, I felt at home among the subs. Almost all had been journalists once, but had, for one reason or another, decided against it and come here. In this way the subs desk reminded me of the Buddhist centre: it was a place to recover, to lie low for as long as you needed.

The other interns thought I was crazy to leave the programme with only three months to go. It was difficult to explain to them that reporting was now the last thing in the world I wanted to do. Subediting, on the other hand, gave a sustaining rhythm to my life. Afternoons and evenings were the paper's; mornings were my own. And now that they were mine *contractually*, I guarded them well, and tried to get as much out of them as I could. I sketched out a short story about a famous graffiti artist who gets writer's block; I bought drawing pencils; I continued to meet my grandfather, usually early on a Wednesday.

He was taking me chronologically through the war. We were up to the six-month officer's course he did in Potchefstroom – returning, after a year and a half of active service, to the place he'd arrived as a 'complete greenhorn' to do his basic training. Stories from the course took a full session, and his first two postings as an officer (in Barberton and Carolina) another. The outrageous tale of the six months he then spent in Madagascar, protecting the island from a threatened Japanese invasion, took one more. Each time I laid another transcript, dated and stapled, at the bottom of the pile in the cardboard box in my cupboard, I felt like I was conducting a private religious ceremony.

Allied victory parade at Monza, Italy, 14 July 1945
Jules Browde (front) in his tank, nicknamed 'Flippy'
Photo coutesy of the Bourhill archive

After six months in Madagascar, my grandfather returned to South Africa, where he joined the Sixth South African Armoured Division – the famed Sixth Div – preparing to cross the Mediterranean to join the war in Europe. (He was one of only a few soldiers to serve in all four major theatres that the South Africans were involved in: East Africa, Madagascar, North Africa and Italy.) He described the emotional return to the northern desert. The final preparations. And then the boat trip they took that night. The conversation he had with a priest. The way the moonlight scribbled on the water. He shook his head. 'It's like an absolute dream,' he said.

This was something he'd said a few times while telling me stories from his childhood, but he said it more often now. He said it while describing his first morning at the artillery school in Potchefstroom. He said it while speaking about his time in a hospital in Nanyuki. Something so strange, perhaps, a war, that it was like a dream held in the parenthesis of civilian life. Every detail was stamped into his brain: the way the mosquitoes rose in a black cloud from the Malagasy swamp; how the cold porridge tasted on a frozen evening in the Italian Alps; the coal-black eyebrows of his commanding officer. Many of the stories were threaded through with conversations remembered word for word.

I sometimes wondered if certain details had once been circumstantial elaborations, malleable bits of artifice pressed into the gaps to help the tale's rhythm, which had hardened, over the years, into the body of the story itself. Of course it was possible. But then I thought of how it was also possible that by telling the stories over and over again he had preserved them in a sort of narrative amber. Memories unspoken fade and die from want of breath. These memories, spoken often, might well have stayed alive with all their delicate organs intact.

Inside their cardboard box at the back of my cupboard, the stack of transcripts was taking on a satisfying height. A rich cast of new characters had taken up residence there. Major Galleymore with his death wish; Luigi Coperchini, the Italian bartender in Dekemhare; the taciturn John Louis Gordon-Grey, son of a soldier. Black-browed Herloff Petersen. The friendly mechanics Joe Brough and Koos Reyneke; Rondekop le Roux, Aap Nel – and someone else, too. Someone I had met in the stories from his childhood.

In those stories, with just one or two exceptions, she had been slightly blurred (a gentle and affectionate blur, but still a blur: in her chair, in the carriage). Now she emerged clearly drawn and animated: nervous, anxious, loving – a woman who has only just lost her husband and, painfully aware of the fragility of life, is desperate not to lose her son. 'My mother suffered a lot more than I did during the war,' he had said more than once.

It was one particular story – which ended up being indirectly about her – that gave me a fresh understanding of what we were doing in these sessions in the lounge. I had spent so much time thinking about what this meant to me that I hadn't taken the time yet to consider what it meant to him. What it means to get your stories down; what grand hopes must attend the process, whether you want them to or not.

It happened like this.

The last two sessions contained a surprise attack of stories: how, after Germany's surrender, he skipped over the Italian border and went to Paris with his friend Lynne Cloete; how he and his battery spent a month at Lake Como in northern Italy, almost a hundred of them, swimming in the crystal-clear waters, drinking cold beers in a rowboat, dazed with sun and relief. And then, in the last session, how he almost died on the plane from Bari to the repatriation camp at Helwan in Egypt (crash-landing, on the way, in Crete); his first time in a plane.

And then, at last, how he arrived back, miraculously in one piece, at the military airbase at Zonderwater, near Pretoria.

'My mom was there. And my brothers. And my little nephew, Michael. They were all there waiting for me. My sister Lily couldn't come to meet the aircraft because she was very pregnant – about to give birth, in fact, to her second child.

'The only person I had expected to see, who was not there, was my grandmother,' he said.

'We all greeted each other, my mother crying and hugging me. She told me to my great sadness that my grandmother had died a few weeks before. I had missed her by only a few weeks.'

He drove them back to Daventry Court, where his mother, weak-kneed with happiness, had prepared a welcome-home tea.

'And that, Dan, was that, I suppose.'

I was leaning forward to stop the recorder – feeling a mixture of things: accomplishment, a sense of anti-climax, relief – when he asked if he could add something.

I sat back and said, 'Of course.'

'Have I ever told you the story of Billy Gezundheit?'

I liked the name; I thought I would have remembered it. 'I don't think you have, Broncs.'

'Well then. Now just let me tell you,' he said. 'During the days of going camping with Habonim, I met and became very friendly with a fellow from Cape Town. Went by the name of Billy Gezundheit.'

I settled deeper into the couch.

'Billy was a really remarkable chap,' he continued. 'After finishing high school he became a law student, and a student leader, at UCT. I met up with him once at a Nusas conference in Grahamstown. We shared a room together on that trip, and edited the conference newspaper, if you could call it that, every morning. We both had a bent for lyrics and writing and we got on extremely well. So much so, that when Billy came up to Johannesburg to join the air force – at around the same time that I joined the artillery – we met up, and I introduced him to my mother. And thereafter, whenever he was in Johannesburg, he used to call in to see her.

'I was away much more than he was, you see …

'Then in about 1944, I think it was. Towards the end of the war. Billy had recently completed a tour of duty as an air force fighter pilot in Europe, and had only one more tour to do, apparently. Before he left, he went to see my mom, and they had a long discussion, during which he told her that he'd gotten engaged to a girl from the Strand. I even remember her name, but it's not important. He also mentioned that he wasn't keen on flying this mission, said he felt like he'd done enough. But anyway, my mother was very pleased to see him, delighted at his news, and most appreciative that he had thought to visit her again – to say goodbye.

'Well, some months later there was a story in the newspaper, which my mother saw. About how Billy Gezundheit had been shot down over the Mediterranean. Apparently he bailed out of his plane, into a small boat, and was adrift for so long that he died of starvation and exposure. His body was washed up on the coast of Croatia or somewhere.

'My mother wrote to me about this. I read about it in a letter I received in Italy. In the letter she called him her *dear Billy*. She was so upset about it. My mother was so fond of him.'

I said nothing. He looked away again. The tape spooled, recording currents.

And then he turned and looked me deeply in the eyes, and said: 'And, I would just like to pay homage to her.' He spoke in a voice I hadn't heard before: softer but sharper, like something said at very high altitude. 'Because although she wasn't a highly educated woman, my mother had very deep feelings about family, and I must have been a source of tremendous distress to her in those times. But she didn't show it. She was friendly with my army friends. She always entertained them if ever they came up there. She had a good sense of humour. And ... well ... I just felt like putting that into this, this ... this talk. Anyway, there it is.'

It had taken me a long time to see what was in front of my eyes all along. The rivers of stories had meandered into the margins of the pages, breaking their banks to deposit their gritty sediment in the space created by the dictaphone, the air and the sunlight, by time and the maroon-cushioned, high-backed chair. Perfect stories, with their beginnings, middles and ends, are what we tell to protect ourselves from the truth, which is shambling, fragmented and completely insoluble. The neatly inverted pyramids are what we hide behind with our bags of guts straining at the seams.

THE WATSON BROTHERS

Interview 18
Date recorded: 08/11/2006

I had just returned from a short trip overseas to find that the usual messages had been left with my secretary. There was one she described as being unusually urgent. She said, 'There's an attorney from Port Elizabeth by the name of Leon Schubart who has phoned practically every day for the last week. He desperately wants to talk to you.'

So I phoned Schubart, and it was obviously of great relief to him to have me on the line. And he said to me as follows: he said, 'I need your help urgently. Can you come down to Port Elizabeth?'

I asked him, 'What's it in connection with?'

He said, 'I have clients who are involved in what could be a very serious matter, and they are being *shockingly* treated in jail. I believe that all sorts of things are going on behind the scenes. Three brothers: Valence, Cheeky and Ronnie Watson.'

I told him I'd heard of the Watson brothers. These fellows had all once been very well-known rugby players.

The allegation being brought against them was that they had burned down their family home with the intention of claiming its value from an insurance company.

Now that is essentially fraud, and so could easily have been a civil case. They could have been told to appear in court on such-and-such a date and charged there, but here they were awaiting trial for arson in awful conditions. *Chained together*, Schubart said, in a small filthy cell in the city's most notorious prison.

He persuaded me to travel to Port Elizabeth, where I could personally see how they were being treated, and hear the full story of the machinations of the security police, who, he believed, were intent on bringing to bear on the accused the heaviest punishment they could.

A few days later Schubart sketched in the rest of the background in person. I had flown down to Port Elizabeth in the morning, and he came to see me at my hotel that afternoon.

The Watson brothers – who were now all in their mid and late twenties – had been some of the best schoolboy rugby players in South Africa. After high school both Cheeky and Valence Watson had played for the senior Eastern Province team, and everyone expected them to go on to play for the Springboks. But then, in 1976, these boys started playing in the so-called black league in the New Brighton township.

Their father, who I ultimately got to know very well, by the way, was a lay preacher, and he had inculcated in his four sons and daughter the idea that people are equal – black and white. These kids had grown up speaking Xhosa fluently. So, as they got older, they naturally did not feel at home in the white rugby establishment.

But remember that in those days, sport, like everything else in this country, was strictly segregated, and this sort of thing – white and black playing together – was forbidden. So the police would regularly disrupt the games that the Watsons played in in the townships. And when Cheeky was selected by Eastern Province to attend the Springbok trials, Danie Craven, then president of the South African rugby union, famously said that Cheeky Watson would play for the Springboks 'over his dead body'.

By that time the whole Watson clan had become known as enemies of apartheid. The harassment went beyond the disruption of rugby matches. The parents owned a couple of clothing shops in Port Elizabeth that were frequented mainly by black customers, who supported them in part because they knew of the Watsons' political affiliations. Schubart showed me a photograph he had of uniformed policemen standing menacingly inside one of the shops and crowding people out.

They also received all *sorts* of threatening letters. Death threats and that sort of thing. The brothers lived in fear of what might happen and took precautions to protect themselves and their families. Valence was married but he still lived with his parents. Cheeky and Gavin both lived within walking distance of the family home.

Which brings us to the night in question: a Saturday night in October 1985. Schubart explained that Valence, Ronnie and Gavin were going to stay for that weekend at Gavin's in-laws, who had a little place in Kenton-on-Sea, not far down the coast. The Watsons' parents were also going away for the weekend, which meant that the family house would be empty.

Valence asked two friends of his – Archie Mkele and Geoffrey Nocanda were their names, two former teammates of his – to keep an eye on the house. Geoffrey owned a car and Valence asked him and Archie if they wouldn't mind stopping by once or twice, just to see that everything was all right. Archie and Geoffrey agreed, and Ronnie, Valence and Gavin went off on their weekend away.

On the Saturday night, Cheeky was at home when he heard a great deal of commotion outside in the neighbourhood. And when he went into the street to see what was going on, he could see flames coming from what looked to be his parents' house. He raced over there to find that indeed it was, and that the firemen were failing to bring the flames under control. By the time the others got back from Kenton, the house was destroyed.

Now, what none of the brothers knew, but what they found out the next day, was that Archie and Geoffrey had been caught in the fire. When they tried to visit them in hospital, they were not allowed to see them. But later they did manage to speak to them, and Archie and Geoffrey told them what had happened to them that night.

They were sitting in their car in the driveway, they said, when a panel van came up behind them and men in balaclavas jumped out of it and dragged them out of the vehicle. The next memory they had was of being in the house, which was now in flames. Archie remembered stumbling over Geoffrey, helping him up, and escaping the burning house. They ran down into the creek, which ran alongside the house, and back onto the road down below. Here they were picked up by a passing car and taken to hospital. Because the hospital was reserved for whites, they were put in an ambulance and taken to Livingstone Hospital, which was a so-called black hospital. In that ambulance, in terrible pain, they were questioned by the police. In the hospital, having been just admitted, Archie was questioned again.

The Watsons could do nothing with this story. They couldn't go to the police with it: the police, for them, were the enemy. They knew this had been some kind of punishment from the authorities for playing 'black' rugby. So they simply went through the process of claiming from the insurance for the damages and tried as best as they could to put their lives – and the lives of these two chaps – back together.

But things were about to get worse. In May of the following year, Archie and Geoffrey were arrested under the emergency regulation that had just been passed, and were taken to separate jails and held in solitary confinement. The Watsons didn't even know which jails they were being held in. That was how it was under the states of emergency: the police did what they liked and didn't have to tell you anything.

And then, a few months later – in August 1987 – the police arrested Ronnie, Valence and Cheeky on charges of arson and burning down the house for the insurance money. Geoffrey had signed a confession saying that the brothers had asked them to set fire to the house.

Schubart had on several occasions tried to get them bail, but the courts had refused on the grounds that they might abscond. Where these chaps, who had spent all their *lives* in the Eastern Cape, would abscond to heaven knows, but that was the reason given. And that, Schubart said, was when he approached me.

The next day he took me to see these guys in Port Elizabeth's notorious North End jail. And I found these young fellows indeed in terrible conditions – chained to each other and very hostile to me. They were in a state of mind, as you can well imagine, in which they didn't trust anyone.

But Schubart was desperate to have me on the case, and a long discussion ensued in which he tried to give them a sense of who I was and where my allegiances lay. Ultimately he convinced them that I was the best person for the job, and they seemed to take to me. And I, in turn, told Schubart I would take their case.

As soon as I left the North End jail that morning, I did something: I went to see the chief of police, and I told him I wasn't prepared to consult with my clients in such conditions. I said that they had to be unchained and they had to be moved to a decent jail.

He told me, 'We haven't got better accommodation.'

So I said, 'Then I'll have to tell the press that I can't interview my clients because they're being held in such terrible conditions.'

The apartheid government liked to keep up appearances. Of fairness and justice. They were playing a double game. And it was that desire to be *seen* to be doing the right thing that I was trying to manipulate. Well it had the desired effect. The very next day the brothers were removed from their chains and taken to a more central prison in Port Elizabeth, Louis le Grange Square, where they were held under better conditions.

And that, I think, was the first light the Watsons saw at the end of the tunnel. It was a long tunnel, I may tell you, a very long tunnel. But this helped. The brothers warmed to me and from then on they trusted me implicitly.

The State's case against the Watsons was to be founded largely on Geoffrey's signed confession. In the confession Geoffrey said that the Watson brothers had hatched a plan to defraud the insurance company. He said that Valence had put the plan to him and Archie. And the plan was this: Valence had bought a whole lot of petrol and was going to leave it in the house when the family went away for the weekend. What Archie and Geoffrey had to do was to go into the house, douse it in petrol, and strike a match. Which he said they did. But this had caused a huge explosion that had taken them by surprise. The Watsons denied all this categorically.

A date was set for the trial to begin some months later. The Watsons, meanwhile, remained in custody.

But before I tell you about the trial, I must tell you this: a week or so before it was due to begin, Geoffrey smuggled out of prison a letter he had written on a torn piece of a milk carton. His girlfriend – whose name, I was told, was Nola – had been allowed to visit him, and he had managed to give her this message undetected. She had shown it to Gavin, the only brother not arrested, who told her to take it straight to Schubart. Schubart flew up to Johannesburg to show it to me. In the letter, Geoffrey said he was being tortured by the security police to give false evidence against the Watsons.

After we had consulted, Schubart flew back to Port Elizabeth. Because he had spent only one night here, he brought with him just his briefcase and a small overnight bag, which he put in the overhead storage compartment on the plane. When he arrived in Port Elizabeth he stood up to find that the overnight bag was there but the briefcase was missing. Naturally he was very concerned and he reported this to the authorities. Later that night, the airport people phoned him to say they had located his briefcase. He went to collect it the next morning and discovered that the letter was missing.

Now, what happened to that letter is a matter for surmise, but you can imagine what we thought. That this letter had been stolen by the same people who had framed the Watsons: people in the know and in *authority*.

This gives you an idea of the atmosphere in South Africa at that time. And it was under these circumstances that I went down to Port Elizabeth to fight the case.

chapter eleven

In which the young storyteller takes a different route home

Before we finished recording the war stories, I was already thinking about his courtroom tales, eager to capture them with the dictaphone. After all, it was Judge Malan's 'tongue like a whiplash' that had caused my brain to flip to record in the first place. When I thought back to those early experiments, where I had relied on my memory, I felt mainly frustration. So much had been lost.

There were a few things we needed to fill in first, though, in the period between the end of the war and the beginning of his career as an advocate. I thought we'd hurry through this period to get to the good part: the cases.

Three weeks after the final war session (his homecoming; Billy Gezundheit), we sat down again. He told me how a few days after he'd landed at Zonderwater he already realised he would need to 'get down to doing something', and so went to ask the law professor about writing the first-year exams at the end of that year. The professor let him do that. Which meant that only a week after a five-year-long military odyssey had ended, he started studying for a set of exams.

This second phase of my grandfather's university career, during which he completed his LLB, coincided with a crucial period in South Africa's political history: the decline of Jan Smuts's United Party and the resurgence of the Nationalists, led by the bespectacled, heavy-jowled churchman, DF Malan.

The Nationalists were running for the 1948 general elections, the first post-war poll, promising the all-white electorate that if they got in they would enforce rigid racial segregation in all areas of South African life. Malan called this plan apartheid.

My twenty-eight-year-old grandfather-to-be and some of his classmates discussed what would happen 'if the Nats get in' with the same sense of trepidation, he said, as some people would speak, fifty years later, about what would happen 'when Mandela goes'.

And there is some kind of irony in that comparison, considering that one of these classmates was a politically minded student by the name of Nelson Mandela.

Mandela was living in Orlando, Soweto, at the time and was also doing his LLB part time. The University of the Witwatersrand, my grandfather had explained, still admitted a few black students each year, although they were not allowed to stay in the residences or use the sports facilities.

'I was told that he'd come from the royal Xhosa family,' he said. 'And he looked the part. And acted the part. He had a sort of majesty about him. I don't wish to say that he had a superior attitude, but ... well, he gave me the impression of being a really worthwhile human being. I nurtured a friendship with him. We often met in the evenings at the university and spoke about politics, spoke about prejudices in this country, spoke about what was going to happen if Smuts fell.'

That morning I stole a few nervous glances at the dictaphone in a way I hadn't since our earliest sessions. I felt oddly grateful to my grandfather in the same way I'd felt grateful to my friend Daniel, who was already living in New York when the Twin Towers came down. Because he had seen it with his own two eyes, I felt I was only one step removed from that immense buckling vision. So it was that now I felt just once removed from a twenty-five-year-old Mandela, that lean kid from the photographs yet to be swallowed by history. Having studied at the same university, I could also project myself easily onto the wide grey steps of the Great Hall, which was where I imagined the two young men chatting in the twilight.

In the stories from this period, I found a beguiling argument: that a person can be understood as the end result of a chain of events. The idea that if we look closely we can see the seminal moment, the where-it-all-began. So Bruce Wayne puts on a mask and hunts criminals because two of them murdered his parents one night in Gotham, and so on – one thing leading to another according to an ultimately decipherable logic. In this way, we give coherence to the blind swarm of the past.

Even when I was a little kid, I knew what my grandpa's superpower was – what he was the best at. It was called *cross-examination*. This, he would often tell me, did not mean 'examining crossly'. It was more difficult than that, more artful. It was a way of asking questions so that the weaknesses of a story would reveal themselves. It took special skills of listening and memory.

'Just a minute, sir, didn't you say earlier that …' was what I imagined him saying to a lying witness, having fed him enough rope and now watching him tie himself in a knot.

My father told me how law students would sometimes skip their lectures to go and listen to my grandfather cross-examine witnesses; that was how good he was – and I was always proud of him for it. But back then I just assumed that it was his natural superpower: as a bee knew how to make honey, so he knew how to get you to say what he wanted. But now I listened with increasing excitement as the flow of his narrative suggested that he was leading me to the font of this talent. Here it was, if I wanted it: the origin story.

'My mother,' he said, 'had not a great income, and therefore I had to work. And I decided that any job I could get I would take, in order to try to make some contribution to the household.'

Ultimately (his word), he found work as a judge's clerk, assisting two judges in the Witwatersrand Local Division. One was a man by the name of Leslie Blackwell, and the other was Harold Ramsbottom. Most of the time he worked for Blackwell, but when Blackwell went to hear cases on the circuit in Pretoria, he stayed in Johannesburg and worked for Ramsbottom. In the mornings he clerked for one of these two in the High Court on Pritchard Street, and in the afternoons he attended classes at the university in Braamfontein.

The tale was cleverly cast: Blackwell, an Australian by birth, had 'a gnarled face with a big bulbous nose and hooded eyes. He was a very rough character indeed,' while Ramsbottom, 'or Rammy, as we called him, was a gentleman to his fingertips. To me he was the soul of courtesy …'

Rammy, my grandfather explained, had been an officer in the artillery in the First World War, and took a special interest in the progress of this young artillery veteran. 'Every afternoon after work, he would drop me at the library. When Blackwell was here, I used to go by bus. But Rammy insisted on taking me in his car. On the way, he spoke to me about my studies and any difficulties I was having, and when I had problems I would talk to him about them. He really was a most gracious employer.'

So Blackwell and Rammy, the shadow and the light, provided the vibrant chiaroscuro that animated the background of the period.

Sitting in court, clerking for either one or the other, the young law student 'was privileged not only to learn the requirements of judgeship, but also had the opportunity of listening to and watching the giants of the Bar at that time carrying out their duties in court and conducting themselves in the best tradition of the profession of advocacy.'

He mentioned two giants in particular. The first was Harry Morris, who had become famous for his work on the Lord Erroll murder trial in Kenya, a case that caught the world's attention and would later become immortalised in the book *White Mischief*. 'Morris was an absolutely brilliant cross-examiner,' my grandfather said. 'He had a real flair for it. And I learned a great deal from him, just sitting and listening to him question witnesses.'

The other was Harold Hanson, who was only fifteen years older than my grandfather and so still a relatively young man when my grandfather first saw him in action. Hanson would go on to become one of South Africa's most well-known advocates, representing FH Alexander (of the Alexander Technique) and Bram Fischer, whose words he would famously read out on the last day of the Rivonia Trial. I read up a little about him and discovered that other lawyers spoke of 'Hansonian eloquence'.

'This led,' my grandfather said, 'to a determination on my part to follow in this tradition. In particular, I was attracted to the art of cross-examination, and its application in trials, whether civil or criminal, in eliciting from hostile witnesses evidence that would be of benefit to my clients.'

Students of myth call it The Road of Trials, when the hero is frustrated at the critical moment by forces beyond his control.

Blackwell, with his reptilian eyes, asks my grandfather-to-be to type out the handwritten pages of his autobiography after hours. Thinking he might make some extra money, our young hero takes on the job. So now, not only is he clerking for half the day and attending lectures for the rest, but there he sits, night after night in his bedroom, typing out with two fingers his hard-hearted employer's life story. ('I was virtually hamstrung …')

And it is exactly then, suitably hindered, that he meets the Girl, a medical student from Cape Town who has come up to Johannesburg for a few days to attend a student conference.

Of course, this story I'd heard before – a few times – from both of my grandparents. I'd always enjoyed hearing it, had enjoyed identifying the slight variances in their accounts. Something I had not thought about before, though, was how near the physical coordinates of that intersection were to where they, and I, lived now – sixty years in the future. The block of flats where they met was less than ten minutes' walk from where he sat telling me the story one more time, the dictaphone turning between us.

Going home that day, I took a route that was slightly longer than the one I usually used. I turned left on Osborne Road instead of right, and went the other way around the golf course, so I would pass the block of flats from the story.

Peering up through the windscreen as I drove slowly past the building, I thought about how the world may be wide, but our lives are less so. Most of us spend our days in one place. This was his place, here: these roads, pavements, houses and hidden gardens. And so far, at least, it had been mine too.

On the wall of the passage outside my grandfather's study hangs a gallery of photographs: our family in frames. On the left, near the door to the guest room, are two black-and-white contact sheets. Small square images in columns and rows. The first shows different shots of my father and his older brother when they were babies – my father a year old, and Ian a protective toddler of about three. My grandmother, then just a new mother, sits with them, proud and also obviously *curious* about these boys.

The second sheet shows them all a few years later. My father and Ian are now five and seven, maybe six and eight. Strong mischievous faces, their jet-black hair cut short on the back and sides.

Next to these are two portraits of my uncle, Paul, aged six or seven, alone. Paul is ten years younger than my father, so these must have been taken a long time after the others. Paul's dark, straight hair is cut neatly across his forehead, his gaze as clear as water freshly melted.

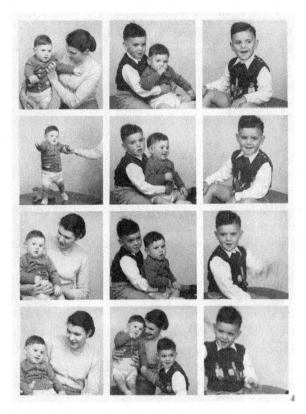

Selma Browde with sons Ian and Alan, 1952

Jules and Selma Browde with sons Alan, Paul and Ian, 1969

To the right of these is a photograph of the three boys, all together now, with their parents – this one taken a few years after Paul's solo portraits. The two older boys, now in their late teens or early twenties, stand with their arms folded, sideburns fully grown and smiles that are fierce, almost angry. Paul, a boy of about ten, stands in front of them, his eyes hopeful.

Next, the grandkids. First, Ian's children, my Californian cousins: little Carrie with her large, expressive eyes; and Tristan, a long-haired boy of about nine, in an oval wooden frame.

Beside these hang the portraits my father took of my sisters and me when we were little. Cara stares up into the camera with a feral grin. Kate smiles from more straight on, eyes scrunched into diamonds, a red heart painted on her cheek. Emma and I stand in similarly composed shots amid the shrubbery of the garden in Shipston Lane. (It was a phase my dad went through.) Emma looks pointedly into the distance, her hands behind her back. I'm holding a cricket bat and glaring into the lens: brooding, or perhaps just impatient. The picture of Micaela is a school portrait, sincere, her hair pulled back into a tight ponytail.

There are more pictures – my grandfather arm in arm with Oliver Tambo; cousins in Australia; and some fading sepia prints of olden-day people in hats and coats, whose identities I can never keep straight in my head. But it was those other images, of my father and my uncles and my sisters and me, that had always pulled me in. In the nine months I lived there, I spent quite a bit of time in that passage just standing and looking. I was drawn to these pictures even if I half hated them. When I looked for longer than a few seconds, a nostalgia would come over me that really was nearly physically unbearable. It seemed we had all lost something important in the years since childhood, and I didn't see how we could continue to live without it.

But after transcribing the story about how my grandparents met, and reading it through repeatedly over the next few weeks, something changed in the way I looked at these photographs. I found myself inspecting them with a forensic interest – as documents, as documentary evidence of the fruits of chance. Life's possibilities are endless, but that endlessness is constantly being nudged into line by something that likes a line more than a swarm, meeting more than never-meeting; some force that shepherds our minds from doubt to momentary certainty so that at last we choose, for better or worse. Is this a definition of fate – I started to wonder – or simply biology? Clearly there is something that prefers, even if just for one fractured life-giving second, order to chaos and togetherness to flying apart, so that of all the infinite permutations there might be *this* and *these*: these bodies and these faces, this love and this fear, this pride and this shame.

A PARTY AT MRS GAFFEN'S
THEIR STORIES

Interviews 14 & 31
Dates recorded: 22/02/2006; 04/08/2013

I had been back from the war about eight months. I was living with my mother and younger brother in Killarney, and doing the second year of my LLB part time. For the rest I was working as a judge's clerk for Judges Blackwell and Ramsbottom, both of whom I've told you about.

One day my mother came to me and told me she'd been invited to a party by a friend of hers named Mrs Gaffen. Mrs Gaffen, who lived in a block of flats opposite the Houghton golf course, had two daughters who by common consent were very attractive young women. My mother had suggested to me on a few occasions that I could do worse than take out one of those two girls. I wasn't particularly interested in them so I'd never got round to doing that. Now it seemed one of them was getting engaged.

It was 1946. I was doing third-year medicine at UCT, and I decided to go to a national students' union conference that was being conducted in Johannesburg.

It was the beginning of July, and I was turning twenty later that month. And I had a boyfriend, by the way. My first boyfriend. A very nice young man who was also an ex-serviceman, funnily enough. We'd arranged that I'd be back in time for my birthday and that he and I and some friends would all go out.

So I took the train to Johannesburg, where I stayed with my aunt and uncle, whom we called Uncle Berman and Auntie Berman, in their house in Kensington. Uncle Berman was a character. Leon Berman. Well known in Johannesburg. He had been a city councillor and considered himself a communist. And they had a son: my cousin, Monty.

Monty and I got on very well. We both were scornful of what we called 'the Johannesburg rich'. In those days there was a certain crowd in Johannesburg who were ... They were nice people, don't get me wrong, but they were very elegantly dressed and had these big parties and they didn't have the same political attitudes that we had. There were two sisters in that crowd. Relations of my Aunt Berman. The elder one had become engaged, and they were going to have a big party for her in an apartment opposite the Houghton golf course. And Monty and I were invited to the party. But we didn't want to go. We said to my aunt, 'We don't like those sorts of things. Fancy parties where everybody dresses up and there are dozens of people milling around. It's not for us. It has no content.'

So my mother said, 'Won't you come with me to the party? Mrs Gaffen would like you to come.'

I said, 'If you don't mind, I'd rather not.'

This party didn't interest me. Besides, on the night in question I'd arranged to get together with some of my old army friends. Not all of those relationships lasted, but at that time we still arranged to see each other relatively often.

But my mom had a way of twisting my arm. She said, 'I know why you don't want to come.'

I said, 'Why not, Ma?'

She said, 'Because *I've* asked you.'

She made me feel guilty.

So I said, 'Very well. I'll take you. But if somebody else will give you a lift home will it be okay with you if I left early?'

She said, 'All right. That's fine. But please do come with me.'

My aunt got very upset with us and said we would be letting her down badly if we didn't come, so we agreed to go. But to show our rebellion, Monty wore a sheepskin waistcoat and very casual pants, and I put on a green suit with a skirt and the ugliest jacket I have ever seen. A bright-green jacket with wide sleeves and huge white rings around each sleeve and around the bottom. And clumpy shoes that I used to wear to university. And off we went. On the way we picked up Monty's friend, Sydney.

It was one of these northern suburbs cocktail parties. A lot of people there in whom I wasn't particularly interested. I stood around for a while, settled my mom in, and was about to leave to go and meet my army friends when there arrived two young men whom I knew: Sydney Kentridge and Monty Berman. And with them was a girl wearing a dark-blue University of Cape Town blazer.

The first thing I see when we arrive are these exquisite girls dressed in black, with little cocktail hats. In 1946 the fashion was cocktail hats with little veils on some of them. But instead of feeling out, in my green suit and clumpy shoes, I actually felt good. I felt good about it. We were different. It was very immature, but that is how I was at the age of nineteen.

Monty and Sydney went and stood out on the stoep where some people were sitting, and I sat in the lounge – there were a lot of people around, I forget who I was sitting with – when suddenly everyone in the room, particularly the women, looked up. I looked up to see who they were looking at and there was this man I'd never seen before. I thought, Huh! That is a typical Johannesburg man, not my type. That was my first impression. He walked through the lounge and went out onto the stoep, and I didn't give him another thought.

Sydney Kentridge was younger than I was, but I knew him quite well. He had also grown up in Yeoville. He lived on Regent Street and we often passed each other. We had also been at King Edward's at the same time. Monty Berman I had met only cursorily, but I knew who he was. The girl in the blazer I had never seen before. But as soon as I saw her I was drawn to her.

There was nobody really for me to talk to inside. So I went out onto the stoep, where Monty and Sydney were sitting with a group of people. There wasn't an empty chair, so Monty said, 'Sorry, cuz, there isn't a seat for you.' That was his sense of humour. I said, 'All right,' and turned around as if I were going to go back inside, when this man – the man I'd seen earlier – said, 'But there's an empty seat next to me. Why don't you sit here?'

So I sat next to him, and we got talking, and to my absolute amazement, we got on very well. He was nothing like my first impression of him. He was entirely different.

I don't remember everything we talked about. If he says we spoke about rugby, then I'm sure we did, because there were always university matches and I do remember, I think, talking about how at UCT games everybody linked arms and sang and swayed. I know he always says that it was my talk about rugby that interested him so much. But in fact we spoke about all sorts of things.

Eventually he said to me, 'Look, I'm going to a party with a group of people I was in the army with. Wouldn't you like to come with me?'

She said, 'Well, I've come here with Sydney Kentridge and Monty Berman.'

I said, 'What if I fix it with them? Would it be all right?'

Once she said that that was all right, I realised I was obviously on a very good footing with her.

So after that night he asked me to come out with him again, and I went out with him a few times and I really fell for him. I really did, and it seemed to happen mutually. And then he asked me if I would put off my going home and not make any other dates – because I used to keep asking him to drive me back to my uncle's house to fetch letters from my boyfriend in Cape Town, which I received every second day.

In the end I did postpone my trip home, and on my twentieth birthday a crowd of us, which he organised, went to a nightclub and we had a lovely evening. We had supper and danced and it was really a wonderful twentieth birthday, and then I went back to Cape Town.

And Jules wrote me a letter, asking if this boyfriend of mine – I don't know if I should mention his name ... He was called AJ. Jules wrote me a letter to say, 'Well, have you made up your mind? Is it J? Is it AJ? Is it neither? Is it both?'

Which I found very amusing.

So I wrote back – because the strangest thing had happened when I arrived back in Cape Town. AJ was really a most terrific person. I mean, you couldn't find a nicer human being. But I can't explain what it was that made me feel that as much as I liked him, I could never marry him. So I wrote back and I said, 'It's J.'

And then the letters started, which I have still got. He started writing to me. He wrote me the most wonderful letters. My mother made me keep them. She said you must always keep the letters. I don't think anybody should see them.

Jules and Selma Browde in Milan, Italy, 1959
'So I wrote back and I said, "It's J."'

chapter twelve
an interlude

In which a child watches his grandfather enter the sea

I can see two round lights in the darkness. These belong to Bronco's car, which is waiting for us in the road. My father reverses the Volkswagen kombi down the driveway, four little bodies lying side by side in the back, all whispering the word *holiday*. Minutes later, my sisters have fallen back asleep. I sit up and watch the dark empty city. I like to see how it ends. Past its edges is a wilderness. After travelling through the wilderness for a while, I lie back down and close my eyes. I lie close to my sisters, the engine turning over beneath us, and it feels as if my parents' low voices are coming from a long way away, but I know they are right there, inside the kombi, and will be there when I wake up, in the light, and we'll be a million miles from home.

My father and my grandfather take turns to lead the way. I pay close attention. The main rule says you have to stay *in sight* of the other vehicle. You also can't go too fast. I spend most of the journey in the kombi. When I'm not keeping a close eye on our progress, I read or play Twenty Questions with the others.

I spend about an hour or so of every trip in the back of Bronco's car, usually with Emma. This feels something like spending the night at a friend's house: fun, but not of a simple kind. To be in a city car, as I think of it, on what my father calls the *open road*, is strange. This problematic fact – the city car in the wilderness – seems to reflect an essential difference between these two people and my parents. Another is that they don't have long conversations in the car, like my parents do. In here it is quiet. Bronco drives with both his hands on the wheel and occasionally hums softly to himself. Nana's silence is a part of his concentration, and she only rarely turns around to talk to Emma or me. So mostly the two of us sit at the back and have our own earnest discussions. The seats are made of a rubbery, grey material that has lots of little holes in it, and while we discuss the facts of the natural world ('Clouds don't have shadows,' I remember telling her once) I trace patterns in these holes with my thumb.

Something else happens every time: Nana turns around and tells us in a semi-whisper, as if in confidence, that the reason my grandfather can drive these long distances with such ease is because he drove a truck in the war. Pressing my forehead to the window, I'd wonder what a truck could be used for in a war. I'd also wonder how my father learned to drive long distances with such ease, seeing as he never drove a truck in a war. My father didn't even go to the army, because he hurt his neck. Which I know wasn't hurt that badly. (I know the real reason he didn't fight in the army; that is one of the secrets.) I decide that driving long distances is simply one of the talents my father possesses naturally, like being able to catch a ball no matter how hard you throw it at him.

When we stop to fill up the cars with petrol, Allie and Bronco stand together near the cars and measure our progress against the plan. There is always a plan, although the plan can change. We plan to stop over here, but we end up stopping over there. We aim to refill in such-and-such a town, but we decide to *push on* and refill in some other town instead.

What seems to be an infinitely flexible strategy narrows, invariably, to one main concern: where we are going to stop over. Or, as I get older, if we are going to stop over at all. My father usually wants to push on, stop later; Bronco doesn't want to take the risk of driving in the dark. He prefers to stop where we planned to stop, even if we arrive there at three in the afternoon, sun still blazing. It doesn't matter to him if we have a longer drive the next day.

I pay close attention, thinking about the details of the disagreement, the kilometres to go, the hours until sunset. Sometimes it turns into a proper argument, tempers fray, and I wish it was not happening. I don't like to have to choose between them.

One evening we arrive at a motel in a small town in the wilderness, where we are going to spend the night. The sky is already a light purple. I am sitting in my grandfather's car. I am about nine or ten years old.

The motel has a steep curving driveway and Bronco has to go very slowly and turn the steering wheel a lot. I am leaning forward between the front seats, watching him operate.

After we are at the top, and he has parked the car, he turns around to me and says, 'Okay, now tell me. Who is the best driver in the world?' He has a big smile on his face.

I remember the smile falling from mine. The thing is I know he's a good driver. I also know he honed his skills in a war. But he is asking me to commit a betrayal: a *war crime*. (This is a story my grandfather tells if he's telling stories about me. He laughs when he tells it. And I remember it too, how difficult it was.) With my heart skidding, I say, 'You're a very good driver, Bronco. But you're not the best. You're the second best.' My heart hits an oncoming vehicle.

'Who's the best?' he says. He is still smiling, which I don't understand.

'My dad is,' I tell him, and wait for his smile to disappear, which it never does.

Theirs is a white house in a swale, on the inland side of a hill, beside the sea. To get to the beach you have to walk up the hill. A short steep road takes you to a long road that winds with the coastline. This is Millionaires' Row. It has that name because in these great houses overlooking the bay live millionaires. I regard these palaces with passionate curiosity. In the details – the window frames, the number plates on their cars, the way they cut their lawns – I look for clues to some unfathomable secret: money. Millionaires are a mythical race, like actors or sports stars, and Millionaires' Row represents some kind of limit to my grandparents' ineffable powers. Of course, the fact that they own this second house at all is impressive to me, but I'm still sharply aware that it is *down here* and not *up there*. My grandparents' powers are more mystical than money, their reach is broad.

This three-week holiday at the coast, which happens each December, is the only time I see them at all times of the day: first thing in the morning, buttering their toast and sipping their coffee; and late at night, past bedtime even. I stay up with everybody in the big room downstairs and don't get sleepy, until I do.

Certain things are turned upside down on holiday. For instance, my father becomes a son and my grandfather becomes a father. What this adds up to is a new vision of myself in the order of things, reinscribed and updated every year. I like being the youngest in this particular line. Allie and Bronco are both awesome to me, in different ways. Bronco has a wider head and less hair, and he doesn't get cross with me. My father is younger and funnier, with his big freckled hands and straight black hair. I know he is a kind and fun dad. I have already met some boys at school whose fathers are not kind to them. I know Allie is always kind, even when he is cross. And he's funny: sometimes he makes me laugh so much my stomach hurts.

One holiday, after my gran tells him to put on a jersey because it's cold, he says to her, 'Mom, please do me a favour. At my age most of my friends' parents have been dead for twenty years.'

This makes everyone laugh.

They laugh even more when she says, 'Yes, those are the boys who get into trouble.'

These are jokes I don't completely understand, but I think they are funny anyway.

We go on drives in the kombi for no other reason than to stop somewhere and look at whatever we can see. What you can see when you do that is called a *view*. My mother likes to go on these drives to look at views and I know she would like to go on more of them. My sisters and I find enough room in the back of the kombi. The mood on holiday is one of generosity and compromise. A time for deepening connections. My mother also likes to go on walks in the forest or near rivers, places like that. When we go on walks she says, 'Look around you.' (Especially if anyone whines.) She says, 'Just look around you, guys. Be aware of where you are.' At the house she likes to make coffee, and sit on her bed and read.

My dad is more relaxed away from the pressures of his work, which is always changing. Each new job seems to bring with it a new set of problems. Sometimes, late at night, he talks to my grandparents about changing his job. One year he fixes a dartboard to a pillar on the bricked patio and we play long games of darts in the late afternoons. My father is better than my grandfather at darts and at beach cricket. My grandfather is better than my father at chess.

When they play chess, I like to sit nearby and watch. Sitting over the board, staring down at the pieces in the game, my grandfather looks confident but also, somehow, quietly respectful. He tells me that chess is an excellent game because it demands *concentration* and *lateral thinking*. He explains what it means to think *laterally*. When he makes a move he does it with a little whistle if he's confident, or, if he has been forced to make it, a shrug. He does not look away from the board until the game is over.

After supper, on most nights, there is a card game at the white plastic table, which is brought inside especially for the purpose. My mother, my sisters and both my grandmothers always play. My father doesn't have the inclination. He reads on the couch. But my grandfather often plays. I sometimes play, and sometimes I don't. When I don't, I lie on the couch near my father and read.

I like to play cards when my grandfather plays. His eyes are always moving between the cards in his hand and the ones on the table. But I notice he doesn't mind if someone else wins. I learn from his warm involvement with the game, in the strategies he is always working on, that games are not that serious, but are still worth every last drop of your concentration.

But I like these late-night card games mostly because Ma is a part of them. Ma is usually the odd one out. She is the only one on holiday who has her own room, for one example. It makes me sad when I think about that, or when I see how she sits silently at the edges of conversations. But she is a full and equal member of the After-Supper Cards Club. She is good at cards – knowledgeable – and I like to hear her voice like this, cheerful and confident, and I like to hear her laugh, as she does during these games of cards, while insects bash against the big glass sliding doors, trying to share this light.

In the early morning I am usually awake and waiting for him, but sometimes he wakes me. One morning I am still asleep when I hear the word *heaven*. I swirl to the surface of my mind. My eyes open. He has his head in the doorway, his wide head with its silver hair. 'It's like heaven out there, laddie!'

The air at this time of day has a different quality from any other time. Cool and fresh and open, it is like the air itself has just woken up. This is six o'clock. The two of us walk up the steep hill and then along Millionaires' Row for a couple of minutes, and then we cut down through the heavy gorse, going in single file down the sandy path that leads to the beach.

To our right is the wall of a Millionaire's house; to our left the dark-green thicket that seems possessed of nameless dangers when I walk here alone. But now I am not alone. My grandfather, walking just behind me, wears faded canary-yellow shorts and no shirt, his towel around his neck like a scraggly scarf. The closer we get to the beach, the louder the noise of the ocean becomes: a pure low roar. The path becomes sandier and softer, until we are walking on sand only. The gorse ends and we can see the sea stretching away to the mysterious horizon. We walk a short way down the beach and stop. There is usually no one else about at this time. If there is, it is a solitary man with a dog, or a pair of women in tracksuits, marching.

My grandfather folds his arms low on his chest and just looks out. The ocean seems to have been smoothed down by a giant hand.

He says, 'It's *marvellous*, isn't it?'

'It is,' I say. 'It is!'

I have taken off my T-shirt and now I am running down to the sliding edge of the sea. I do a little involuntary hop as the briny water touches my toes. A brief, skirting look around tells me that he has put his towel on top of his shoes, and is coming in after me.

A little way out I dive under a low wave and stand up again, shaking the water out of my eyes, turning around to see his progress, and to see if he saw my dive. He has arrived at the edge of the water. He nods: he saw my dive.

I watch as he walks out until the water closes around his shins. Then he stands still, hands on his hips, and scans the horizon. Once he has seen what he needed to see, he starts coming in again, taking small steady, even strides, his hands still on his hips, until he is a little more than knee-deep. Then he stops again. The water has made a narrow band at the bottom of his trunks a darker yellow than the rest. Bending slightly from the waist and slightly at the knees, he cups seawater in his hands and throws it over his shoulders, *ooopss*, like that, tossing it first over one shoulder and then the other, making a sound each time he does it, *ooopss*, a low plain physical syllable that makes me happy, his eyes glittering like the new sun's reflection on the surface of the water.

I am watching him, carelessly thinking about him, taking a child's picture with my eyes. Bronco, Allie's dad. His skin is different from mine. I know that this is something that happens to you, your skin changes, it goes brittle and falls, and it has happened to him before it has happened to anyone else. Nothing has happened to me yet. I am still suspended in childhood, watching these giants move above me, waiting for them to take me in, show me around, hold me up to see whatever it is that they can see.

THE WHITE PANEL VAN

Interview 18
Date recorded: 08/11/2006

The prosecution called Geoffrey Nocanda as its main witness. The magistrate, by the way, was a senior magistrate in Port Elizabeth by the name of Steyn.

The prosecutor, Henning van der Walt, led Geoffrey through his evidence, in which he repeated his story that Valence had asked him and Archie to burn the house down. He said the other Watsons knew about it but that Valence was the one who did the talking, bought the petrol, and so on.

He answered the questions like a zombie: in a lifeless monotone. Mostly looking down. Obviously *terrified*. Looking up nervously every now and then.

There was a man sitting in the court, a very thin, sunken-cheeked man by the name of Nieuwoudt. Gideon Nieuwoudt. Who was subsequently exposed, by the way, as one of the cruellest members of the security establishment. Did terrible things to people. And he was in the court, watching this all very closely. And Geoffrey clearly *knew* that he was in the court watching, because often he looked at him and then looked away.

The court was packed, by the way. In those days there was a black side of the court and a white side of the court, and both sides were packed. Everybody knew that the Watsons were on trial here. You must remember that these boys were celebrities, especially here in the Eastern Cape.

When Van der Walt had finished with Geoffrey, I stood up and began my cross-examination. I put a number of things to him. And one of them was this; I had prepared the following scenario: I said to him, 'Do you have a girlfriend by the name of Nola?'

And he said yes, he did.

I said, 'Is this her?' And I turned to the public and I said, 'Nola, will you stand up please?'

She was in court. We had asked her to come to court, and she stood up. And Geoffrey looked at her. And he looked away again. And he said, 'Yes, that's my girlfriend.'

Then I said to him, 'Are you still in love with her?'

He looked at this young woman who was standing in the public gallery. Then he looked down into his lap, and he said, 'Yes, I am.'

I said, 'Did you write her a letter while you were in jail?'

You see, I wasn't sure what he knew; had someone told him the letter was no longer in our possession?

Geoffrey looked at this fellow Nieuwoudt, and then back at me. For a long time, maybe half a minute, he said nothing.

'Did you or did you not write Nola a letter?' I asked. 'This is not a very difficult question.'

He said, 'Yes, I did.'

'I'll tell you what,' I said. 'I want to put to you what you said in the letter. You said in the letter that the Watsons were innocent, and that you were being tortured to give false evidence against them. Did you say that in the letter?'

He paused, and then he said, 'Yes, I did.'

And then, of course, I did the whole thing. I put it to him that now he was being terrorised by the security police; I said, 'And this man sitting in court is watching you!'

I pointed at Nieuwoudt, who went as red as a beetroot. There was consternation in the court. Everybody started talking all at once, and over the racket I then said loudly to him, 'Now, what's the *truth*, Mr Nocanda?'

At first he didn't say anything. The magistrate called for order; the court quietened down. There followed another long period of silence as we all waited for him to speak. Then he said, 'Well, I *was* tortured while I was in jail, but now I'm telling the truth.' He said this very softly. Even in the silence it was difficult to hear him.

I asked him to repeat what he had just said.

'The truth is ... they did tell me to burn the house,' he said again.

'So why did you lie to Nola?' I asked him.

No answer.

'There must be a reason why you would have lied to Nola,' I said to him. '*Surely*. Why did you tell her that they were innocent if they were guilty?'

No answer.

I said to him, 'So you're not going to answer those questions?'

No answer.

Now that's one of the worst things a witness can do, who is asking to be believed. To remain silent under such circumstances, to simply refuse to explain such a radical contradiction, is a concession of defeat. I told the magistrate I had no more questions for the witness.

An extraordinary thing happened next, and I'll tell you what it was. After Geoffrey stepped down, I applied for bail again, and Van der Walt again opposed the application. The next morning we waited two hours for the magistrate. The court was even fuller than usual that morning. The fact that he was to give his bail ruling had been published in that morning's newspaper. He wasn't ready by nine o'clock. Came eleven o'clock, he still wasn't there. It was a Friday. After this, whatever happened, we were going to adjourn for a week or so and I was going back to Johannesburg.

At last Steyn came in and said, 'I have decided, in the circumstances of this case, that the accused should be granted bail.'

And I tell you, there was pandemonium in the court. An *enormous* cheer. People were on their feet.

About three-quarters of an hour later, when I tried to leave the court building, I couldn't get through the doors because of the television cameras. The whole of Main Road, Port Elizabeth, outside the court, was packed with people. There were *thousands* of people there. These chaps were real heroes in the black community for the stand they had taken. All the traffic had been stopped in the central part of the city, and the brothers were lifted onto people's shoulders and carried down the steps of the court building.

Now I didn't really want to get involved in all of this, so I left by another door, a side door, and I stood on the street corner, about fifty or sixty metres away from where they were, and I watched as these young fellows were carried shoulder-high on this sea of people, to *tremendous* roars.

I waited until the last of the brothers was put down, and I made my way through the edges of the crowd to say goodbye to them. I had a plane to catch, and I wanted to be at the airport in good time. But Cheeky said to me, 'Please, man. Come with the family for two minutes. We're going to celebrate at Nelson's Arm.'

I said, 'Well, you know, I *was* going to the airport ...'

He said, 'Please come with me. Do me that kindness.'

So I said, 'Okay. But I have to be very quick.'

We went into Nelson's Arm, which was a seafood restaurant owned by their sister's husband. The boys' mother was there, and their sister, Sharon. They were all so happy to have the brothers out on bail, man. They'd been in jail now, remember, for six months.

When the waiter came around, he said, 'What can I do for you?' And I said, 'Please, I'm in a hell of a hurry. Just bring me four prawns.'

'Prawns!' cried Valence. 'Haven't you read Leviticus?' And he gave me the chapter and verse. In Leviticus it tells you what you can eat and what you can't eat. And one of the things that you can't eat is prawns, you see.

So I said to him, 'Look, you brought me here, you buggers. I'm going to have some prawns now, and then I'm going home.'

Which I did.

When I came back, about a week later, the State introduced a lot of technical evidence from the insurance company's expert, who spoke about the chemical properties of petrol, which they said had been used as an accelerant in the fire. They had an absurd number of experts in the trial, and the technical evidence went on for days as the prosecution tried to take the momentum of the case away from us.

And then they closed their case. And the trial was then postponed again for another week or so. During that time I stayed down in Port Elizabeth, working with Schubart and my junior colleague, Richard Buchanan, on the defence.

One day I received a phone call from Cheeky. His wife, Tracy, had been to the hairdresser and had apparently overheard something. I asked him to stop right there, because who knew who was listening on the phone, and I hurried over to where the Watsons were staying in a townhouse on Park Drive, near the house that had burned down.

It turned out that a woman in the block of flats next door to the Watson home had seen something just before the fire started. There was a ten- to twelve-storey building next to the house, a very sought-after apartment building.

So I said, 'Who is she?'

133

Tracy said, 'I don't know her at all. But I want you to go and see her.' (By asking around at the hairdresser she had ascertained the number of this woman's flat.)

So I went off, like Perry Mason, with Schubart, and we called at this block of flats next door to the house, which was still a blackened shell.

At first, this woman's husband didn't want to let us in. They were English people. I mean, from England. A man and his wife. He said, 'Look, I don't want you to have anything to do with her. She's already had a nervous breakdown.' And he wouldn't let us talk to her.

I stood there in the passage and pleaded with him. I said to him, 'You know, if there's any relevant evidence that she can give to help these three young men in this predicament, then she owes a *public duty* to do that. And I can promise you one thing,' I carried on, 'I won't in any way cajole her to do anything. I just want to hear what she has to say.'

At last, he very reluctantly said, 'Well, come in.' And then he introduced me to his wife, who looked very apprehensive.

I said to her, 'Come on, let's go and talk.'

And she told us the following story. She and her husband had been out to a club that Saturday night, and had come home just after midnight. It was a beautiful night, she said, and instead of going to bed, as her husband had, she went out onto the balcony for some air. They were on about the third or the fourth floor. She took us out onto the balcony. From there you could see the burnt house and the driveway.

While she was out there, she said, she noticed a white panel van driving slowly with its lights off down the driveway. And just as it reached the street, she said, there was a huge explosion, and that was when the fire started.

She said, 'Please don't ask me any more questions. That's really all I can tell you.'

But she did tell us that she'd heard that there was a woman on the sixth floor of the building who had also seen this van. From her balcony, she pointed out the exact location of this other woman's apartment.

So we went up to the sixth floor and knocked on the door. And this woman came to the door and opened it slightly.

I told her we were lawyers and explained briefly why we were there. She said, 'Oh no, *please!*' She was also from England, funnily enough. She said, 'You know, I really don't want to be involved with this.'

So I said, 'Well, we're not here to offer you money. Unless you take a credit card.'

And she laughed. She just laughed.

Then I said to her, 'We're not here to offer you money. What we want to know is the truth about one matter. One point.'

She said, 'Oh, all right. Come in.'

And she led us into her bedroom, where she told us her story.

She was lying in bed on that Saturday night when she heard an explosion down below. She jumped up and ran out onto her balcony to see what had happened. Her bedroom led straight out onto the balcony. When she looked down to the street, she said, she saw a white panel van turn from the driveway into the street without its headlights on. She said she had phoned her son immediately to tell him what had happened and what she'd seen. Her son told her to call the police, which is what she did. But the police had come only the next morning. They came up to her flat, a couple of them, and stood on her balcony, took photographs and a statement from her, and left. She'd mentioned the explosion. She'd mentioned the van. But she hadn't heard anything more about it.

I asked each of these women if they would be prepared to give evidence. The first woman was *very* reluctant, but in the event they both ultimately agreed to do so, and did. When the trial resumed, I called these two witnesses. They both testified under oath to the presence in the driveway that night of a mysterious white panel van, driving with no headlights away from the house that was now on fire.

And after they gave this evidence, it was Valence's turn to give *his* evidence. He told his version of the story. How Geoffrey owned a car and that was why he had asked him and Archie to keep an eye on the house. He spoke about the intimidation of the security police. The threatening letters the family had received. And I asked him about all that the family had lost in the fire. His father's collection of Bibles, his mother's jewellery, not to mention every one of the family photograph albums. Highly sentimental things they could easily have removed if they were planning on burning their house down. The state prosecutor tried but could not find any inconsistencies in Valence's testimony.

Once Valence had finished giving his evidence, and after almost a month of trial, we were given a chance to address the court in argument. That is when the prosecutor asks for a conviction and attempts to justify it with reference to the evidence as he saw it. Which he did.

Then I was called upon to answer on behalf of the Watsons. One of the important points I made, in reference to the case against the brothers, was the evidence of the two women regarding the panel van.

Because this was incompatible with the State's case. Nor had the prosecution attempted to explain it. I also pointed out, as strongly as I could, the obvious unreliability of the State's main witness, Geoffrey Nocanda, and why he gave the evidence he did. And I reminded the court of what the family had lost in the fire. The magistrate reserved judgment, to be given later.

After a relatively short period – a few days, in fact – he pronounced his judgment, in which he acquitted Ronnie and Cheeky of any crime, but, unbelievably to me, sentenced Valence to six months in prison for arson and insurance fraud.

He dismissed as unfounded the Watsons' assertions of political persecution and concluded that 'the totality of evidence leads only to one inescapable inference – that there was a conspiracy' to burn down the house and file an insurance claim.

In his summation, the magistrate said he accepted Geoffrey Nocanda's evidence. He said it most likely had been obtained after police torture, but this did not mean that it wasn't true. He made only a very brief reference to the testimony of these two women, saying it was unreliable because of minor discrepancies in their accounts. Namely, whether the panel van had driven away just before or immediately after the explosion at the house.

It was a very poor, cursory judgment. But, unfortunately, it was the sort of judgment typical of that time in South Africa – taking the side of the government and its security establishment against its political opposition.

I had no problems getting Valence bail, however, pending an appeal, which was heard a few months later in the Grahamstown High Court.

Now, by the time the appeal was heard, this case had really become a *cause célèbre*. It had been all over the newspapers, here and abroad. Selma came down to Grahamstown with me, and we stayed together at the Wagon Wheel, which was where I always stayed when I went down to handle cases there.

The case came before what they called the 'full bench' of the Eastern Cape Division. Two judges. I knew them both. Frank Kroon had been my junior in a case in Grahamstown before he'd taken silk. And Jimmy van Rensburg I knew quite well, since we'd occasionally been pitted against each other in cases down there, before he became a judge.

Once again, the court was packed. I didn't know it at the time, but apparently a lot of the people there were law students – many of them students from Rhodes – who later became practitioners and told me that they'd come to hear me argue this appeal.

I argued it fully. I argued again that the Watsons had little motive to burn the house down, and reminded the court of all they had lost. And I stressed the evidence of these two women particularly. I reminded the court of their testimony, so cursorily dismissed in the first judgment: the unrelated witnesses who both testified to the presence of a white panel van driving away from the scene without its headlights on. I asked the court to find this to be a sinister piece of evidence against the prosecution's case. And, of course, I stressed the fact that Geoffrey Nocanda's evidence could not be relied upon because of the methods of the police by which it had been obtained. After I had completed my argument, the prosecution argued its very thin case.

And well, the judges did an unusual thing. Judges usually reserve judgment in an appeal, but these two simply said, straight after the prosecution had finished, that they would give judgment after a short adjournment for tea. And after the adjournment, they came in, they sat down, and they gave their judgment. And Valence was acquitted. The judges spoke in the broadest terms and got it over and done with quickly. They said there was no proved motive for the brothers to have done this; that they were not there, and the destruction of the house could have been caused by an unknown party, that sort of thing. And the main state witness had been discredited.

They pronounced their finding in a summary way – in very general terms. They simply said, 'He should have been acquitted, and the conviction and sentence are set aside.'

Their judgment was extraordinary in that it made no reference, *none at all*, to the two women's testimony or to the panel van. This they left untouched.

Regardless, a cheer went up in court. The judges had to ask for silence before they could make their final remarks. The whole thing ended with Judge van Rensburg saying, 'And therefore, Mr Watson' – who was sitting next to me – 'You are found not guilty, and discharged. And you can consider yourself *very lucky*.'

He said that, and then they both stood up to leave.

As they were leaving the courtroom, there was a scream in court. You know who screamed? Just guess. Your grandmother. She was on her feet in the public gallery. She said, 'What *right* does he have to say that? He has NO RIGHT to say that!'

And when the court was finally adjourned, I left Valence and his brothers in the courtroom and went to Judge van Rensburg's chambers. Judge Kroon was with him. They were standing together in the middle of the room.

I said to him, 'Jimmy, what right did you have to say that? After you've found that there was no motive, no evidence. Having said all that, why did you say that he's lucky? What's *lucky* about it, Jimmy?'

Van Rensburg came over and patted me on the shoulder and said, 'Come on, Jules. He'll sleep well tonight. Forget it.' Kroon stood looking at me. I was so upset by that response that I simply turned on my heels and left them without saying another word.

chapter thirteen

In which the old storyteller recalls the acrid smell of the past

Some of the stories from his career at the Bar were no more than short anecdotes. Many of them, especially those from his early days, had in fact been told to him by his older brother, Len. Like this one, for instance. One morning in the lift at work Len saw an acquaintance of his, Mr Hurwitz, a Lithuanian immigrant of their parents' generation. Len greeted him; he said, 'How are you, Mr Hurwitz?' In his thick Lithuanian accent the old man replied, *'Vhy do you ask? Are you a healt' inspector?'*

'Len thought this was *so funny*, man. He ran all the way up to my chambers to tell me about it. He was laughing so much he had to catch his breath.' (This was during the brief period in the 1960s when Len and my grandfather both worked in Innes Chambers in Pritchard Street.)

It was his cases, though – the cases 'involving all sorts of human activity' – that kept us busy for the next six months.

We got together to record less frequently now. Sometimes three or four weeks would go by between sessions. But I'd always look forward to the next session, and whenever we saw each other we would discuss the case, or cases, he was going to tell me about next.

Settled as I was into the late-night rhythm of my job, I enjoyed the counterpoint of these interviews, which I still associate with the light of morning, the light streaming in through the large window behind him and getting caught up in his silvery-white hair.

He told me the story of the mine owner, who, after being cross-examined, came up to him outside the court and told him he was so useless as a lawyer that he was essentially taking his client's money for nothing. He told me about the fire at the furniture repair shop and the witness who claimed to be an expert on everything. And about Mevrou Schultz and the 'shortest, and perhaps most successful', cross-examination of his career. He told me the story of the magistrate who almost got trampled to death by a horse, and of *Ex parte Cassim*, where his client was a young Indian man who wished to become a member of the all-white Pretoria Bar. He told me about the case that arose out of an attack on a police station in Rustenberg, a case in which his client was sentenced to death, and how he managed to get this sentence commuted on appeal. He told me the story behind The State vs Adams, the case that challenged the Group Areas laws in Johannesburg and had the indirect effect of opening up the CBD and Hillbrow to all races in the 1980s. He told me about the Trojan Horse trial in Cape Town and the Magopa people in Rustenberg and about going to Botswana to represent the feminist activist and writer Unity Dow.

Something I perceived while reading through the new transcripts was how many of his stories had, over the years, developed wormholes, openings in their polished surfaces that were the mouths of tunnels that led to other stories, other surfaces, equally polished and similarly wormholed.

So, for example, when he was telling me about the human rights convention in Cape Town in 1979, at which he and Johan Kriegler and others from the Johannesburg Bar first discussed the possibility of starting Lawyers for Human Rights, he mentioned that 'one of the people at the convention was a man by the name of Louis Henken,' a professor from Columbia Law School in New York.

'When it came Professor Henken's turn to talk, towards the end of the conference, he started off,' my grandfather said, 'by saying that everything he wanted to say had already been taken out of his mouth by others.

'"Which reminds me of a story," said Professor Henken. "And I know," said he, "that if I tell this story, it will be all that will be remembered of this address and the paper I am about to present will most likely be forgotten. But I'll tell the story anyway."

'And Henken then went on to relate the following story,' my grandfather said – and he repeated the joke that Henken had told, a long story involving a bossy Scottish vicar and Jonah's adventures with the whale. 'And Henken was right,' he said, laughing, once he'd reported the punchline. 'That story is all I can remember of his address.'

A tunnel leads both ways, of course, and some stories led me back to others I'd heard months, or even years, before. One example of this was an incident that took place after he argued a case in Germiston in 1959.

'The case finished early,' he told me. 'And the attorney – a fellow by the name of Herman, who had taken us there in his car – wasn't yet ready to come home. So he asked me if I wouldn't mind taking a train.

'I said, "Of course I don't mind."

'The attorney said, "I'll send my clerk to take you to the station." Which he did. And on the short ride to the station I got talking to this clerk, who, it turned out, was from the town of Bethlehem in the Orange Free State.

'So of course I thought of Ivan Booyens,' he said. 'You remember Ivan Booyens, the chap who fell under the wheels of U636 in the mountains in Abyssinia? Of course you do. Well, he was from Bethlehem.

'But this was now 1959, fourteen years since the war had ended, and eighteen years since the incident.

'I asked the clerk if he knew anyone by the name of Booyens in Bethlehem. To which he replied, "I don't know anyone by that name. But my father has lived there all his life and he will know, I'm sure."

'So I gave the clerk my telephone number, and he promised to phone me if he learned anything from his father.

'There was some time to spare before the arrival of the train which was to take me to Johannesburg, so I decided to go get a cup of coffee at the small coffee shop on the lower platform.

'Just as I got to the bottom of the stairs, I heard my name called. Someone behind me shouted, "Jules!" And I turned to see who it was, and to my absolute amazement I saw Ivan Booyens.

'I nearly died when I saw him. I really got a *hell* of a fright. I said to him, "*Ivan! Good God!* I mentioned your name not five minutes ago!"

'Booyens was there, apparently, as the inspector of catering on that particular line. He worked for the Railroads. He was at the station to do a routine check, he said, and had decided, against his usual habit, to come down to the lower platform to get a cup of coffee. It was *unbelievable*, man.

'At the coffee shop we sat and spoke about our experiences in the regiment, and I was delighted that he was completely recovered – and that was the last time I saw Ivan Booyens.'

And so it went.

But these stories were mostly about cases, each setting out a problem and tracing a course to its resolution. Which would be either in his favour, or against – by luck, skill or otherwise. Dramatic tension was built in: there were ready-made protagonists and antagonists; you knew what everybody wanted; and there he was in the thick of it, trying to achieve a clearly established goal. Meanwhile, up on the bench, like a king or a god, sat the judge, who would decide the fate of the characters.

The fifty years he spent working at the Bar were almost exactly coterminous with the years that the National Party ruled the country. The beginning of his practice, in the early 1950s, coincided with the first rash of apartheid race statutes, and the shape of the rest of his career was determined in these years. While he did other work in the magistrates' court – criminal and civil cases – he also began, early on, to do a lot of work, much of it without fees, to help those ensnared in this new and fast-growing web.

'I was briefed in many cases arising out of the iniquitous legislation then being enforced in this country,' he told me. 'I mean the race classification cases; criminal cases arising out of aspects of the struggle: for example, raids by activists on police stations and their being charged, and so on; and allegations against people for what was known, in those days, as "furthering the aims of communism".'

One morning I asked him why he thought his career had taken this particular direction. It had struck me that this was by no means self-evident: there were many young lawyers with exactly his background who did not take this route.

'That's a good question,' he said, and took a moment to ponder it. For the first time he told me he would come back to me.

A week later he handed me two pieces of foolscap paper, with his handwriting on both sides of each. In answer to my question he had listed three people whom he called 'ethical inspirations': 1). His father, who taught him by his own example 'to treat people fairly and decently, irrespective of the colour of their skin'; 2). Colin Gluckman, later Colin Gillon, one of the early leaders of the Habonim youth movement in South Africa, who had introduced him at a very early age to Jewish thought and ethics; and 3). Selma, my grandmother: 'the third and thankfully most prolonged source of inspiration.

'Caring for others,' he wrote, in a deliberate cursive, 'has occupied most of her days, and indeed even the hours when one might have expected her to be asleep. It is her example of service to others that was directly responsible for most of the worthwhile activities in which I became involved during the course of my career as an advocate.'

I put these pieces of paper into the box with the transcripts, then changed my mind and filed them with the earliest stories in the pink translucent folder.

Selma Browde in her study at home, 2015

In the last few law sessions his stories took on new shapes. He told me the story of how he and some of his colleagues had formed the Bar's first non-racial group of advocates, and how the members of this group had chosen to stay in Pritchard Street when all the other major legal groups moved north to Sandton. He told me how in 1998 Nelson Mandela, then the country's president, asked him to lead a commission of inquiry into the administration of South African rugby. He recounted the story of the scaled-down Truth and Reconciliation Commission he chaired at the Wits Medical School the following year.

On a morning in April he told me about the party the Bar Council had given to mark his fiftieth anniversary at the Bar in 1989. While he was telling this story I realised I had my own memory of the event. I recalled looking out of a high window at the tall city buildings in the glow of an early evening, and later sitting cross-legged on the floor, listening carefully as a man with a rich, soothing voice made a speech praising my grandfather.

The man in my memory, it turned out, was Ismail Mahomed, and he was then the Chief Justice of South Africa – the first black person to hold that position. He had come up from Bloemfontein to be present at the party.

And that speech I remembered, my grandfather told me, was one that he would cherish for as long as he lived. He told me that Ismail printed out a copy of it, bound it in red velvet, and gave it to him a few months after the party, as a gift for Rosh Hashana.

Remembering the speech and the circumstances of the gift left my grandfather pensive, and he deviated from his plan for that session to tell me a string of stories about Ismail Mahomed, who became a close friend of both my grandparents.

One was about how Ismail had taken care of my grandmother when she found herself without accommodation in Windhoek, where she'd gone to attend the inauguration of Sam Nujoma in March 1990.

Grimacing now and then, he recounted other stories: how Ismail had sometimes carried on his practice as an advocate in Innes Chambers in the 1980s; how he had been allowed to work there, but, because of the Group Areas Act, was not permitted to have his own chambers or eat in the common room.

The last story had the three of them – him, Ismail, and my grandmother – in Pretoria in the eighties. Ismail was my grandfather's junior colleague in a case that involved a young man charged with 'furthering the aims of communism'. Because the two of them were not allowed to have lunch together in any of the restaurants in the area, they used to take sandwiches and eat them in my grandfather's car.

One day my grandmother went to Pretoria for a day to watch the trial, and when it came time for lunch she wouldn't hear of anyone eating in the car. She insisted that they go to a hotel nearby. The proprietor of the hotel restaurant, as expected, refused to seat them.

'When you think about it ...' my grandfather said, shaking his head.

'Anyway,' he continued, 'Ismail decided not to make a public dispute about it. But your grandmother made such a fuss – shouting at this chap – that ultimately he agreed to put us in the corner.' He paused. Then: 'Which just shows you.'

I waited. What did it show you?

'We could have done more,' he said, and pursed his lips.

The look on his face was one of distaste. It was as if he was smelling some sharp odour that these thoughts had conjured. The awful smell of the past. His eyes narrowed slightly to see again through a dimness vividly remembered.

On some nights the newsroom felt like the cabin of a plane crossing the ocean at night: the slightly unnatural hush; the pale fluorescent glare; the close-pressing blackness outside the windows. On one such night – soon after the Ismail Mahomed stories – I got to thinking about his study at their house in Houghton, and what it meant to me when I was a child in apartheid South Africa.

That something was wrong in the land was one of the first things I remember knowing. Even if I didn't understand it, I learned to see it around me, in presences and absences. A presence: the yellow hippo-shaped trucks that sailed down Grant Avenue to and from the Norwood Police Station. An absence: no black children at Norwood Primary School. I learned to hear it in the strains of *Die Stem*, the country's national anthem, which we were supposed to sing in school assembly and I didn't sing; and in the names some children used for black people.

Though we didn't use those words – and even despised them – still we were part of what was wrong. I could feel it was wrong that Di slept in a small room on the other side of our yard. That she spent more time with us than she did with her own daughter, Mapula, who was only a few months younger than I was. Di's 'proper home' was in a place called Hammanskraal, almost an hour's drive away. That was where Mapula lived. In the hour's drive between Mapula and me was everything that was wrong.

Something else I knew was that in his study, bent over his papers, Bronco was trying to do something about it. Even on the brightest afternoons it was cool and shaded in that room. Like how a shul was always shaded. *Solemn* – though I would not have known that word yet. I felt it in there: a mood commensurate with the task at hand. When people came to see him, they sat in there. They parked their cars in the bricked driveway outside, came in through the heavy wooden front door, and then sat and spoke gravely in this room. The thick, brown and black books that crammed the shelves looked like rows of *siddurim*, stippled black or brown with gold writing embossed on their spines. I knew as soon as I knew anything that these books had to do with his work, the Law. I knew the Law was important because it was connected to what was wrong.

I thought of his study as one of a pair of twins. The other twin was the courtroom. I knew that in *this* room, the study, he made his preparations for the battles he fought in the other room. Court, I imagined back then, was a sort of indoor sports arena: a highly controlled combat zone where he went to face the monster of what was wrong, in the hope that the monster would be made weaker by the confrontation.

Something else I thought about that night was how as a child I wanted to be a lawyer. It wasn't something I thought about much, but for many years I wanted to do what he did. I wanted to go to court to fight against what was wrong. That lasted through most of primary school, a dream I swept into some muted corner of my mind along with my plans to climb Mount Everest.

In the next session – one of the last of the law recordings – he started to tell me stories from the years after he retired from the Bar. Some of these concerned his early experiences as one of the judges of the Supreme Courts of Appeal in Swaziland and Lesotho.

When we finished that day, I went, as usual, to put the large hardcover books back on the lowest shelf in his study. It was a part of the business I always enjoyed, something like covering my tracks.

This was a smaller house than the one in Houghton, but what I realised as I looked around it that day was that this was essentially the same room, transplanted. The brown swivel chair in the corner was faded and cracking now, but it was the same chair, and the corner it stood in was still cluttered reassuringly with the same objects: a large cardboard box with a Dustbuster in it; a white tube envelope that had a pink ribbon wrapped around it; and, leaning against the side of the bookshelf, a large framed black-and-white photograph of his younger brother, Bernard, smiling confidently, an unlit cigarette slotted expertly between two slender fingers. And in the middle of the room his desk still stood like a sign. Perfect as a sculpture, its golden wood reflected the same swimming light. The desk promised that whatever work you had to do – school homework, an important case, even the filling out of tax forms – it wouldn't be as bad as you thought. *Just as long as you sat down.* In his voice it spoke.

In Loco

Interview 16
Date recorded: 22/07/2006

In a criminal prosecution, particularly, it is often important for a court to see for itself exactly where an alleged offence was perpetrated. This may be vital in addressing the evidence given by a witness. So on some occasions the court goes out to examine the site and surrounding circumstances. This is known as an inspection *in loco*, which simply means *at the site*.

When, for example, you are an advocate acting on behalf of an accused, you know that if you have an inspection *in loco* you are opening your client up to a rigorous test of his evidence. So it is often a bit of a gamble. Which can sometimes have unexpected results.

This is what happened in a case I want to tell you about now – a case heard in the Johannesburg magistrates' court, in which a white man was charged with having sexual intercourse with a black woman.

This was in the latter part of the 1950s, and it was not the first time, nor was it the last, that I appeared in a matter concerning an alleged contravention of the Immorality Act. I had several such cases: police saying they broke into a house in the middle of the night and found a white man in bed with a black woman, or else that they followed some chap to a township and caught him with his pants down. The Nationalist government's police were obsessed with this sort of thing.

Many of these cases – though not all – had to do with white men visiting black prostitutes. They would pick them up in their cars and take them to wherever it was. Sometimes it was alleged to have happened in the car. Sometimes in a strip of veld. Sometimes it was in the room of the woman in the township. Anywhere, really. After all, you are dealing with sexual intercourse: very often opportunities are seized without careful consideration of time and place.

There was a division of the police that specialised in this: the so-called Vice Squad, whose members went around with binoculars, ladders, recording devices. *Spying*, essentially. They would receive tip-offs: 'This is a man who frequents this sort of place.' And they would go and lie in wait. The fellow would arrive and they'd wait a bit longer, and then break in, and they'd find him nude, or with his pants around his ankles, or whatever it was. It was a most disgusting piece of legislation. And a sick sort of voyeurism, if you think about it. And the impact on human beings was terrible.

The penalty was up to five years in jail for the man and four years for the woman. But they hardly bothered prosecuting the black woman. In nearly all the cases I know of, white men were hounded by the police. (The case of a black man and a white woman was so rare that I can't remember encountering one.)

The white man's defence was usually some sort of convoluted denial. Merely preparing to have intercourse, but not to a degree where it became an *attempt*. This was my client's defence, as you shall see. In applying the law relative to criminal offences, the line between *preparation* and *attempt* was often what the court had to decide.

The State's only witness in this particular case was a young policeman, an Afrikaans chap not much older than you, who told the following story. He said he'd been driving one afternoon on the Eloff Street extension when he'd seen the accused (a white man) and a black woman, walking 'suspiciously' together along the side of the road. The policeman said he saw the two of them enter a field surrounded by a corrugated iron fence, and thinking it his duty to observe what happened next, he pulled the car over to the side of the road.

He said he was able to follow what he saw happening next through a small hole in the fence. What he saw through the hole, he told the court, was the accused having intercourse with this woman, the two of them pressed against a tree on the far side of the field.

Not only did he witness this, the policeman concluded triumphantly, but when the man came back to the road, his fly was open. When he arrested the accused, the policeman told the court, he was still desperately trying to button his fly.

148

My client, who was out on bail, said that indeed he *had* gone into the field with this woman, and admitted that he'd had an idea that he would do something with her, but he'd changed his mind, he said. As to the question of his fly, he gave the following explanation. He did not dispute the policeman's evidence; he said, 'It's true, I was doing up my fly, but it had nothing to do with the woman.' When he came out of the field, he said, he had to pass through a narrow gate in a barbed wire fence, and a piece of wire sticking out from the gatepost had pulled open the buttons of his fly.

It was, of course, a most unlikely story, but these were the sort of hopeless excuses brought about by this mad legislation. Defending people in this position was a pathetic exercise. You did what you could. This was my client's story and he seemed intent on sticking to it.

He also told me that he doubted very much that the policeman could have seen anything through that hole in the fence, and that, in any event, from where the policeman was standing there could have been no clear view of the tree. He suggested to me that we should apply to have an inspection *in loco*.

And so I took his word for it, and applied for an *in loco* inspection. It was a real roll of the dice. If there is no hole in the fence, or if indeed, as my client said, it was impossible for the policeman to see the tree, it would be decisive against the prosecution's case. But if we arrive there and see the hole, and from the hole we see the tree, then that would corroborate the evidence of the policeman and it would be another nail in his coffin.

Things were not looking good for us, and I felt we had little to lose. So I made the application. The prosecutor was only too pleased to go out, and did not oppose the application, so the magistrate said, 'Very well, we'll go.'

Sometimes the *in loco* inspection would be scheduled for the day after the application was made, or at least the next session. But in this case, the magistrate said we'd go immediately. There was a short adjournment of the court to organise motorcars. The magistrate went in one car with his driver and the court clerk. And the prosecutor went in his car, and I went in my car with the attorney. So three cars in all left the magistrates' court on West Street.

We drove out to where the Selby turnoff is. There you go under the bridge and travel south on the Vereeniging Road. It was somewhere near the Turffontein Racecourse, that's where this had taken place. And we stopped there. It was a very bare and almost desolate scene. Today it's quite built up there – with warehouses, car dealerships, factories and that sort of thing. Then it was still very empty – a few low sidings, barns, but mostly dust and veld.

The policeman took us to the fence. We all followed him. It was a high corrugated iron fence, in places brown with rust. The magistrate took out his notebook, and he turned to the policeman and said, all in Afrikaans, he said, 'Where's the hole?'

The policeman pointed it out.

At first I couldn't see any hole at all. Only by walking up close to the fence did you discover a short horizontal tear, a little above eye-level. I recall that the magistrate had to stand on his toes to get his eye to the spot. I also took a turn. A few metres away there was another fence – a barbed wire one, with the small gate my client had spoken about. Beyond this barbed wire fence was an empty field, a few thorn bushes, and about a hundred metres in the distance was a solitary tree.

The magistrate asked the prosecutor if he wouldn't mind going to stand next to the tree, where the policeman said it had happened. The prosecutor walked around the end of the corrugated iron fence, through the narrow gate, and then made his way across the veld to the tree.

Now I have no clear recollection of what exactly we were able to see through the hole, but I do recall that it would have been difficult to see exactly what was going on at the tree. It was a gloomy day and the sun kept disappearing behind clouds and re-emerging. I remember being struck by how ridiculous and cruel it all was. What were we all doing there?

In the end, the peep-hole test was inconclusive. Only the question of the fly remained. Why was my accused buttoning his fly when the policeman arrested him? That remained the glaring piece of evidence that seemed set to convict him.

The group of us now went to the other side of the fence and waited for the prosecutor to come back from the tree. When he came back, he again passed through the narrow gate, and what do you think happened?

A piece of wire that was jutting out of the one side caught in his pants and ripped open his fly. There in his dark pants was suddenly a shock of white: his shirt-tail showing through.

Well. At first we all stood there mute with incomprehension. But as he started buttoning his fly we all collapsed laughing, including the magistrate, who rocked his head back and roared with laughter. All, that is, except the prosecutor, who stood there shaking his head and looking suitably aggrieved. When he'd recovered, the magistrate turned to the prosecutor and said *'En nou meneer die aanklaer?'* Meaning: And now, Mr Prosecutor? *'Waar is you saak* nou?' Where is your case *now?*

And as a result of this extraordinary coincidence, my chap got off, which meant that the gamble of the inspection *in loco* paid a handsome dividend. And, of course, I wondered for a long time afterwards, to this day really, what force – if indeed that is the right word for it – opened the prosecutor's fly that afternoon on the Vereeniging Road.

Which is not to say that things always turned out that way. Sometimes the gamble went the other way. And I'd just like to tell you now – very briefly – about another *in loco* inspection, which didn't turn out so well for my client.

This one happened, fittingly enough, at the Turffontein Racecourse itself. Not very far from the site of the strange story I've just related.

In this case, I was briefed by the Johannesburg Turf Club. This is the group that ran the horse racing at Turffontein, the oldest racecourse in Johannesburg. It was started in the early years of the city. The Turf Club generally administered racing there.

What had happened was this: a woman, the plaintiff in the case, had come to spend a day at the races, and she had entered the main gate, which is a very beautifully constructed feature of the property. Unbeknown to her, when a race is over the jockeys bring their horses around and ride past the main gate, along the inner road inside the course to the paddock, where they dismount. Now she had apparently arrived in between races and had entered the gate, but didn't see a horse and a jockey coming along before it was too late. The horse collided with her, and injured her. Not terribly badly, but she sustained some injuries, and she decided to sue the Turf Club for damages, arguing that they did not give people proper warning of the potential risks involved in entering that gate.

My instructions from the board of the Turf Club were that anybody could see if there was danger coming there. They were all very dismissive of her account. It was very simple, they said. All one had to do was to keep one's eyes open, which was something this woman obviously hadn't done. They said they'd never had trouble like this before and denied all liability.

Well, there was a dispute in court about whether it was safe or not, and I applied for an inspection *in loco*. Which was granted.

We all went out the following morning. It was a fine day, I recall, with no racing on. We parked the cars in the lot and made our way towards the main gate. I was walking with the magistrate and the chairman of the Turf Club. The plaintiff, who had by now recovered from her injuries, followed a few paces behind us with her attorney and advocate.

As we got to the gate, I stepped aside – politely, I thought – and said to the magistrate, 'After you, sir.'

He thanked me and went in ahead of me.

No sooner had the magistrate stepped foot through the gate than he had to *leap* backwards to avoid being trampled by what was a *huge* horse with a rider in the saddle advancing along the road at high speed. He grabbed hold of me to steady himself; he had gone quite pale. The thumping of the hooves got fainter as the horse and rider appeared to gallop off towards the paddock.

The magistrate let go of my arm and looked directly at me. Even though *he* wasn't smiling, I couldn't help doing so. It was *so* funny, man. I put up both my hands, as if surrendering, turned to the Turf Club chairman and told him, in a stage whisper, that I thought we should probably settle this case. Which they did.

And so it was that an inspection *in loco* had the opposite effect. It sunk us. The Turffontein Club paid this woman out a sum – I don't remember what it was, but they could afford it – and subsequently put up a very big sign at the gate warning people of the possibility of horses approaching on the inner road.

chapter fourteen

In which one journey ends and another begins

Sometimes on Thursday nights I'd go out by myself after work. This always felt like a better idea in my car driving out of the building than it did once I was actually out. Then it would become clear to me what I was doing out there. I wanted to meet someone. Often I'd find myself trying to catch the eye of a girl on the dance floor, and I didn't like how that felt: another guy on the prowl. Coming back to my flat was always a relief. I'd sit in the La-Z-Boy with a bowl of Coco Pops and read.

By this time my grandfather had told me the last of the law stories. In the second-to-last session he spoke of a judgment he wrote in Swaziland in 2002 in which he found one of King Mswati's decrees – making fraud an unbailable offence – to be unconstitutional. The king accused him and the other judges of being pawns of 'external forces' trying to derail the country, and instructed his authorities to ignore the judgment. In protest my grandfather and the other judges resigned, and Swaziland had no Court of Appeal for more than two years. It was only after a lot of international pressure that King Mswati climbed down and released a statement unconditionally accepting the ruling and retracting the accusation. My grandfather and the others went back to work in early 2005.

In the final law session he used two case studies to explain the work he'd been doing as the integrity commissioner at the provincial and city legislatures. In these stories he spent more time describing the nature of his relationship with his assistant in the city legislature, Aubrey Ncongwane, than he did on the cases. The last story he told me was not about work at all but about Aubrey's son and the difficulties Aubrey and his wife had had finding the right school for him.

I clearly remember the moment, on that morning late in winter, when we turned the corner and entered the home stretch. I have the transcript in front of me. 27 June 2007. 'Now just tell me something,' is the first thing he'd said once the dictaphone was rolling. 'Is it on now? Did I mention how I met Selma?'

'You did.'

'I did. Yes.'

'At the party,' I said.

'Yes, that's quite right. Absolutely right. Very well.'

'You spoke about your courtship, and you spoke about the wedding, *um*, but after that …'

While telling me the stories of his cases he had occasionally mentioned, just by way of providing context, a few monumental developments, like 'We had the boys by that time', or, 'That was around the time of Ian's accident'. But since he'd spoken about the early years of his marriage, he hadn't said much about his life at home. It was as if at a point near the beginning of his career his life had split into two different lives that had subsequently run parallel to one another, related but never touching.

He had just spent months talking about one of those lives, and I realised I was craving to hear him speak about the other one. I think he was craving it too.

That day he told me, again, about the early years of their marriage, explaining in detail how my grandmother had 'kept them afloat' in those early years, when briefs were 'few and far between'. How she left medical school in Cape Town to live with him in the hotel room on Commissioner Street. How, prevented from continuing her medical studies in Johannesburg because of university red tape, she sold advertising space in a cricket almanac and painted vases to 'make extra coin' while he battled to get work. How he came *this close* to quitting the Bar, but she persuaded him not to.

These were stories he'd told me before, almost word for word, but I didn't interrupt him. In this context they were different stories because they were about something else; they were about the foundations of a family. And soon he headed off into brand new territory. He told me how they moved out of the hotel when a friend found them 'simple, fairly cheap accommodation in a newly built block of flats called Eliana

Court in Norwood'. Which was where they were living when, on the afternoon of the first night of Pesach in 1949, their first child was born.

Entranced, I listened to his story of my uncle's birth – at the Princess Nursing Home in Hillbrow. The doctor emerging to tell him that mother and baby were safe. The tale ended with him looking for the first time into the face of his newborn son and feeling that his own father, who had died eleven years before, had somehow been 'replaced' by this little boy. They named him Ian.

This was exactly the sort of thing I'd been hungering for.

A year after Ian was born, the little family moved out of the flat in Norwood and into their first house, on George Avenue, in the suburb of Sandringham. Here, on farmland to the east of town, an organisation called the British Empire Service League was helping Second World War veterans buy houses at affordable prices. And a year after that, my grandmother gave birth to their second child, another boy. Alan.

When I was a child the stories I liked to hear my grandfather tell more than any others were the ones about my father as a boy. So now I leaned in a little closer. I knew the ones he'd tell, and he told them. The one about how, as a kid, my dad strung up a cricket ball in a stocking in a tree and stood in the garden every afternoon, for hours, hitting the ball back and forth, back and forth, until my grandmother took him to see a psychologist. The one where he threw the tennis ball over the heads of the judges at the school sports day at the Balfour Park grounds. The one where he dived, fully clothed, into a hotel swimming pool in the middle of winter, a teenager watched by chance by a conference of psychiatrists.

Once he'd told all of these, he told another story – also familiar, but one I hadn't, until that day, considered to be part of the same catalogue. This one started with the same boy, now a little older, unhappy in his early twenties.

'He had no ambition,' my grandfather said, setting the scene. 'He had no guiding star of any kind. He seemed just to drift along. But then he met Suzie, and they went down to Cape Town, and they – what was called in those days – 'shacked up' together, in a little house in Observatory. And they lived there together for a while.

'It wasn't long before the two of them joined a *garin*, a crowd of young people, and went to live on a kibbutz in Israel, called Nir Eliyahu. A kibbutz very near the Palestinian town of Qalqilya.

'Then, in their second year away, we received news that Suzie was pregnant. And we were thrilled, of course. And so began a countdown of sorts, to the beginning of a new generation.

'I heard the story only later,' he said. 'How the doctors at the nearby hospital wouldn't allow Alan to be present at the birth, and how Suzie and Alan adopted the attitude that they would have to find a doctor who *would* allow him to be present.

'And how, ultimately, they found a South African doctor who was practising at a little hospital called Poriah, overlooking Lake Tiberias, who said that he would do the job and that of *course* Alan should be there. I forget that doctor's name. You can ask your parents. But the point of the story is that your father was allowed to be with your mother when you were born.'

Alan and Suzie Browde with their son, Daniel, 1979

I had a peculiar feeling, listening to this. I felt grand and simultaneously about as small as a grain of sand. I sensed something I could
put into words only a few days later, after I'd typed out the interview.
Once I'd stapled the printed pages and slipped the document under the
pile in the cardboard box, I went out onto the balcony and looked down
at the cars in the parking lot next door: my father's white Camry; my
mother's orange Yaris. I thought about those two people working under
that corrugated iron roof. I was beginning to understand that whatever
else I am, I am also just another character in their stories.

We did the last planned interview on 1 December 2007. A blue sunny
day in the middle of summer. He wanted to use the session to speak
about my uncle Paul, my father's younger brother, their last-born child.
My grandfather said he'd been thinking a lot about what he wanted to
say, and while he had no notes, his first few sentences had a rehearsed
quality.

The first paragraphs of the monologue – for that is what it was –
dealt with Paul's childhood. He told stories that illustrated his talent for
kindness. Like the time he befriended an outcast boy in his class even
though he knew he would lose friends as a result. These were clearly
not just random stories he'd thought to tell; he was going somewhere
with this. This was plotted. The stories were tending towards a room
in a house on the Californian coast, where he learned that his son was
HIV-positive.

'You must remember, Dan, that this was 1987. In those days it was a
death sentence. I was told effectively that Paul was going to die. And to
me it was absolutely shattering. Shattering. But, uh, thank ... you know,
whoever it is ... thank God ... that he was ... that it turned out ...'

I remember that morning, that moment, eight years ago. I remember the beauty and the light as he looked down at his hands and tried
to steady himself, to concentrate. This was the story he wanted to tell.

'I just realise how much he's meant to us, and what ... and I can't
really, I can't ...'

With his forefinger and thumb he pinched the bridge of his nose,
and could not, for the time being, say any more.

I let the tape spool in the silence.

When he looked up, he said, 'You know, recently I went with Selma
to Poland to attend a wedding. Margie Hellman's eldest boy got married

to a Danish girl there. Because her father was Polish. Now, why I'm telling you this,' he said, 'is that in the middle of everything, I went to Auschwitz. We, the three of us – Ronnie Hellman and her husband and I. Selma didn't want to go, and I wouldn't have let her go, anyway. Because she doesn't sleep as it is thinking about hungry children, let alone Auschwitz.'

He was looking at me carefully, as if searching my face.

'And as I came out, Ronnie's husband – he's an Australian chap – said to me, What did I think of it? And I said to him, I said, "I make a vow, now. I will never try to describe my feelings – either my feelings, or Auschwitz itself – because I don't believe that I have the ability to put into words the effect it's had on me." And, in a way, if you ask me to describe exactly what Paul has meant to me, personally, and the whole drama of his HIV-positive situation, and his emergence from it, I can't. Because I don't believe I can do justice to it. And that's why I'd rather not say more than I've said.'

'That's fine,' I said.

The tape rolling, rolling.

'I can't wait to see them,' he said. 'Paul and Simon. They're coming out in about two weeks' time.'

'Three weeks,' I said. 'Aren't they arriving on the twentieth?'

'They're coming on the twentieth, that's right. Yes.'

'I can't wait to see them either,' I said.

'Anyway, so that's it. Now look here, if we can just stop this thing, I want to ask you a question …'

I must have leaned forward and turned the dictaphone off, because that is where the recording – the last full recording – stops.

I can't remember what he wanted to ask me. I like to think the missing question held a message. Either way – this I do remember – I took the machine off the pile of books and put it back into its sock and put the sock into my backpack. Then I took the big books back to the study, and, after saying goodbye, I went in to the newspaper, dropping the tapes back at my flat on my way to work. I typed out the interview over the next few days and slid it under the pile in the box at the back of my cupboard.

It had been two years and two months since we had started recording. We had done twenty-five interviews. I had typed out 450 pages of transcripts. We had set ourselves an ambitious goal: to start from his earliest memories and bring ourselves to the present day. And we'd achieved that. We needed a sense of completion and we got it from this fact. But of course it was arbitrary. There were more stories to get down.

My grandfather would often say, 'I'm sure I've told you about So-and-So' and would then be disappointed if I told him he hadn't. A short, hurried pick-up session, aimed at recording one or two stories, would follow, to remedy the sense that something precious had slipped past and lay abandoned on the road behind us.

But it happened too often. There were too many stories. Once, and then twice, we just left it, said *too bad*, and a tale he wanted to tell, and I wanted to record, would remain behind, untended to. I would criticise myself for this, especially in the beginning, since it seemed a failure of will. But I reminded myself that it was impossible to get every single story down. Recording all the stories of a life is an un-finishable task. Without discussing it openly, we found a way to let the exercise be; and things, as much as was possible, went back to how they were before we started.

I went to their house for other reasons, the reasons I used to go there. This felt strange at first, but less and less as time went by. If I popped in there on a Saturday afternoon I could enjoy the lull of simply being a welcome guest. My grandmother loves the well-worn ritual of after-noon tea, and performs it with the respectful relish of an anthropologist in a foreign land. She would bring out a tray with all the paraphernalia – sugar dish, tiny milk jug, small plate with biscuits – and set it down with a not-unironic smile.

Weeks and months passed, and whatever strangeness I'd felt at not being there on recording business receded completely. In its place there came a species of relief: a superficial kind, marbled with raw nerves.

My sisters were all still in Joburg. (This was before Emma moved to London to study psychiatry and Kate took a training position at a hos-pital in Cape Town.) They all still lived with my parents in Sandringham and we'd see each other every Friday night, either there or in Orange Road. Around the table we'd make each other laugh or cry while the candles silently melted. I couldn't help thinking that these were the times *we* would tell stories about one day. We wouldn't have this, or it wouldn't be so easy. I could feel the waters around us rising.

Quite often on these nights my grandfather would lean forward on his folded arms and say, 'Now look *here*. That reminds me of a story' – just as he always had. But now, when he did, he'd add something new. Shooting a look at me, he'd say, 'This is a story Dan will recognise.'

And I'd wait for him to start, praying it was.

[II]

chapter fifteen

In which we meet the young storyteller two years later, and discover that the interviews sit in a box under his desk, gathering dust

The transcripts and the cardboard box grew into each other and became one thing that followed me from place to place. When I moved out of the flat to house-sit for a few months in Troyeville, I stashed it among the rest of my things in a spare room. When I moved from Troyeville to a new flat in Killarney, I put it under the desk in the lounge, which for a year doubled as my flatmate's bedroom. When my friend moved out I shuffled things around and took it into the walk-in cupboard off my bedroom. There it sat on the lowest shelf, an uncertain treasure beside a pile of phone books left behind by the previous owner.

The name of the building was Earls Court, one of many 'courts' in the suburb of old apartment buildings. Next door was Mentone Court; Dukes Court was diagonally opposite; and just a block away, along Riviera Road in the direction of the zoo, was Daventry Court, where my grandfather lived with his mother and brother after his father died in 1938.

From the street Daventry Court looks like a gigantic paper maquette: a precise arrangement of white rectangles and cylinders with pale-grey decorative strips that appear to have been stuck on with modelling glue running the height of the building. When I walked past it, if I was in that sort of mood, I would stop on the pavement, pick out any first-floor window, and think back to the stories he'd told me – the stories we'd stopped recording three years before. I'd picture him inside, a young man of twenty tossing and turning in bed, ashamed because he hadn't yet joined the army. Or I'd see him sitting by lamplight at his typewriter in the early hours of the morning, squinting as he struggled to decipher Judge Blackwell's longhand scrawl.

My flat was on the third floor of Earls Court. Its lounge and bedroom windows looked out onto the plane trees that grow on the side of Riviera Road. At the beginning of each summer, as the branches sprung their first luminous-green leaves, a weaver bird would build a nest at the end of a thin branch near to the lounge window. I'd sit on the couch and watch as he went about his business. In the next tree along a hadeda would build a nest of his own, though I never saw him do it. The nests couldn't have been more different: where the weaver's was a small, meticulous construction made of long thin strands of grass, the hadeda used large sticks, which he laid down like kindling in a fork of branches.

The turnover of subeditors at newspapers is fast: after four years at *Business Day* I was one of those who'd been there the longest. There were people who'd been there much longer than I had, of course, but I was definitely not a newbie any more and could confidently join in the conversations about the golden era that had just passed.

During the financial crisis of 2008, when a lot of regular advertisers stopped placing ads in the paper, the company tried to cut costs by retrenching employees and consolidating once-separate divisions. The staff of a financial magazine had recently come down from the floor above to share our newsroom, which meant that those of us who still had jobs had to squash up on one side of the room. In spite of all of this, the work of subbing still felt more like a pastime than a chore.

The more closely-felt changes and realignments in my world had happened closer to home. To start with: my great uncle, Bernard.

Younger than my grandfather, Bernard had aged faster, and throughout the past decade his health had been declining. I saw Bernard seldom, but when I did – mostly on Friday nights – he usually seemed in high spirits, despite his growing frailty. The family put his high spirits down to his finding a close friend and companion at Our Parents' Home. Hans, a German Jew and Holocaust survivor, was short and portly and spoke in a thick, German-inflected, Old World accent. The two of them acted like a pair of mischievous children, always together and usually laughing at something no one else understood. Every other week my grandfather took the two of them for lunch at Alexander's

Deli on Grant Avenue. Even as his face grew thinner and his movements became slower and more laboured, Bernard seemed happier and more confident than I – or I think anyone – had ever known him to be.

When he died that winter, the winter of 2008, after a minor fall, no one saw it coming. My grandparents were not even in the country: they had gone to India for ten days to attend the wedding of a friend's daughter. I remember feeling perturbed by this. I knew it would be particularly difficult for my grandfather because of what had happened when his older brother died. I remembered that he'd been out of the country then, too. That was a story he hadn't told me, and thinking about this now, after Bernard's death, I was surprised he'd left it out. But I didn't make a note to ask him if we could get it down. I didn't think like that any more. I'd stopped thinking like that a long time ago.

Bernard Browde

I counted eleven people at Bernard's graveside. I thought of the stories my grandfather had told me about his little brother, the awkward child who struggled to make friends. Aside from my father, me, Hans and the rabbi, there were no other men there, so the gravediggers and some other employees of the Chevra Kadisha came to make up the *minyan*, the ten men necessary to hold a prayer service. I can't remember what the rabbi said in his eulogy. All I remember was cold air sliding off the bare yellow koppie and Hans looking distractedly down at his shoe throughout the whole thing. When the first spade-load of soil hit the coffin, he grimaced as if he'd been punched in the stomach.

On the long walk back to the *ohel*, I thought more and more about the little Bernard in my grandfather's stories. The boy my great-grandfather called '*Lange Loksch*', which is sort of like 'beanpole' in English. I thought particularly of the story about the stamp collection and wondered again about Bernard's role in it.

That night, I went with my father to visit Hans in his room at Our Parents' Home. Hans was restless and talkative and poured whisky after whisky into tumblers he kept in a tall wooden cabinet at the foot of his bed. Even as my eyes widened at how much he was drinking, my heart swelled at the heavy music of his words. Here, I realised, was one of the old men from the stories – a living relic, part of a dying breed. Here was Sharpie, the shammas. Here was Mr Sacks from Turffontein Wholesale. Here was old Mr Hurwitz, saying to Len, '*Vhy do you ask? Are you a healt' inspector?*'

The only person missing was my grandfather. Bernard's passing meant that he was the only one of his siblings still alive. First Len, then Lily, and now Bernard, all had gone, leaving him the last remaining planet in their solar system. I couldn't stop thinking about this, and I traced a line back through the night sky to myself and my sisters.

Things were changing with us, too, and I couldn't work out whether it was me changing or if my family was changing around me. I supposed it was a bit of both. I saw them less now that I was living at Earls Court. Often the only time I'd see them in a week would be on Friday night.

Sometimes I thought about the pact my sisters had made one distant night. Lamenting how my parents' siblings were scattered all across the world, they promised each other they would never let this depressing fate befall them. They would always live in the same city, they swore. They were fourteen, twelve and nine at the time. I was seventeen and didn't take part in the pact, but I was there, at the table, nodding inside. They were speaking a secret sibling language I understood. But the pact had been broken. After finishing medical school Emma had gone to London to study psychiatry. Kate had also qualified as a doctor and was working at a children's hospital in Cape Town. Cara was still in Joburg. So was Micaela, who was only a toddler when the others made the pact – the pact that, I guess, *had* to be broken. There is the spell of secret languages, but there are stronger spells: the spell of movement, the spell of finding your own place in the world.

When my grandfather came back from India, he looked tired and grey, and he was distracted, lost to his thoughts. The one time I tried to talk to him about Bernard he was impossible to reach. It was hard to see him like that, but it didn't last long. Soon things were back to normal between us, or what passed for normal now.

Stopping the recording had left a hole – a tender space that itched sometimes, a nostalgia for those mornings with the dictaphone spooling between us. We were like two travellers who had gone off to a distant land and returned to live among our countrymen. Something connected us that only we could understand. But from time to time I wondered if we understood it in the same way.

The stories were down now; that objective had been reached. But, in the silence after the interviews, that wasn't enough. There was a new lack – an absence strangely shaped at the edge of my vision. What was missing was a book, the book my grandmother had named all those years before. That was the idea spoken only in passing and only now and then: to turn the transcribed interviews into a biography. A biography I should write, or assemble, or however it was biographies came about.

So the cardboard box in my cupboard was both a treasure chest and a difficult question. Occasionally I'd take the first interview from the top of the pile and read the first paragraph. 'Let me tell you this,' it began – and it ended with the Freemasons throwing rose petals into his father's grave.

Sometimes I sat on the end of my bed with the transcript and imagined those words as the starting point of a biography. 'Let me tell you this,' the book would begin. But then things went dark. Looking ahead from that point was like looking into a dark room. I could see the outlines of certain things, but I couldn't tell if they were the things I thought they were or other things with similar outlines. So I left it alone. I carried on working at the newspaper – occasionally fiddling with one of my poems; reading about the rose petals, now and then – and left the difficult thing to work itself out.

It came to mind though, usually out of the blue. I remember one day, driving along Oxford Road on my way to work, reading the headlines strapped to the street poles – OBAMA SURGES IN POLLS; SELEBI SUSPENDED – and thinking that I didn't know where I stood in relation to politics and history, when suddenly the door to the dark room was open and I was peering inside. Is that what a biography is, I asked myself, changing lanes. Placing a person's life in relation to politics and history? Did I even know how to do that?

But I never looked into that room for long, let alone dared to edge my way in to take a closer look around. Before I could do that I needed to know what I was looking for. And I didn't know. All I knew was that whatever it was, the answer was no. No, I wasn't able to do it – not now, not like this. So I kept turning away from the door and the teeming darkness behind it.

Then this happened: a few weeks later, in July of 2008, Ma was admitted to the hospital for the third time in six months. She had slipped and twisted her ankle, and the pain and swelling weren't going away. She was in a wheelchair; she was losing weight. My mother was worried; her eyes would pool with tears whenever we spoke about it. And while I can't say for sure, it is possible – as the poet said – that years from now I will be telling this story and I will say that it was what happened next that sent me back to the box of transcripts to see what I could make of them.

HARTMAN

Interview 19
Date recorded: 25/10/2006

One day in 1985 I received a call from an attorney in Grahamstown. He asked me if I'd be interested in taking a case on behalf of a young Afrikaner by the name of David Hartman, who was refusing to serve in the army on the grounds that he was a Buddhist and his conscience would not allow him to be associated with violence of any kind. I told him this case did interest me – a lot.

South Africa really, at that time, was at war. PW Botha was the president, and he had declared two states of emergency. The army was on the streets of the townships and on the border. And for young white men there was compulsory conscription: they had to serve two years in the army after they finished school. Those who refused to do so were subject to imprisonment.

The attorney, whose name was Nettleton, said, 'Well then, if you take the case, would you mind if I nominated the junior?'

I said, 'Of course not. On the contrary, that's what you *should* do.'

'Well, there's a young man by the name of Cameron,' he said. 'Edwin Cameron. He has very recently joined the Bar in Johannesburg. Would you mind if he was your junior?'

I'd met Edwin once or twice. He was quite friendly with your uncle Paul. He seemed an extremely intelligent young man. So I said, 'Not at all. I'd be delighted to have him as my junior.'

Shortly thereafter, David Hartman, a tall good-looking young man, came to see us, and told the following story. He had gone before the

Board for Religious Objection in Bloemfontein – which consisted of a judge, an army chaplain and four theologians – and he'd told them he was a follower of the Buddhist philosophy and wanted no part in violence of any kind.

One of the members of the board had suggested he serve in a branch of the army in which there wouldn't be any fighting. He had said no, he didn't want to do that, because this would be assisting in violence.

While he was explaining this point, the judge had interrupted him and had said, 'Tell me, Mr Hartman. Do you believe in *God*?'

To which he'd said the following: 'If someone asked me if there is a god, I would say I do not know.'

'So you don't believe in God?'

'I neither believe, nor disbelieve, in God,' he'd said. 'God plays no part in my philosophy.' That is what he told them.

This meant nothing to them. The board came to the conclusion that if you don't believe in God, you can't be a conscientious objector on religious grounds. So they denied Hartman his application and said that if he still refused to serve in the army he would have to go to jail. According to the Defence Amendment Act, non-religious objectors were sentenced to six years in jail.

In preparing for the presentation of the case, I asked Edwin to research the matter carefully in relation to conscientious objectors in other countries. He had done a number of these sorts of cases. The End Conscription Campaign had been launched a year or two before, and he was very involved with that. It was something he was particularly interested in.

And I remember that when Edwin came to my house one afternoon, to show me what he'd done, I understood why people said he was one of the most promising lawyers in the country. I couldn't have been more impressed. He had done meticulous research, and I told him so.

He had looked into this and found that while the board's decision followed decisions in many other countries, including the United States, and several cases had turned on whether or not a person believed in God, and whether you had to believe in God in order to be considered a conscientious objector on religious grounds, there was still a powerful argument to be made that it was the wrong decision.

The Act demanded that a religion be a recognised world religion. We would argue that Buddhism was such. Where it required a religion to have a book of revelation and an article of faith, we would show the canon of teachings to which this particular Buddhist tradition subscribed. And we would direct the judges' attention to a test for religious conviction as it had been formulated in the Supreme Court of the United States, which pronounced that a belief that occupies in someone's life a place *parallel* to the one more commonly filled by the God of theistic religions should enable a person to qualify as a religious objector. So we would review the decision of the board on the basis that it was actually a wrong decision, that they hadn't applied their minds properly in terms of the Act.

And so we went down to Bloemfontein a short time later, feeling relatively confident that we had a good review. We were to appear the next day to argue the case before three judges in the Supreme Court of the Orange Free State, as it was called then. We stayed overnight at a hotel in Bloemfontein, and the following morning we walked to court.

Near the entrance to the court, on a fenced-off lawn, we noticed what appeared to be a bright-yellow mound. Almost like a tent. A buttercup yellow. And sticking out of the top of it was a human head. This head was completely shaved, so you couldn't at first see whether it was a man's head or a woman's. And from this figure emanated a sound like this: *tongtong, tongtong, tongtong.*

We stopped and looked more closely, and I saw that it was a woman wearing yellow robes, and that she had a little instrument, a sort of lute with only one string, and as she plucked it, it went *tong, tongtong, tongtongtong.*

The two of us stood and watched this for a while, and then I said, 'Edwin, do me a favour. Just go and find out what this is all about.'

So Edwin hopped over the fence – which was about knee-high – onto the lawn, and went over to this yellow mound. I watched in amazement as he had a short talk with the person. Then he came back and he said, 'She's a Buddhist.'

I laughed. I said to him, 'Well, alright. Now please go and tell her that we'd like to speak to her later to ask her what she is doing here.'

Edwin said, 'Well, you'd better go and ask her this time.'

So I climbed over the fence, and I went up to her and said good morning. She smiled and greeted me very affably.

'Tell me, why are you doing this?' I said. I looked at the lute; it was a very beautifully carved instrument.

She said, 'I've come from England because word has spread about this case. And I'm here in an effort to put some wisdom into the minds of the judges.'

I said, 'Well, good. That's fine. Carry on.' And I turned around and went off and, as I did, I heard *tongtong, tongtong, tongtong*.

Well, we went into the court building, we robed, and then – as tradition had it – went to say good morning to the presiding judge. The presiding judge was Frank Smuts, a well-known judge in the Free State. I had appeared in front of him before, and the moment he saw me he said, 'Oh, I'm so delighted to see you.' He didn't look at the others, he said this just to me.

I said, 'Why are you so delighted, Judge?'

He said, 'Because I want you to put an end to that racket that's going on outside. I know you can do that, Jules.'

I said, 'Well, I must tell you, I *can't*. It's got nothing to do with me.'

The judge said, 'What are you talking about? I thought she was part of your team.' He was being facetious. He said, 'It struck me that she might be a mascot for your team.'

I said, 'Not at all.'

'So why do you think she's doing that, Jules?' he asked me.

I said, 'Oh, I know why she's doing it, but I can't tell you, Judge.'

'Of course you can,' he said.

I said, 'No, I'm afraid I can't. Really.'

'Oh *come on*,' said the judge.

All the while I could see Edwin's face flushing redder and redder. He had very little experience and here we were trading banter with this leading judge in the Free State.

I said, 'No, I can't tell you.'

The judge said, 'Look, I saw you talking to her. What is she trying to do?'

Now very seriously I said, 'All right, now that you ask. She's there in the hope that she'll put some wisdom into the minds of the judges.'

Frank Smuts roared with laughter. 'Oh is that the reason? Well then, you'd better tell her to carry on.'

Came the luncheon adjournment and we still hadn't finished our argument. So we went outside and she was still there on the lawn. She had put her lute away and was now standing and speaking with another woman who also had a shaved head. I invited the two of them to lunch, and we all went to a little café nearby, where we had a very interesting talk.

I remember we were both surprised when the nun ordered a chicken sandwich. Hartman was a vegetarian and we had naturally thought all

Buddhists were. But she explained that this was not the case.

The woman from England was a Buddhist nun who had arrived by ship in Durban, and had made her way up from Durban by hitchhiking.

'Why do you hitch lifts?' I asked her.

She said, 'I've got no money.'

'You've got no money?' I said, 'What do you mean you've got no money? Have you come from England without money?'

She said, 'Yes.'

I said, 'But how can you do that?'

She said, 'We believe that with the right intention things will work out. And so far they have. We've got lifts here. We've been hosted by people. And,' she said, 'we even have a bit of money now. We've got a little bit of public money from Buddhists in South Africa. They heard about our presence here.'

Her friend was a South African woman, also a Buddhist, from Johannesburg. They asked us how we thought it was going. I said I thought it was going very well. I looked at Hartman and at Edwin. Edwin said, 'Yes, I think we've had a good reception so far.' The nun and her friend seemed very interested.

When we went back into court, I finished with our submissions. Then their opponent presented his case. He was a very well-known lawyer from Pretoria, JP de Bruyn. His case rested on a *later* judgment in the United States, in which the test for religious conviction that I mentioned had been criticised. The judge in *that* case had said that it had been wrong to remove the need for a god, because then there is no distinction between a religion and what is simply a moral code; it leaves the door open to all sorts of abuse. For instance, someone could say, 'I believe in a tree.' De Bruyn argued that belief in God or in a Supreme Being was a fair line to draw, to make sure that not just anybody who didn't feel like fighting could say look, this is what I believe. We replied briefly and the three judges reserved judgment.

Outside the court we found the nun and her friend. 'Now we wait,' I told her, 'to see if you managed to put some sense in their minds.'

The nun laughed. She said she was very sorry, but they had to hurry off. They were on a flight back to Johannesburg early that afternoon.

I said, 'What flight are you on?'

She told me. Whatever it was.

I said, 'Well, you'll probably need a lift then.'

By some coincidence – although *they* didn't think it was a coincidence, mind you – we were on the same flight. So Edwin and I and the nun and her friend all went to the airport in the taxi Nettleton had hired for us, and we flew back to Johannesburg together.

When the three judges gave their judgment a few weeks later, they did so in Hartman's favour. They said that the drafters of the Defence Act, with its exemption clause for religious objectors, had to have been aware that the country was home to people of diverse faiths, and that if the legislature was serious about protecting the freedom of faith and worship, it could not exclude those of the non-theistic traditions, such as the one to which Hartman subscribed. It was to the credit of these judges that they gave a well-reasoned decision, a very fair decision. And David Hartman was excused from going into the South African army.

chapter sixteen

In which we learn a few things about Ma

When Ma came to live with us for the first time, I was in primary school. Young enough to be excited at the prospect of her visit, but old enough already to feel sorry for her. In her flat in Cape Town, Ma lived alone. I thought about this dreamily, in the way kids do, pondering the facts of a world gradually coming into focus. No one else in the world lived so alone. She didn't even have a dog. Sometimes I would purposefully make myself miserable by comparing her life to Nana and Bronco's lives. Theirs seemed so full and busy. They had so many friends. They had each other.

She lived with us for a few months then, because she was ill. I remember the metallic shimmer of her lavender-blue nightdress against her heavy, cumbersome body when I saw her in the mornings before school.

Ma moved up to Joburg for good when I was fifteen. She bought a flat in a large dark-brick block near the Killarney Mall called Seven Oaks. It was three flights up, at the end of a long closed-in corridor, the floor of which was always polished to a fierce blue sheen.

And aside from the fact that they were both on the third floor, there was something else her flat in Seven Oaks had in common with her old flat in Cape Town: it, too, was haunted. I found this out when I stayed with her for a month in my last year of high school. I was having trouble studying for my matric finals and I imagined that her flat – which I associated with stillness and quietness – would help me concentrate.

It did. I studied consistently there. But I also became sadder by the day, and when I was alone I felt the same strange fear I felt as a little kid in the room in the Newlands flat where she kept her photograph albums, the room dense with an invisible presence. That presence was as palpable here as it had been there. I understood that my grandfather had never died. He lived on in her empty rooms.

Alec Sanders with his grandson, Daniel Browde

She looked at it the other way around. She told me many times that when he died (she was only fifty-two at the time) half of her died too. She would say it briskly, just a fleeting remark, but with a certainty that permitted no further questions. Her bottomless grief didn't stop her from loving us. No, she was gifted at that. She loved me and my sisters with every cell of her riven heart. But her sadness gave to her love the same heavy contours it gave to all her gifts, big and small.

Her name was Joy.

My relationship with her, so powerful in the first years of my life, changed ineluctably as I got older. Sometime in my teens I forgot how to listen to her. Even though I visited her in her flat in Killarney, and then in Pembury Lodge – the assisted-living facility where she spent the last few years of her life – I would put off such visits, put other things first, and when I did go I'd struggle to stay there very long. Ma would speak endlessly about events in the lives of a bewildering network of distant family relations: illnesses, engagements, bar mitzvahs, bat mitzvahs, marriages, graduations. She was like some obsessive collector of miniatures showing me her inventory: here was a car the size of an ant; here a vase no bigger than the head of a pin; and other things so ponderously small I had to take her word for it that they existed at all.

I made a vow to visit her at least once during the week. In the many weeks I failed, I saw her on Friday nights. Occasionally we would have Shabbat supper at her flat – she would serve either fried sole or leg of lamb – but mostly we alternated between my parents' place and Orange Road.

At the Shabbat table she would listen distractedly, often wringing her hands, working one thumb over the knuckle of the other. On the rare occasions that she did speak, people found it difficult to listen. Her contributions offered no easy purchase. After she spoke there would be a gap of silence, until someone else steered the conversation back to more engaging waters. I often thought about how it must have been for her to be there, in the warmth of my other grandparents' home, in the bright light of their love and their friendship.

In April 2008, Ma twisted her ankle in a fall and had to go to hospital. When she was there the doctors did other tests, and found other things wrong. Her blood pressure was high and there were problems with her lungs. Nobody said it, but we all knew – with an improbably familiar knowing – where this would lead.

During that year she spoke to me at last of the currents that had shaped the flow of her life. One night she gave me her perspective on the relationship between my late grandfather and my mother's older brother – my uncle, Johnny, who now lives in New Zealand. She was back in hospital. I used to go there after work sometimes and sit with her for an hour or so. Her body – always too much of it – was shrinking, and the skin was hanging in places. Her head was turned sideways on the pillow as she told me that my uncle had been unnecessarily afraid of his father's judgement. I knew it had been a complex relationship (not least because Johnny had become a paediatrician like his father), but the remarkable thing was that I had never heard her say anything like this before.

Joy Sanders (Ma)

Another time, during one of the increasingly brief periods when she was out of hospital, I took her to the Rosebank Mall for lunch, and she told me in full a story I'd had only glimpses of before, the story of her early childhood. I listened carefully to every painful word. The white noise of the mall disappeared, and for about twenty minutes all I could hear was the sound of the words. I don't remember either of us touching our salads.

After I dropped her back at Pembroke and spoke a little with the nurse, I went home and wrote down as much of her story as I could remember. There was a lot I couldn't remember, and the story I wrote down was full of gaping ellipses. I wrote it in a seventy-two-page, lined A4 exercise book that had all sorts of nonsense in it (to-do lists, phone numbers, et cetera), but once I had finished getting down what I could, the exercise book felt changed, consecrated even, and I looked around for somewhere special to put it. At last I went into the walk-in cupboard and laid it carefully in the box on top of the pile of transcripts.

Through the winter Ma's condition deteriorated. She spent longer periods in the hospital. Her mind was not right; in the trees outside the hospital window she saw monkeys no one else could see. Some days she'd be lucid, and she would speak about the big things and not the parade of minutiae that had been her distraction for all those years. Some days she'd only be able to complain about her pain; some days she would be too tired to talk at all. On those days I'd tell her about my life, and she'd drift off into a hard, sweating, uncomfortable sleep.

One afternoon I was sitting on the blue hospital chair next to her bed, holding her hand while she slept, when I slipped into a doze. I couldn't have been asleep for more than a minute, if that, but when I woke up she was wide awake, looking at me questioningly. Her hand, soft and warm, was still in mine. She had mostly stopped talking by then, but now she said, 'Did I wake you?'

I said, 'No, Ma. You didn't.'

She nodded, relieved, then closed her eyes and went back to sleep.

My grandmother, Joy Sanders, died on 2 October 2008. One thing I'm grateful for was that she was home when she died, and in her own bed – away from the hospital, away from the doctors who never looked in her eyes, and the nurses, who (all but one) treated her like a burden.

She hadn't been well at all the day before. She'd stopped talking altogether, and then she'd stopped eating, and then drinking, and I woke up just as the sun was coming up half expecting to find the messages that I did find on the phone: one from my aunt, one from my mother.

It was a bright morning in spring, still cool at that hour. My mother and her sister, Jennifer, who had flown down from Harare, and Kate and Cara and Micaela were sitting on white plastic chairs around a white plastic table on the stoep, surrounded by the pot plants my gran had tended so assiduously. My mother was wearing sunglasses and weeping gently, on and off. I went around the table to her and hugged her and then everyone else. Something I kept thinking was this: it has happened; nothing else can happen.

'Is she inside?' I asked my mother, though I knew she was.

My mother nodded.

One of the many things I remember in clear isolation from that morning is that small nod my mother gave. Which meant so many things and also just the one, inarguable thing: the body inside the room.

The first time I went in, I went alone. The curtains were drawn and the light in the room was low. I found a sheet covering her face. I pulled it back. It slid off her nose and then off her chin. My gran had died with her mouth open and her nurse had tied a black scarf around her jaw and knotted it at the top of her head. Death had frozen her features solid. The scarf had squashed her lips into a shape that was unnatural, the slightly wavy line between them becoming the darkest moment in her face. Her eyes were closed.

She reminded me of a friend of mine, the last time I saw him. He had been on a motorcycle when he was hit by a car, and, after spending days in the hospital in a coma, he had died. His was the only other dead body I had seen from so close up. The serious expression, the absence of colour, the dark between slightly parted lips: they looked like each other now, resembled each other like members of the same family.

I stood for a long time in the dim room with my heart beating forcefully, almost painfully. When I felt like it was time for me to go back out to the balcony, I didn't feel like pulling the sheet back over her face, and so I didn't. The sheet was not put back over her head until they came to get her. Not by me, nor by anyone. Outside, my mother was crying as she spoke on the phone to my father. A week before, my dad had come down with pneumonia and he was speaking from a hospital bed up the road.

I went into the room again about half an hour later with Micaela, who had asked me to come in with her. She was fifteen then, a wide-eyed and curious teenager. We stood close to the bed and together we looked at Ma's inert face. As it turned out, she had wanted me to come in with her for a specific reason. After a minute she told me what it was. She asked if I thought Ma's eyes were completely closed.

I bent over my grandmother's face and looked closely at the eyes; it was hard to tell. So I leaned in even closer and I agreed that, no, they probably weren't.

'It makes me feel so weird,' Micaela said, and my heart dipped and overflowed and I wanted to hug her for her honesty. She wasn't talking about Ma being dead. That was simply what had happened. She was talking only about her eyes not being totally shut.

So I bent over again and tried, being as careful as I could be, with the tip of my right index finger, to pull Ma's eyelids down, to close her eyes completely. It was extremely difficult. I think I moved them half a millimetre down, if I moved them at all. But even half a millimetre was some distance, then, in eyelid terms. I don't think I've ever been more gentle doing anything. When I stood back, we looked again. Micaela said it was better.

Over the next few weeks, I opened the thin exercise book almost every day to read the story, and when I did I usually cried. The story she told me in the mall, about her childhood, lying now in the box of transcripts in the walk-in cupboard. Though it was a sad story, one of the saddest I know, I felt very relieved to have got it down.

SHIPS AND FAIRIES
MA'S STORY

Written from memory
Story told (approx.) 11/07/2008

My father died when I was only very little. I think you know that. But do you know that some people in the family used to say he took his own life? Oh, you *have* heard that? But I don't think so, I really don't. He had a little baby, just a few weeks old, why would he take his own life?

My point is that it was just the two of us. Just my mother and me. And my mother took me *everywhere* with her. Everywhere she went. Until everything changed when I was six. That was the year she took a voyage by ship to England for a short holiday. She did all *sorts* of things that women didn't usually do on their own. And I went with her.

On board the ship she met a man by the name of Charles Edmond Perceval Rowe, CEP Rowe – sixty, divorced, retired, with children from a previous marriage. He was a large man who resembled a bloodhound, and he took a real fancy to my mother and decided to woo her. But he thought I would be in the way of his wooing. So once we got to England, they took me to a lodge in the countryside – a boarding lodge for children, run by a married couple. And they left me there for a month while Charles wooed my mother in London.

I was quite afraid at this place in the country. It was very beautiful, but I thought there were elves and fairies in the garden, and I was afraid. I was not on my own there; there were three or four other children staying there too. But being from a foreign country, I felt separate and had difficulty finding things to say to them.

Charles wined and dined my mother like no one had ever been wined or dined in England. He took her to the Lord Mayor's and the Queen's tea parties, as well as the Ascot races. Do you know that my mother's family back in South Africa was surprised to see, on the newsreels at the bioscope, images of my mother at the Ascot, at which she and Charles arrived in a coach and four?

One day, he came to get me to take me into London for a day. But he did not try to relate to me. In fact, he had no *idea* how to relate to me. He bought me an Edinburgh rock. Do you know what that is? It's a sort of long hard sweet. I didn't enjoy it very much. The only other thing I remember about that day was that I fell in a rose bush.

When we got back to South Africa their relationship persisted, and Charles and my mother decided to get married.

My mother's sister and especially my mother's brother-in-law were dead against the marriage. They pleaded with her not to marry him. They said, 'Why can't you just *live* with him, why do you have to marry him?' And this was around 1930, remember.

Nevertheless, the marriage went ahead, and the two of them moved into a building called Castle Mansions, on Eloff Street.

Charles said there was not enough room for me in their apartment, and insisted I be sent away to boarding school. I was six years old. My mother tried to enrol me in Grade One at Kingsmead Girls' School, here on Oxford Road, but Kingsmead was very new and was only taking sixteen applicants that year. I was not one of those accepted, so instead I went to a school in Durban.

On the train back to Johannesburg, at the end of my first term there, I decided that from then on I was going to be nice to Charles. I made a vow that I would take him his slippers and call him Daddy. But it didn't matter what I decided, because he had already decided that he wasn't going to be nice to me. I think I must have done something to offend him.

Soon I stopped going home even for holidays. Charles didn't want me in the house at all. So over the holidays I remained at the school.

He was a man of wealth – mining – yet he was very tight-fisted. My mother and he used to play in a school of bridge, and when it was their turn to host the game he would make my mother buy the snacks with her own money. Would you believe it? My mother was a schoolteacher and Charles was sitting on a fortune, yet he would make her pay for the snacks with her own money. He would also drive her car and not give her money for petrol.

Charles was a sod. One whole room in Castle Mansions was full of whisky and gin. He used to buy whisky by the case and store it in that room. One whole room for liquor, but no room for *me*. And when he died, Charles left my mother 140 pounds a month – absolute peanuts, even then.

My mother fell for him, she told me, because of his perfect command of the English language. He apparently spoke effortlessly and wrote beautiful letters.

chapter seventeen

In which the young storyteller receives help

This was my theory of death: the energy cradled in a living body, shaped into personality by the brain, is returned, when the body dies, to the atmosphere.

But in the days after my grandmother died I had the sense that what had departed from her body was not simply energy but in fact a distinct being – calling it a *soul* made sense – that had come to earth to see through human eyes (her eyes) and feel all the things she felt.

Ma's soul was out in space, animate and still interested. It liked the candle my mother had lit and put on the bookshelf, next to a photo of Ma smiling in New Plymouth, where my uncle Johnny lives. And it liked the funeral service at Westpark Cemetery (Ma was buried not very far from Uncle Bernard), where we asked the rabbi, who never knew my grandmother, not to deliver a eulogy. And it liked the prayer service we had at my parents' house in Sandringham, where the rabbi *did* speak – he asked us if he might talk about what he'd learned in the past few days.

After making a few observations about how each of us had spoken about Ma, the rabbi said that the departed soul of my grandmother would now be a 'good intercessor on High' for us, the living. That made sense to me in terms of what I was feeling then. I felt she was out there like a star.

Core-deep, but short-lived. Almost as quickly as those feelings came they disappeared, popped like bubbles on blades of grass. All of it,

I reckoned, had just been wishful thinking. *The energy cradled in a living body, shaped into personality by the brain, is returned ...*

But these years later, I don't know. I don't know what I think. Because although all those feelings still make no sense to me, certain things happened quite soon afterwards that make me think that maybe there might have been some truth in the rabbi's words after all.

The first was this: three months later, on Ma's birthday – 15 January 2009 – I met Thenji at a party in Newtown, and I knew within five minutes that something had changed in my life, some latch had fallen. A person had arrived in the middle of my life, to stay.

She seemed to feel the same way, and we made plans to meet up again a few days later. After that, we started to make as much time as we could to see each other. Thenji made me feel un-alone, but she didn't seem to interfere with the helpful parts of my loneliness.

And that was the first thing.

The second thing happened like this: every couple of months or so my grandfather or my grandmother would ask me if I thought that 'something should be done' with the transcripts. They would often lead up to this question by telling me that one of their friends had remarked, after hearing him tell a story, that my grandfather 'should publish his memoirs'.

I'd answer by saying that I *did* think something could, *should*, be done with them, and – jumping ahead – that I would like to do it. But, I'd say (jumping even further), a book like that was not something a person could do in his spare time. A person would need to spend months on it, I'd say.

I didn't think I could do it in the mornings before work. Or at least – though this I didn't say to them – I didn't *want* to do it in the mornings before work. I liked the idea of giving myself to a book full time, being a full-time writer. It seemed romantic, and the only way I was going to be able to make great things happen.

Now, for the first time, I really wished that I had those months: to spend with Thenji; to work on a book. For the first time since I'd started working as a subeditor, I felt – to use my grandfather's word – 'hamstrung' by the job. I also wondered if, on those nights at the paper, I might be hiding behind something.

I took out the transcripts and – for the first time in years, since I'd deliberately stopped doing so – began to think about them as *material*: things incomplete in themselves, loose strips that could be cut, reversed, stitched and sewn into something else, something more complex and altogether finer. This was now the early summer of 2009. When I spoke to Thenji about the idea of using the interviews as the starting point for a biography, she was enthusiastic and encouraging.

I started to think about how the stories would sound retold as biographical anecdotes; and I began reading through the childhood stories closely, wondering how the book might begin. Once or twice I even took out a pen and experimented with opening paragraphs, but nothing ever led to anything. I told myself that if I was really going to do this I'd have to leave the whole newspaper situation – and the opportunity to do so arrived very soon after that.

But before I describe this part, I have to backtrack a little and explain something about my grandparents and their circle of friends and acquaintances – the people who came to supper at their house, the people who left copies of *The New Yorker* behind in their guest room.

I could tell, for instance, the following story (something that happened a week or two after they got back from that wedding in India).

It was early evening, dark enough outside that the lights in their house had been turned on. My grandfather and I were in his study, and he was telling me about someone he'd 'got talking to' at the wedding. 'A writer,' he said, 'a lovely fellow who has written a number of very good books, by the way.' He was sitting in his brown swivel chair; I was standing close to the door.

'We discussed the state of South African politics,' he told me, 'and this man had really remarkable knowledge and understanding. Name of Hochschild,' he said. 'Adam Hochschild.'

'*Adam Hochschild?*' I repeated.

The book *King Leopold's Ghost* had changed the way I thought about my life. It deals with the horrific colonisation of the Congo, and changed my sense of what colonialism was – and is – and consequently my sense of what it means to be a white person living in Africa. In the story he tells, Hochschild, an American journalist, shows how colonialism created a negative force field – an enduring blight – that will affect the world for centuries, if not forever. The book sits in the small bookshelf next to my bed, like a Bible or a gun.

'The man who wrote *King Leopold's Ghost?*' I said, incredulous.

He pointed at me the way a conductor might point his baton at a musician who's just hit the right note. 'That's the very chap,' he said. '*King Leopold's Ghost*. Yes, a fine chap, Hochschild. Nana spoke to him too. He lives in California. Said we should go and visit them if we are ever out there.'

I was surprised, but I shouldn't have been – and that, I suppose, is the point of the story. Since they have both been successful in their respective fields, my grandparents have come into contact with a lot of people who have achieved success in their own. And since my grandfather strikes up conversations with people wherever he goes, and since his conversation is mostly unburdened by the need to be right or to display erudition, people respond well to him and want to keep talking to him. And when they meet my grandmother, she will ask them so many questions – usually well-informed, difficult questions – about their work or their lives that they will want to find the time to answer her. And so it is that over the course of their marriage they have attracted a wide and impressive group of friends, many of them pre-eminent in their fields, all with fondness and regard for my grandparents.

One of these friends (to get back to the main story) is a man by the name of Allan Greyling. Allan first came into contact with my grandfather in the 1990s, when he, Allan, was a young man working for a giant accounting firm. Despite his youth, he already had a relatively senior position in the company's forensics department, and was called upon to give expert evidence at the legal inquiry into the collapse of one of South Africa's biggest business conglomerates. My grandfather had been appointed commissioner at the inquiry, and he was so impressed with the work that Allan had done, and the way he presented his evidence, that he said so in his report.

The affirmation stayed with Allan, and when a few years later he left the huge firm and went out on his own, he asked my grandfather if he would sit on the board of his fledgling company.

I sense that in my grandfather Allan saw more than simply the name of a prominent legal personality to associate with his brand: he saw a sensitivity to the nature of the world that he appreciated, a warmth and a wisdom he wished to keep close.

Every couple of months the two of them had lunch together in an Italian restaurant in a small shopping complex in Oaklands, the suburb bordering Orchards to the west. And it was at one of those meals that my grandfather and Allan got round to discussing the interviews that we had done, and the possibility of turning the transcripts into a book.

My grandfather related to Allan what I'd told him: that I couldn't give the book the attention it needed if I had to do it in my spare time.

To which Allan apparently said, 'How much time would he need to complete it?' (My grandfather told me about this conversation later.)

'I'm not really sure,' my grandfather admitted.

'Why don't you ask him how much time he needs,' Allan said. 'And I'll pay him whatever he's earning at the newspaper to work on the book.'

When my grandfather got to this part of the story, he stopped and held my gaze for a moment. Was I really serious about doing this, he wanted to know.

I was, I said. I didn't want to work as a subeditor forever, I told him. I said I felt like I had plenty of other things to do. One of them being this.

He nodded slowly.

When he asked me how long I thought I'd need to write the book, I didn't know what to say. Quickly, I tried to work it out. I'd already done the interviews so I supposed it would just be a matter of editing the transcripts and doing some research to be able to place the salient moments in his life in historical context. How long would that take? I guessed I could do it in three months. But to be safe I told him four.

'Four months,' he repeated back to me.

I nodded. (Four months full time? I checked in with myself. Yes, that was quite a lot of time.)

My grandfather said he would speak to Allan and organise a meeting for the following week, a meeting where we could, all three of us, sit and chat about it. I thanked him, and I did feel grateful – to him and to Allan, who I had met once or twice before – but I also felt quite unsettled. Things were moving quickly.

The dining-room table wasn't covered; it was just a wooden table, painted a gloss white. A heavy grey ceramic bowl stood in the middle of it. It was lunchtime, but none of us was eating. We each had a tumbler of ice water in front of us. Condensation marbled the outside of the glass.

Even sitting down, Allan gave the impression of forward movement. His close-cropped hair and the sleek contours of the frames of his glasses added to the kinetic effect. I smiled, feeling clumsy. I'd spoken to Thenji and a few other people, and the general agreement had been that four months was not enough time to write a book – even one for which I'd already done a lot of the legwork. The consensus was six months. In fact, Thenji didn't even think that six months would be enough.

But I went ahead and suggested six months. I could do it in six months, I told Allan, but I'd do it for the money he was going to give me for four.

Allan smiled warmly. He said, 'Don't worry about that. Let's just say six months.'

I nodded and said, 'Well, that's …' But I trailed off. Instead I just looked at him and hoped he could read the gratitude on my face.

The three of us said our goodbyes that day in the tiled area next to the front door. Shaking Allan's hand, I said, 'This really means a lot.' I realised that for the moment he was standing directly between me and my grandfather, so I leaned in towards him and added, in a whisper: 'It means a lot to *both* of us.'

A few days later I gave my notice at the newspaper, and exactly one month after that, I drove out of the underground parking lot for the last time, feeling buoyant and committed to my new task, to my new girlfriend, to my new life. With some timely and generous intercession, I had been released from the comfortable chains of my full-time job.

STAMPS

Interview 4
Date recorded: 21/05/2005

At that time I shared a room with my brothers. Len was eight years older than me, and was approaching the end of high school. He slept in the bed nearest to the window; I slept in the bed next to Len's desk; and Bernard, who was still a little boy of about six, was in the bed across from mine, closest to the door.

Bernard was ... How can I say? ... As a result of a difficult birth, he was cognitively and, as it turned out, permanently emotionally immature. Consequently, he did very poorly at school and was treated with kid gloves by my parents. But he had a lovely kind face and could be very affectionate towards anyone who expressed any liking for him.

Len – my older brother – was a complicated fellow. He was extremely good with his hands. He understood electricity and made all sorts of contraptions, handmade wireless sets that could pick up the radio broadcasts. He also fixed up a bell at the gate, which would ring in our room. He did all sorts of things like that. But Len also had a strange quirk about him, which I've often thought about. He could be a very warm person and was often very amusing, but he also did things that seemed almost cruel, in a way.

Let me tell you the story of my stamp album, for instance.

In those days I was very keen on stamp collecting and I had quite a good collection of stamps. My dad would sometimes give me pocket money and I would walk down to the CNA on Raleigh Street and buy a sheet that contained stamps, which I studied carefully before inserting them on the appropriate page of the album. My dad had also bought me a beautiful album. It was made by the Stanley Gibbons Company in England. It had a thick, heavy grey cover, and each page had pictures of stamps from a different country in the world, and you would try to match them. My particular album also had a section with a travel theme. All the stamps in that section showed different modes of transport. Locomotives, motorcars, ocean liners, all of that sort of thing, including even canoes and other primitive means of travel. I kept the album in a drawer in the cupboard beside my bed, and I would often take it out to study it.

Now, Len had done the same thing before me – and he still had a lot of stamps, which he was no longer interested in. His stamps now lay discarded in his desk drawer. Some were loose and some were on sheets specially made for stamp collection. He had lost interest in stamps, which I think he now considered a waste of time. I sometimes opened his drawer and looked at them, taking care to close the drawer afterwards and leave everything exactly as I'd found it.

One evening I decided to ask him if he wouldn't mind giving me his stamps, so that I could take any I didn't have and put them in my album.

I recall he was at his desk that evening, studying. He turned and looked at me. He thought about it for a while, and then he said no. 'There's no question of me giving you stamps just like that,' he said. He said, 'If you want a stamp, you've got to do something to earn it.'

I said, 'What do I have to do to earn it?'

He said, 'I'll give you a flip.'

A flip was a hit on your bottom with the sharp end of a ruler. Rulers in those days were made mainly of wood, but they had a strip of metal down the one side, you see, for getting the line straight. So a flip was a very painful thing.

But there were stamps in there that I really wanted, stamps I coveted, and I agreed to this arrangement.

Len opened his desk drawer and pulled out the tray of stamps. He brought them over to where I was sitting, on my bed. 'We can start right now,' he said. He sat down on the end of his own bed.

I remember carefully tipping the stamps onto my bed, pretending that I was looking at them for the first time. I sifted through them until I found the one I needed most. I said, 'This one,' and I held it out to him. My older brother took it and inspected it with exaggerated care.

'Two flips,' he said.

And that was how it happened from then on. If I wanted a stamp from his collection, I would have to take it to him and say, 'What about this one, Len?' He would then take some time inspecting the stamp, and then he'd say, 'One flip.' Or 'Two flips.' And we would go through that whole ritual of payment: the lowering of the pyjama trousers, the clenching of the jaw, and the flips, which drew blood sometimes.

And at that time I took it. It was very painful, but I wanted the stamps. I know it may be difficult to believe, but I still looked up to him as much as I ever had. It didn't really affect my feeling for him in any way; although, looking back on it later, I came to think that it was an extraordinarily harsh thing to do to a youngster.

Of course, I would try to get hold of stamps in other ways too, buying them occasionally from the CNA or swapping them with other boys at school, but if I needed a particular stamp and he had it, I earned it in this way.

And after a while – that is, in about two years – I had a fine collection that I was very proud of. I had stamps from almost every country in the world. I had stamps from Romania and Bulgaria, I recall. Even from China and Japan. And I tell you, I was absolutely mad about that collection. I really was very proud of it. And then one day, when I was about fourteen years old, it disappeared. The album and all its beautiful stamps simply disappeared. I came home from school and it was gone. The drawer where I usually kept it was empty.

At first I told myself I'd simply put it somewhere else. Although I was sure I'd left it in the drawer. I looked around the room, under the bed, behind the desk. I looked in Len's drawer, saw the few stamps left in the tray. I looked through all the other drawers too, and through the wardrobe, under the piles of clothing. I looked everywhere in the whole house that afternoon, even in my parents' and sister's rooms, but I found nothing. It had simply vanished.

Later that afternoon, I developed a strong feeling that I knew who had taken the album. I didn't know how, but I knew. This was a few hours later, when I'd had time to think.

I went to my younger brother, Bernard, who was playing outside, and I said, 'Where is it?'

He ran inside, into the bedroom. I followed him. I said something like, 'You'd better tell me where it is!' But he just buried his head in the pillow and said nothing.

When my dad came home that evening, I asked him if I could speak to him about something serious. I remember that he called my mother and the three of us sat in the entrance lounge. I told them the story. My father listened carefully; he knew exactly how much I treasured my stamp collection. I told them I had a feeling that Bernard had taken the album. I said please, they must ask him if he had taken it and, if he had, to give it back to me.

I could see that they were very upset by this, but they asked me please just to leave it be. They spoke in voices I almost didn't recognise, and they told me they understood how upset I must feel, but they asked me please to just leave it. I could see they were both very distressed by this. But they said, 'Please, just leave it and forget about it.' By the looks on their faces there was a lot I understood about my brother that my age didn't allow me to put into words, but that I understood nevertheless – and so I just left it. And it was never recovered.

A few months later I learned that Bernard *had* taken it, and had, in fact, given it away to someone at his school. He had given it to a boy who had been bullying him. It seems Bernard gave this boy the album as protection from further bullying.

From top to bottom:
Leonard, Jules and Bernard Browde, circa 1930
'At that time I shared a room with my brothers.'

chapter eighteen

In which the young storyteller has his first stab at writing a book

I did a few things right away. I made a list of the books I wanted to read and I bought a thick hardcover exercise book from the CNA in the Killarney Mall. Prof. Kariithi said all writers should have a writer's diary, a place to write in every day, free of judgement, editing and self-criticism. A place to experiment and analyse and just write – a kind of a self-therapy. To make the transcripts easier to access, I punched holes in them and slotted them into a big lever arch file, which I put on a bookshelf near the computer. The file sat on the shelf like the Rosetta Stone: it needed deciphering.

I blamed the false starts I'd made before on trying to be too clever, too idiosyncratic. I told myself not to be scared of writing a straightforward (even corny) biography, illuminating one central theme – like 'the search for justice' – and finding moments throughout my grandfather's life that connected to that theme. I imagined I could use as a template one of those illustrated biographies of famous figures written for children. Something like *The Value of Kindness*, a book about Helen Keller I remembered from childhood. That could be a good idea, I thought, if only because I'd be able to measure my progress, day by day, as if I were building a house.

The first list of books to read looked like this: 1). *The Jews of Lithuania* by Masha Greenbaum, and 2). *The Jews of Johannesburg* by Leibl Feldman, translated from the Yiddish by Veronica Belling.

The Jews of Lithuania is a heavy book with a hard mustard-yellow cover and pages so thin they are almost translucent. I'd seen it a hundred times on my grandparents' shelves and had often wondered about it. Now I borrowed it and started to read it every day, copying down relevant passages into the exercise book. It was very comprehensive, tracing the story of the community from its beginnings in the fourteenth century through what Greenbaum calls the Golden Era of the 1700s, to its destruction in the 1940s. I started to skip the parts that were too comprehensive, because there wasn't enough time – especially since this was just supposed to be background research.

The Jews of Johannesburg – also yellow, but with a soft cover – is written in a humorous style and contains many black-and-white cartoon illustrations. One morning, in the third week, I read in this book something that made me get up and stand at the window. The chapter I was busy with concerned the Anglo-Boer War and contemporary Jewish attitudes to that conflict. The Jews' loyalty was divided. Some English Jews fought on the side of the English, but most of the Jews in South Africa (several hundred families by that time) sympathised with the Boers. The South African Jews 'knew full well', Feldman writes, 'that were it not for the gold mines, the British would not have laid a finger on the Boers'.

Basing his claims on reports in Jewish newspapers from the time, Feldman tells of how about 300 Jewish men joined the Boers in their fight against the English. Several Russian Jews were apparently also 'among the many legendary heroes of the Boer army'. Veldkornet Herman Judelewitz, for example, whose 'heroic deeds were legendary'; as well as Joseph Segal, who was a 'loyal scout' of the formidable guerrilla tactician General Christiaan de Wet.

This reminded me of something I hadn't thought about in ages. Hadn't my grandfather told me that his father rode a horse for the Boers against the British?

Excited by the connection, I phoned him and asked if we could meet to talk about it. I wanted to learn more about the wartime exploits of this teenage Talmudic scholar and cavalryman.

At his house my grandfather looked over his glasses at me and smiled. It was a broad rock of a smile, with a very old vein of mischief running through the middle of it. 'Well, that's what he *told* me,' he said. 'But my dad like to pull your leg, you know, and he took great pleasure if you took him seriously. He was a lot like *your* father in that way. For all I know my dad couldn't even *ride* a horse.'

I was disappointed to hear this but I had to admit I found it funny, too. Also, I always enjoyed it when my grandfather compared his father to mine. In the meantime I'd thought of some other questions for him. The first part of a biography, I'd realised, where you paint the family background, doesn't necessarily have to be exhaustive, but it is supposed to have things in place going back at least a few generations.

I was worried because he'd given me two conflicting pieces of information regarding his mother's birthplace. The first was his memory of his mother's trip to Europe in 1936. Her sister – my grandfather's aunt – had married a wealthy man, and that year she took the two of them to England. It was the first time since she arrived in South Africa as a teenager that his mother had left the country. While in England, she apparently became so 'distressed' at what she was hearing about Hitler and 'how he was riding roughshod over everyone', that she decided to travel from England to see her family in Suwalki, a small town in Poland.

Her sister said she would pay for her journey east but could not accompany her since she was expected back in South Africa. So his mother went alone.

He remembered sitting in the kitchen of their house on Page Street and listening to her tell them about the train ride across Europe. How one night, while the train was travelling through Germany, she was woken by a hammering on her compartment door. Frightened, she opened the door and saw a gang of men standing there: policemen. She told how these policemen wore on their uniforms the sign of the swastika. They demanded to see her documents.

He sat wide-eyed and listened closely as his mother told them of her relief at arriving at last in Suwalki, and about her relatives, the Bernsteins, each of whom played a musical instrument. 'And I can remember my mother,' he'd said, 'describing how wonderful it was to be with them, and what a feeling she got when they all played together in an ensemble.

'That family was wiped out by the Nazis. Each one of them killed. Except for one son, Lovka,' he said. 'Lovka Bernstein. Because Lovka had joined the Polish navy and when the Germans entered Poland he wasn't home. He was away with the navy. Lovka lived out his life in London, ultimately. But that's another story,' he'd said. 'The story of Lovka Bernstein.'

He told me that he'd once had a photograph of his mother sitting with her relatives in their house in Suwalki, but that he wasn't sure where it had got to.

The other piece of evidence, the conflicting piece – sent to him by his nephew, Michael, in the United States – was a photocopy of a death notice for his grandfather, which appeared in a Yiddish newspaper in Johannesburg in 1936. He had given it to me on the day we did the last interview, and I had inserted it with the transcripts in the file. Above a picture of a handsome middle-aged man with a full-bodied goatee and light-coloured eyes staring straight at the camera, is the name Reb Yehudah Leib Meyers. The obituary underneath is in Yiddish, written in Hebrew characters. Translated by a friend of Michael's, it reads as follows:

> On Shabbos Shuva, Reb Yehudah Leib Meyers, son of Dov Meyerowitz, passed at an age greater than seventy-five years. On the second day of Rosh Hashana he was in the Yeoville Shul and in the middle of praying he did not feel well and was carried out. The next day he passed away. The deceased was from a very well-known family from Kovno Gouberna.

Kovno Gouberna, my grandfather explained to me, means Greater Kovno. Modern-day Kaunus, in Lithuania. In other words, not Suwalki in Poland.

'So which is it?' I asked him. 'Poland or Lithuania?'

He shrugged. 'It's still a mystery to me,' he said. 'I've sometimes thought perhaps it was the *region* of Suwalki, and not the town. Suwalki was also the name of a region, right on the Polish–Lithuanian border. Territory I believe the countries disputed.'

Online I found nothing to solve the mystery, although I did find some interesting facts about the town of Suwalki, which remains a small town in north-eastern Poland, about thirty kilometers from the border with Lithuania. Pictures of it show pretty grassy squares and parks with trees. A river runs through the middle of it.

Suwalki, I learned, had a sizeable Jewish population at the outbreak of the Second World War, about 10 000 people, almost all of whom were murdered in the camps. On the Wikipedia page I saw a picture of the memorial at the Suwalki Jewish cemetery to those who died. It is constructed partly from fragments of graves smashed by the Nazis.

*Exhibit A: Ida Browde (third from left) with her cousins,
the Bernsteins, in Suwalki. Leon 'Lovka' Bernstein on far left.*

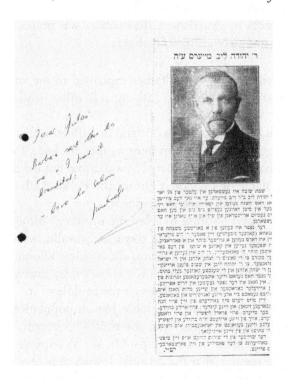

Exhibit B: The death notice of Louis Meyers

While I was online, I Googled some of the things I'd been reading about in the Lithuania book. I read an article in the *Jewish Virtual Library* about the Pale of Settlement, the territory in the west of Czarist Russia (including modern-day Poland and Lithuania) where Jews were legally allowed to stay.

On the buzzing screen I read about the pogroms in the late nineteenth century that saw Jewish families fleeing the Pale, some going to America, some to Europe, some – like my grandfather's parents – to South Africa. I Googled 'South African Jews' and saw thumbnail pictures of Nadine Gordimer, Arthur Chaskalson and Phillip Tobias.

After some more random searching, I found another book to add to my reading list: *The Fox and the Flies* by Charles van Onselen. This book tells the story of Joseph Silver, a Polish Jew involved in the Johannesburg underworld at the turn of the twentieth century. I gathered from the blurbs and summaries that Van Onselen suggests that Silver might have been Jack the Ripper.

Thenji had moved into the flat by then. This was a little more than a year after we had met. We were lying in bed one night, talking with the lights out, and I was telling her about Suwalki and the pogroms and Joseph Silver. I still didn't have curtains, and the leaves of the trees outside, lit from below by the streetlights, filled the windows. She said she liked hearing me talk about the book; she thought it was a great project, she said. She also said she didn't think it was going to be what people expected it to be.

I asked her what she meant.

She said, 'I don't think it's going to be an ordinary biography. You know ... a book about a well-known lawyer.'

I said, 'Because I'm his grandson?'

I closed my eyes and had a two-second dream about the pantheon.

'Dan?' she said.

'Aren't biographies for people like Gandhi?' I asked her. 'Oliver Tambo ... people like that?'

'What are you talking about?'

'I don't know,' I said. 'I just ...' I thought about what I was trying to say. My mind was smudged with sleep.

'Do you even *want* to write a book like that?' she asked.

I said, 'What?' though I had a feeling I'd already asked her that.

The next day – and the day after that – I thought about what she'd said, about how she didn't think the book was going to be an ordinary biography. I wanted her to be right. The simple house I'd imagined – doors and windows, locks and hinges – looked a difficult prospect. I knew it was early days, but the basic plans were already looking improbable.

Two weeks had passed and I hadn't made much progress at all. My exercise book was filling up with notes, historical facts, a few of his stories retold in the third person, but mostly it was filled with doubts I expressed only there.

I was finding it difficult to work at home. I found all sorts of tasks to do instead of working; and once I was finally sitting down, I'd keep getting up to fetch biscuits from the kitchen, where I'd stand and stare out the window at the building opposite.

I remember one afternoon, having no luck, I drove to Zahava's Deli on Grant Avenue and ordered gefilte fish and black coffee, hoping for some kind of inspiration.

When I told this story – about going to Zahava's – a few days afterwards to some friends of ours, one of them mentioned that her mother was the librarian at the Brenthurst Library, and that maybe I could work on the book there.

I'd heard about the Brenthurst Library: it was right around the corner from our flat, close to the highway, on property that I knew belonged to the Oppenheimer family. The library housed a collection of books and maps and drawings started a hundred years ago by Ernest Oppenheimer, the mining magnate. The biggest stash of so-called Africana in the world. Our friend said I should meet her mother and explain the project. Sometimes people were permitted to do research and work there, she said.

The Brenthurst Library sits in a clearing in a forest of tall thin trees. It is a circular building, made from pale bricks and dark space-age metals, surrounded by a raked expanse of smooth white pebbles. A reedy fountain at one edge of this Zen-style moat trickles silky black water over slippery rocks, making a tiny gurgling sound. Walking slowly from my car to the entrance, I breathed in the smell of pine needles and sighed.

Inside the library, ornately framed oil paintings and etchings hung on teak-panelled walls. A tall, narrow-faced woman strode across the carpet to meet me: my friend's mother. She greeted me in a normal speaking voice that boomed in the hush. She then took me to a small boardroom, where I explained the biography project to her and a white-haired old man who, I remember, had a silk handkerchief peeking out of the breast pocket of his jacket. Neither saw any reason why I should not be permitted to work there. Besides, they'd both heard of my grandfather – in fact, they'd both heard of both my grandparents.

The library's desks were arranged in rows on one side of the room, behind a regiment of freestanding bookshelves. This area was far from the windows and had to be lit by electric light even during the day. Looking around on my first morning there, I found all kinds of relevant books. My grandfather's first memory was of bullets falling on the roof of their house during the great miners' strike of 1922. There must have been fifty books about that strike, a whole row practically. But I decided to finish the two books I was reading, and to carry on piecing together the story of his childhood for at least two hours a day.

On my third day there I discovered a shelf of South African Judaica, and spent the whole day dipping into these books. I found one by my grandfather's friend Gideon Shimoni, in which I discovered this description of the character of the Jewish community in South Africa: 'A [...] mode of religiosity that has been characterised as conservative traditionalism and also "non-observant orthodox", an apt description of the reality notwithstanding the apparent oxymoron. It has been well described as the "pouring of Litvak spirit into Anglo-Jewish bottles".'

I liked that; it made sense. I scribbled down the name of the writer Shimoni had quoted – Gustav Saron, *The Making of South African Jewry* – and I added both books, Shimoni's and Saron's, to my list.

I had been going there for two weeks when I had an idea for how to start the biography. It would begin with a sound. A simple sound, coming from above. Something like, 'The little boy lies in his cocoon of blankets and listens: a short sharp *bang*, followed moments later by a rippling clatter – *rat-a-tat-tat, rat-a-tat-tat* – and then a small *thump*, coming from somewhere else, not above him any more, but outside the house, lower, where the ground is ...'

Bullets. Fired by white mineworkers at soldiers, or by soldiers at white mineworkers. His first memory and a formative moment in the history of the city. The Rand Revolt. I started to research the Revolt. I didn't choose any one book in particular, because I knew I couldn't read any from beginning to end. I just read chapters from lots of different titles and took notes in my exercise book.

At three pm every day, a willowy woman named Elsie – wearing a peppermint-green maid's uniform – wheeled out the tea trolley, and I would stop working to have coffee and biscuits on one of the low couches positioned near the entrance.

At the beginning of the fourth week, I started trying to draw connections between the history I was reading and one of the first stories he'd told me: the story about how his father, afraid for their safety, had sent him, his brother and his sister to stay with their aunt in the 'country' for the duration of the strike. What I enjoyed was that the 'country' was St Patrick's Road in Houghton. Something else I found interesting was that his aunt, his mother's sister, was married to a wealthy man named Morris Lipshitz, who was a bookkeeper for Ernest Oppenheimer. There were so many lines and tantalising circles that could be drawn – but they would need to be drawn cleverly, neatly.

I stopped experimenting with those lines and circles on a Friday. I know it was a Friday because I remember realising that morning that exactly six weeks had gone by since I'd started: a full quarter of my six months was over. I spent the afternoon reviewing what I had done so far. It didn't look like much. I'd made hardly any progress at all. I walked home feeling despondent. I felt like calling my father and telling him that something was going wrong, but I didn't. I didn't say anything to Thenji either.

That night, at my grandparents' house for Shabbat, I told my grandfather, when he asked, that so far it had gone really well. He said he was 'delighted' to hear it. I told him about Gidi Shimoni's book and everything I'd learned about the miners' strike. His eyes shone, but I didn't feel the glow. The next day I wrote an email to Allan Greyling, telling him about the privilege of having access to the Brenthurst Library, and about the two different fronts I was working on: my grandfather's memories and the history of Johannesburg. I worked hard to affect a confidence I didn't feel.

MADAGASCAR

Interview 9
Date recorded: 15/10/2005

In May 1942 we set sail from Durban harbour in a troop ship called the *Empire Trooper*. I was an officer now. I had just completed my six-month officers' training in Potchefstroom, and I'd been assigned to a regiment that was going up to North Africa. There, we were to become part of the Fourth Motorised Brigade, a comparatively small artillery force supporting the British infantry battalions fighting the Germans in the Western Desert.

At that time there was a great fear of the Japanese submarines off the east coast of Africa. These subs had already torpedoed ships carrying Allied troops in the Mozambique Channel. So instead of sailing up along the coast – the fastest route – we headed out in an easterly direction to sail south of Madagascar.

A short while after we passed the southern tip of the island, a few of us noticed that instead of turning to head north, we continued sailing east, towards India. When we asked our superior officers why we were continuing on this course, none would explain – if indeed any of them knew themselves. So someone organised a chess tournament, and we played chess and wondered among ourselves at a possible explanation. There was little else we could do. As subalterns in the artillery we weren't involved in greater strategy.

After ploughing east for a day and a night, we received news. By that time we were very near India. We were told that we had sailed east to avoid submarine activity. And we heard that the *Empire Trooper* would not sail to North Africa after all. Instead we would sail back to Madagascar to support the British troops who had, in only the last few days, wrested control of the northern part of the island from the Vichy French. The Allied strategists apparently feared that the Japanese might invade Madagascar to use it as a base in the Indian Ocean. So we sailed back west, and ultimately arrived at Diego Suarez, a port town right up on the northern tip of Madagascar.

We arrived to find that there was peace in the north of the island. Several British battalions were fighting the Vichy French in the south, but here it was very quiet, and the fear of the Japanese invasion seemed to have subsided for the time being. We occupied a position above the harbour that had been created by a British garrison, and in those first few weeks we had what can only be described as a very pleasant time. We organised fruit and vegetables from one of the farmers in the region – I remember his name was Monsieur Parent – and our chaps would hunt wild ducks in the bay. So we ate very well. In the evening we'd sit outside our tents, on the windward side of the hill so we could see the sea, and have a little to drink and a smoke.

The biggest thing we had to worry about was mosquitoes. Between us and the harbour there was a swamp, and I'm not exaggerating when I tell you that every evening, as the sun was setting, there arose from the swamp an opaque black cloud, and that cloud would make its way up towards us, and pass over us. Tens of millions of mosquitoes. Consequently we had very strict rules relating to mosquito nets. As officers on duty, we used to go around in the evening and inspect the mosquito nets of every person. And if they had a hole in their net they were in trouble. So the nights were awful. But the days were beautiful because the mosquitoes disappeared. At dawn they went back into that bog and stayed there.

Now then: we'd been on the island for about three months when one day the battery commander, Major Herloff-Petersen, told me that the Japanese attack might come off after all.

Herloff-Petersen, whom I got to know very well subsequently in Italy, had a prognathous jaw and a big black moustache, and he was a bit of a tiger was old Pete. Or as we called him, Black Pete. He had black hair, a black moustache, and his brows were beetle-black. He was a very intimidating-looking man but was, I learned, a good and gentle soul.

Pete wanted me to take two of our guns south to a small bay on the east coast near Tamatave and hold the fort there until other troops came down. So I went down to the bay with two crews; a couple of sergeants;

and another officer, theoretically junior to me, who was responsible for vehicle maintenance. I was in charge of the outfit because I was good at signals and could keep in touch with the regiment.

And there we really lived the life of Riley for a couple of weeks. Nothing happened. We set up our guns and then we managed to get some very good food. There was a small island in the bay very near to where we were, on which wild duck used to settle. And we fired .303 rifles at them across the water. We never hit one like that, but as soon as the rifle went off they all took off into the air and then our chaps would shoot them down with shotguns. Then we'd sail out and pick them up. Some of our chaps were crack shots. One could shoot rabbits. We had people who knew all about these things. You had men in the army who knew exactly how to cook them. One of the chaps had been a chef in peace time. And we lived really like fighting cocks. We were in that little bay for about three weeks.

Ultimately, the order came through that this had been a false alarm. Rumours of the Japanese invasion were exaggerated, and I should come back to Diego Suarez.

So we packed up everything and I then went to the sergeant in charge, and I said, 'Sergeant, have you got everything?'

He said, 'Yes, sir!'

'All the guns ready to move?' I asked.

He said, 'Yes, sir!'

I said, 'The ammunition, all packed and put away?'

He looked at me strangely and said nothing.

We kept the ammunition in large metal containers; there were about four or five shells in each one.

I said, 'Come on, man. Is the ammunition packed away in the containers?'

He said, 'But we didn't fill the containers, sir.'

'You can't be serious,' I said to him.

He said, 'I'm serious.'

I said, 'Do you mean we've got no ammunition here at all?'

That, it turned out, was exactly what he meant. We had come to stop the Japanese invasion with no ammunition.

My face at that moment must have been a study, I tell you.

When I got back to the regiment I decided that I'd better come clean about this. I knew the sergeant would inevitably tell his mates what had taken place and rather, I thought, that Black Pete should hear it from me.

So I decided to tell him that night – a night I happened to be on duty. The duty officer had to go around inspecting the mosquito nets. That night I was on duty with my fellow officer Jack Chesters.

We were inspecting the tents when we saw the *Queen Mary* arrive down in the bay. The *Queen Mary* was a British ship and one of the biggest vessels afloat at that time. It was a luxury passenger ship that had been converted into a troop ship. We saw it come into the harbour; it had sailed in and moored behind this giant rock in the harbour, so that you couldn't see it from the land. It was very strange how this enormous ship could simply disappear from sight.

When we had completed our duty round, I left Chesters and went to find Herloff-Petersen in the officers' mess. The mess was a big marquee tent with rows of trestle tables and a bar. I hung up my Sam Browne belt on a rail outside the tent, and went in.

There was Pete, sitting at a table with the colonel. So I went up to them, and to the colonel I said, 'You know, sir, the *Queen Mary* is in the harbour here.' I thought I'd just make some conversation first.

The colonel looked at me icily and said, 'Mr Browde. I thought you would know better than to talk about ships and shipping.'

This was a big thing in the Second World War. Big signs all over the place – in coastal areas, particularly – read: DO NOT TALK ABOUT SHIPS AND SHIPPING. Talk was dangerous; the idea was that it would get to the Germans and they'd know where the ships were.

I said, 'I'm sorry, sir. I thought that in here we …'

'Don't *think*,' he said. 'Just don't talk about ships and shipping.'

I said, 'Very well. And now that I've broken the ice, I think I should tell you another story …'

And I told them how we had gone south with no ammunition. I left nothing out. I remember that while I was speaking, Pete just stared at me from under his heavy black brows.

The colonel laughed when I'd finished. He said, 'Well thank heaven we didn't have that Japanese attack.' And then he turned to Pete and said, 'So what do you think of your guns?'

Pete was furious with me; he said, 'I can't believe it!' – and there followed some quiet expletives.

I said, 'But you know, I told the sergeant …'

He shouted over me: 'Don't tell me what you told the sergeant to do! Don't! You carry the buck here, boy. You don't tell anybody anything.'

That was a lesson I have actually remembered all my life. I was in charge so I shouldn't have tried to put the blame elsewhere.

But just then in walked Jack Chesters wearing his Sam Browne belt with his revolver sticking out of his holster. We all knew not to do that. Chesters was committing a serious offence.

The colonel said, 'Mr *Chesters*! Don't you know that you don't walk into a mess with your arms? You leave them *outside!*'

Chesters – and I don't know what had possessed him – said, 'But, sir, my revolver is empty,' and then, to prove it, pulled his gun and fired two shots through the roof of the tent.

Not one shot: two shots.

Well at least that moved the focus from me to Chesters, and what he only went through with the colonel, I can't tell you. The colonel gave him such a *blast*. Jack Chesters was a fair-headed fellow, but he went the colour of a beetroot.

Anyway, there were two holes in the roof of that tent until the day we left Madagascar, which was about two months later.

And I suppose you must be wondering, quietly, how we ever won the war. But that's another story altogether.

Jules Browde in officer's uniform, Alexandria, Egypt, 1943
'And now that I've broken the ice, I think I should
tell you another story …'

chapter nineteen

In which the young storyteller makes a plan and falls asleep

The mistake – I told myself, taking the transcripts back down from the bookshelf – had been to start in the distant past. The distant past is like the middle of the ocean: you can't dive in there and hope to swim to shore. My grandfather was just around the corner. Blinking his eyes. Sitting or standing. Walking from one room to another. The task, I decided, was not to situate his life in history, but to write about him as only I, his grandson, could; and in such a way that he would live through my eyes on the page. I would use his stories as a map and follow him through his adventures in my own imagination.

The other thing I had to do was to delineate the field of the work. Was I writing a history? Making a portrait? What *is* a biography? How long should one be? 250 pages? Should I simply let the scale of the thing take care of itself, be worked out in the doing? I knew I had to answer these questions and work out a plan for actually *writing* the thing, sentence by sentence. I knew the tone was important – to strike the tone of a biography. I had different types of vocabulary to consider too: the language of the court room; the language of war; the language of childhood. To write about a *particular* life and a *particular* world, I would need to write in the appropriate register, using the appropriate words.

So with this vague new impetus, I started in again. To mark the departure I decided to avoid the library for a while and work from home. I gave myself a week to get reacquainted with the stories. I read carefully through the file again, marking with a series of pale-orange Post-it notes what I considered to be the most important or interesting stories. Once I'd isolated these, the idea was to put myself in the shoes of a contemporary bystander and see what thoughts and ideas came.

At the start of my second week on this new path I met my father for lunch at an Italian restaurant at the top of Grant Avenue. It was a small place no more than fifty metres from their office, with room inside for about five tables and maybe two or three more on the pavement. We sat that day at one of the tables outside.

A minute after we sat down, Mario, the owner, came out and stood beside our table with his hands in his apron. 'Alan, how are you?'

He had a sweet spot for my dad, who ate there once or twice a week.

My dad greeted him warmly and then said, 'Mario, you've met my son Daniel?'

It was a routine we went through whenever I was there. None of us tired of it.

Mario put a consoling hand on my shoulder and said, 'This is your *father*? I am so sorry!'

This was my cue to open my hands and shrug, resigned to my difficult fate. Which made Mario break out into loud laughter and whack me playfully on the shoulder for disrespecting my father.

I had just spent another fruitless morning shifting Post-its around, and was feeling a new creeping apprehension. I tried to hide it, and spoke more than I ate; my dad tucked into his pasta and drank an Appletiser in big thirsty sips. I told him I was starting on a new tack, but I stopped short of telling him why: that what I'd done so far felt very thin and not at all like the foundation I had wanted to create by this stage.

I explained my latest plan: to imagine myself as an eyewitness to certain key moments in his life, to write about them as if I'd been there. My father gave this a few moments thought. Then he nodded and said he liked the plan. He even suggested an opening scene: 'You start the book in court. You're in the public gallery and you're watching Bronco cross-examine a witness.'

He told me again about how law students and novice lawyers used to make an effort to watch my grandfather cross-examine. He said the story of his life had to start there. In court. Him and a witness. He said he wanted to be sure that I understood just how central the practice of law had been in his father's life.

'I mean, that was what he *was*,' my dad said. 'He was an advocate. The law was what he gave his life to.'

When we'd finished eating my father ordered us cappuccinos and told me some other stories he'd been thinking about, including a funny one about seeing Bobby Locke on the beach. I laughed to hear this story again, and decided to write it down when I got home. It was one of the stories my grandfather had mentioned but never told in full.

Before I left, my father made me promise to make a new schedule, carefully parcelling out the time I had left. So I went home and mapped out a timetable. I'd read about a famous Japanese novelist who got up at four every morning and wrote until noon – not a minute more or less – seven days a week. I was still feeling slightly rudderless and I found the thought of such monastic discipline appealing. So I gave myself the same writing schedule: four am until noon, every day. I would return to the library in the afternoons to do targeted research, I decided, but from dawn's dust I would fashion a life in words.

Sinking into sleep again one afternoon at the library, my head resting in the warm crook of my elbow, I opened a heavy door and entered a painter's studio. The only windows in the room were small and high up on the one wall. A murky, vaguely *coastal* light filtered down through the gloom in narrow shafts swimming with dust motes.

At the other end of the long room was a large table. On the table, a collection of objects the absent painter had arranged for a still life.

I went closer to inspect these objects.

Five or six black-and-white photographs stood upright in tarnished silver frames. Some of the pictures showed my grandfather at various stages of his life: the bold little boy with the fringe he doffed to amuse his father; the soldier with the thin moustache and solemn, almost mystic gaze.

Another picture was of my grandmother as a young woman. Her dark eyes had a look that was at once determined and vulnerable. There was also one of the two of them together, their faces side by side, four eyes staring out at me questioningly from behind glass.

Next to the photographs was a sort of ceramic vase with three flowers in it, and in front of the vase, open on the table, was a large heavy book: an atlas. I was reaching out to touch one of the flowers when someone behind me put a gentle hand on my shoulder. Elsie had become accustomed to waking me like this. When I opened my eyes and turned my head to look up at her, she smiled. I mouthed a thank you, half embarrassed.

On one of the low couches, five minutes later, I dipped a biscuit into a cup of coffee and thought back on the dream. There had been other photographs on the table, dried-out images that now slid through my mind leaving no trace. But thinking about it in this way, I did remember seeing something else, right in the middle of the arrangement: a rectangular box, about the size of a shoebox, both colourless and luminously beautiful. I must have been connected to the dream still by some magic bridge, because I knew at once (with the irrational certainty of a dream) that this box was the Law. I also recalled in that instant what my father had said at the restaurant a week before. About starting the book in court. 'That was what he *was*. The law was what he *gave his life* to.'

If I'd needed these reminders, it was only because I might have taken it for granted. Since I was a little boy, my grandfather and the Law had been one thing in my mind. He was a Lawyer just as my grandmother was a Doctor. On those days when we went to their house, his study was where I expected to find him and where I mostly *did* find him, in that room plastered with extraordinary books – *that's* what it was! I almost shouted it out into the silence. His study's blend of light and shadow – *that* was the colour of the box in the dream. Which was not, I then realised, a box at all, but rather that room, isolated from the rest of the house and shown from the outside. The props designer in my subconscious had painted its outer surface with light from the interior so that I might recognise it.

A family is a fiction created in part by the stories that those living under one roof tell and hear and believe. These are the myths by which we come to decide who we are. The same tales that cast him as the brilliant cross-examiner cast my dad as the tough guy with the soft heart and me as the promising but unrealised drifter. I decided that this box, as sealed and self-contained as a myth, was a calling and an instruction. I had to find a new way into his stories. If I wanted to be a writer – his biographer and not just his grandson – I would have to do more than stand around in the doorway, waiting for him to look up at me and smile.

THE TROJAN HORSE

Interview 21
Date recorded: 20/09/2006

The major part of my education as an advocate was gleaned from personal observation of – and discussions with – senior colleagues of renown in the profession. It adds up to this: one had at all times to do one's best in the client's interest, regardless of what one felt about the client personally. One had to cast aside one's personal emotions and, after thorough preparation of the client's case, eloquently – and with clarity – seek to obtain the judgment sought by the client.

Why must the advocate avoid being emotional when involved in litigation on behalf of a client? The answer is simply this: when consulted as to whether the client should, in the first instance, become involved in a court case *at all*, it is obvious that the advocate must assess the law and the facts, and bring to bear complete objectivity in basing an opinion. To be emotional in approaching the problem can only cloud the issue to the detriment of the client. And during the *course* of the case objectivity is vital also – in regard to every step taken, every question put, and whether or not a particular witness should be called.

But in some cases emotion is unavoidable – based, for example, upon sympathy for a client or upon a question of rights: *human rights*. It can happen. And under the old South African government it often did – that one's client regarded it as a matter of public concern that an issue be aired publicly, win or lose.

And in one such case, in which I acted as a senior counsel, the issues were so emotionally charged that the case has lived with me ever since.

I refer to what is commonly referred to as the Trojan Horse Case, which was the single most disappointing case I was ever involved in.

The case came before the court on an unusual basis: it was what is known in the profession as a *private prosecution*. And I want to tell you a little of the story.

In about 1987 I was approached by a Cape Town attorney, Joe Ebrahim. Joe told me he was acting for a woman by the name of Hilary Magmoed, whose son had been shot and killed by the police in Athlone, about eighteen months before.

Athlone, you probably know, is a so-called Coloured area about fifteen miles west of Cape Town. In the 1980s, like most of this country, Athlone was in turmoil. To show their displeasure with the system, many young people were throwing stones at police, burning tyres in the street to disrupt traffic, and so on. Towards the end of 1985, the police decided – and I think I quote – to 'teach these young people a lesson'. And the incident in question occurred on 15 October 1985.

On that afternoon, a railway delivery truck was seen driving down Thornton Road – which was the main road in Athlone. It passed a large group of young people, who had gathered at the corner of Thornton and St Simon's Road, many of them still in school uniform. So the truck passed this group of mostly school kids and disappeared from view. What these youngsters didn't know was that the truck was being driven by security force members, and hidden in some wooden crates at the back were members of the railway police (a special branch of the police) as well as a couple of soldiers.

A few minutes later, the truck turned around and drove back; they were *taunting* them. This time, one of the kids threw a stone, and the stone hit the windscreen of the truck. At that moment ten men stood up out of the crates and with automatic shotguns started firing into the scattering crowd. And killed three of these young people: a boy called Jonathan Claasen, who was twenty-one; a little chap by the name of Michael Miranda, who was ten or eleven; and Shaun Magmoed, who was fifteen. Another twenty or so were wounded.

Feelings obviously ran very high in Athlone in the days after this, and Joe Ebrahim, who was a man very involved with the issues of the community, took it upon himself to lay a charge against the police.

It took a long time – far longer than it should have, almost an entire year – but ultimately the matter was placed before the Cape Attorney General, who then declined to prosecute.

216

This decision was difficult to understand, but must have been the result of the political views at the time held by the prosecuting authority, who regarded the deaths of Coloured youngsters as justified.

The tactic that had been used that day was obviously part of a strategy that had been decided at a high level of the security forces. Senior people had handpicked these shooters, and they'd obviously been told that if they did this there would be no comebacks. What could be done in the circumstances?

Joe was a tiger, man. He wouldn't let the thing lie. And ultimately he decided it would be a good idea to launch their own private prosecution. Now, private prosecutions are rare in South African legal history and rarely succeed. Under the Criminal Procedure Act, anybody may launch a prosecution if the prosecuting authority declines to prosecute and issues a certificate of *nolle prosequi* (which means: *we shall no longer prosecute*).

Joe consulted with two extremely capable junior advocates in Cape Town: Jeremy Gauntlett and Denzil Potgieter. And then he contacted me to lead the team as senior counsel. My views agreed with theirs: namely, that this was a proper case for the prosecution to be brought to fruition by private citizens.

This involved obtaining the *nolle prosequi* as well as putting up security for the costs that would be involved. These obstacles were soon overcome and I was briefed, together with my Cape Town colleagues, to conduct the prosecution.

This was a case in which our whole team became emotionally involved. We all met this woman who had lost her son. We saw the brazen attitude of the police towards taking any responsibility for what they had done. And the three of us – Gauntlett, Potgieter and I – worked on this with great fervour. We worked very hard on this case. I stayed down in Cape Town and worked out of Huguenot Chambers, a building near the High Court.

Potgieter and Gauntlett had already done a lot of the legwork, collating all the documentation. There is some irony in the fact that the police of the day were very meticulous, and that often this was to our advantage – as it was here. They would record all their movements and planning. So we delved deeply into the police records. Denzil Potgieter was very experienced in this type of work. We also spent time in Athlone, where we interviewed a lot of witnesses – people either present that day or who could refer us to others who might help us. Tensions were still high – wherever this case touched was sore. Children had been killed; people wanted justice.

One crucial piece of evidence that fell into our laps was a short film that had been taken by an American journalist. A fellow who worked for CBS. He was on Thornton Road that day, and his film, which was about a minute long, showed the policemen popping out of the crates and firing at the fleeing children. It had already been seen on American TV, but of course had never been shown here in South Africa.

When I saw this film, it seemed to me to be a cut-and-dried case of culpable misconduct. The police said they had hidden in these crates because they wanted to arrest the ringleaders, and then somehow had felt themselves to be in mortal danger. When you saw the film it was absurd. Two seconds after the stone hits they are standing up and shooting. Instead of getting out and arresting some of them, as they maintained they wanted to do, they chose to shoot them.

We also had medical evidence that substantiated that many of these youngsters were shot in the back, which shows that at the time the police fired they were certainly not a threat to the police. They were in fact trying to get away from there. And forensic evidence showed that bigger ammunition was used than the police claimed: lethal ammunition.

We prosecuted the chief of police, who had designed this scheme, and twelve others involved with what had, in the meantime, become known as the Trojan Horse Massacre.

And we charged them with murder on the basis of *common purpose*, a legal principle that allows a judge to convict a defendant for sharing a common purpose with others to commit a crime – usually murder – even without evidence that the defendant himself directly caused the death. We knew we could charge them with culpable homicide, but we thought they could be found guilty of murder on the facts; and even if we failed to prove the intention to kill, we were confident the judge would at least find them guilty of culpable homicide.

The police had several counsel – also from Johannesburg, by the way. A chap called Flip Hattingh led the team that defended the police. And we knew we were up against the odds. But still we allowed ourselves to believe that we were going to win this case. The judge was a man called Williamson, Deneys Williamson, who had been at the Bar in Johannesburg but when made a judge was transferred to Cape Town.

During the course of this case we showed the film and called a series of eyewitnesses. We also called an expert witness by the name of David

Klatzow, who started off in life as a haematologist, interested in blood. The case took a long time.

The callousness of the police was illustrated by the fact that they chose not to give evidence at all, thus escaping cross-examination.

And ultimately the judge reserved judgment, and we waited a month to hear the outcome.

In the meantime, this generated a lot of press here and abroad. This was the first private prosecution of the police *ever* in South Africa, and a victory would send an important message from the courts. A loss was unthinkable. Because it really would tell the police they could get away with anything.

Now I've told you the story – I think – of the young white man who drove over and killed an old black woman sitting on the side of the road in Fountains Valley, near Pretoria. And I told you what I said to the newspaper then, after this chap was let off – which was that white judges would not have been able to identify with a young black man if he had appeared in front of them, but because it was a young white man, they could identify with him, and say, 'There but for the grace of God stands my son.'

You know what I mean?

And I am sure that this played a role in this case. Because Williamson came back in and, lo and behold, we lost. I still feel frustrated and angry to relate the story. He said in his judgment that the police had very serious problems to deal with. Which they did. But of course most of these were problems of their own making, or the making of their government, anyway. And the solution that they found in Athlone that day, when they decided to use the Trojan Horse, was an unforgivable one. But he identified with the police more than with the children who had been hurt or killed.

And this really took it out of me. And I wasn't the only one who was upset, of course. My whole team – Ebrahim, Potgieter, Gauntlett – we were all devastated by this case. And I believe we have all carried this loss with us ever since.

But that wasn't the last word. We appealed the decision, confident that in the Appellate Division of the Supreme Court in Bloemfontein we would win the appeal. Because of the fine calibre of judges who sat in that court.

And the case came on about a year later. Michael Corbett, who would later become the chief justice, presided. The full bench consisted of Corbett, two judges by the names of Botha and Grosskopf, and two acting judges, HC Nicholas and Johan Kriegler, whom I have mentioned to you on a number of occasions.

The judges knew from the record that we had this film of what had happened, so when we arrived that morning for the case to be heard, I received a message from Judge Corbett saying that he wanted to see me. So I went along there, and Corbett said, 'Look, I want you to have a screening set up, in the small court.' (There are two main courts in Bloemfontein, and they had built a smaller court down the steps from the ground floor.) He said, 'I want it all set up. We want to see that film before we go into court.'

This was very unusual for the Appellate Division – but, hell, I was so pleased about that, man. I was confident that when they saw this film, there could be no doubt in their minds that Williamson had made the incorrect decision. It was there in the clear light of day.

And we showed it. Everybody sat in the dark there. The judges all sat and watched it. And when it was over, they said, 'Play it again.' They played it five times. The whole film, as I told you, took a matter of seconds. Then, after robing, we went into court.

The judges came in, and when called upon I stood up and announced our appearances – my colleagues and myself. And then the presiding judge said to me, 'Mr Browde, we'd like to have a look at that movie again.'

I thought: what *can* they be looking for?

But we put it on again. We set up the projector in the court this time. You could see it, but not as well as you could in the dark. We did switch out the lights. So you could see it pretty well. And there it was again, clear as crystal: the railway truck travelling in one direction, completely unmolested; the return trip; one stone hitting the windshield; and then these men in khaki jumping up, their shotguns pointing down from the height of the truck at these youngsters, who are running away – and *firing, firing, firing.*

And then we argued the case. I argued the facts, and Jeremy Gauntlett argued the legal points involved. We argued for a couple of hours. And anyway, as I say, this was perhaps the single most disappointing case that I ever appeared in. Because we lost there as well. The appeal court judges found that the police were under stress, and that they did what they did in order to defend themselves. Which, for me, was a lot of hogwash. It really was.

I was *bitterly* disappointed by this case. And I still am, to this day. I still think about it: about the children who died; about Shaun Magmoed and his mother, who was there in court. A woman who wanted justice for her dead son, and these policemen who got off scot-free. It's an awful story, man.

I reread the judgment in anticipation of telling you this story, and it still makes me sick to read it. Because it legitimised the callous and unforgivable attitude of the police in the days of apartheid.

And there's an addendum to this story; you can make of it what you will.

Ten years after this happened, in about May of 1997, former security force members and eyewitnesses to the shooting incident presented testimonies at the Truth and Reconciliation Commission hearing. As a result, four or five of these policemen, who were on the truck, who shot these youngsters, were subpoenaed to give evidence. They came before the TRC here in Johannesburg. And these men stuck to their original statements, and they did not offer any apology nor, might I add, did they indicate that they felt any remorse for what they'd done.

chapter twenty

In which the young storyteller changes tack

One way into the box occurred to me a few days after I'd dreamed it. Reading through the stories of some of my grandfather's cases, thinking about how to retell them, I realised they were strewn with the names of people I knew, people I saw from time to time through my grand-parents, or who I could at least get in touch with quite easily.

Why I hadn't considered interviewing anybody else seemed sud-denly incomprehensible. That I took so long to get there still seems odd, although I think I can go a long way to explaining it by describing the sense of trepidation I felt exactly then. In going beyond the safe enclosing walls of our relationship, I realised I would open other doors; enter other, stranger rooms; break down the image we had all conspired to create. The fear was of having the ground pulled out from under our familiar positions.

Still, I was excited to do it. I wrote down some names on a piece of paper. The first was Gilbert Marcus. He had worked with my grand-father as his junior colleague on many cases, and had gone on to be one of the most respected lawyers in the country. He had also stayed in touch with my grandfather and I saw him occasionally at their house. I wanted to talk to him specifically about a groundbreaking case they'd done to-gether, The State vs Adams, which effectively ended the enforcement of the Group Areas Act across a swathe of Johannesburg. Later that day, I added two more names: Edwin Cameron and Arthur Chaskalson.

My grandfather said he thought this was a 'marvellous' idea and suggested some other people I might speak to. Among them: Aubrey Ncongwane, Keith Matthee, Morongwa Seleka and Brian Currin. He gave me some phone numbers and said he would find more. I was ready for him to comment on the fact that it had taken me a long time to get to this, but he didn't say anything about it.

I spoke to Gilbert Marcus the next day and he agreed to meet me the following week. In the meantime I continued to transpose some of the stories into the third person, adding details as if I had been on the scene as a witness. I also experimented with leaving some episodes in the first person but adding a second perspective, a sort of refracted echo, so it would sound like a second person had been inside his head looking out at his life, seeing what he was seeing and hearing what he was hearing. Thenji was sleeping and I was going mad at the computer in the other room.

A week later, I drove out to Gilbert's chambers in Sandton. I'd stopped aping the Japanese novelist by then and had woken up at a reasonable hour, so I was wide awake as I parked my car under an awning inside the office complex.

Gilbert met me in the building's reception area and led me to his chambers. The walls of tall dark books reminded me of my grandfather's study as well as his old chambers in Pritchard Street, where he took me a few times when I was small.

Once I was in there, sitting across from Gilbert at his large desk, my thoughts started doing self-conscious spirals. Had I done enough to prepare? I should have done more. What could I have done?

Gilbert recounted his early days at the Bar, told me how my grandfather had been a mentor to him, an inspiration and a protection. 'There was a very small community of advocates doing this sort of work,' he said (meaning human rights work against the government). 'But the important thing about it was that it included giants of the Bar. It included Jules Browde, Arthur Chaskalson, Sydney Kentridge – people who were of the highest integrity; people who carried enormous respect. For young people like me it was a form of protection to know that the leaders of the Bar were doing this sort of work, and lending their names and credibility to the *importance* of this sort of work.'

Gilbert thought hard about what he wanted to say, but when he spoke he spoke easily, articulating ideas with coil-jointed sentences; his was the firm but flexible narration of a man trained to argue, to *tell*.

'I remember as a pupil going across the road to sit in and watch Jules cross-examine,' he told me. 'He was a legendary cross-examiner. And for good reason. He had a quality that was simply unmatched by any other advocate I have seen, and it was his capacity to make witnesses relax, to engage with them in an almost conversational manner. With absolutely devastating results for the witness.'

He told me about a few cases in particular – cases in which my grandfather had led him – including The State vs Adams and The Case of the Phantom Coup in Lesotho (the only such case in world history), as well as the appeal against the infamous banning of the *New Nation* newspaper (which they lost).

When his cellphone rang – as it did occasionally – he pulled a face and apologised to me before taking the call. And then went back to what he'd been saying. But the frequency of these calls increased, and after about an hour and a half he leaned forward to indicate that he had to get back to work.

But before I left, Gilbert said he wanted to photocopy an article for me. He'd already prepared some documents to give me, articles and chapters of books, but something else had come to mind while we were chatting.

We walked along a long carpeted corridor to the back of the building. The photocopier was in the coffee room. I watched Gilbert lift the cover and I heard the mechanical slide and fetch of the machine. A youngish guy (an articled clerk, I guessed), late twenties or early thirties, came in to wash out a coffee plunger in the sink, and I watched him look across at Gilbert – and blink once – surprised to see a silk at the photocopying machine.

As I walked to my car, my heart swelled to embrace the story I was telling and my own ability to tell it. I could have what these people had. Gilbert Marcus, Allan Greyling, my grandfather. Whatever else they believed in, these men, they believed in themselves. If I was going to write this book, I had to believe that I was writer.

The next person I went to see was Edwin Cameron.

Edwin met me in his chambers at the Constitutional Court, the room as stark and orderly as a monk's cell. He told me that my grandfather 'brought his personal moral authority to the arguments he made'.

I took notes in a black moleskine notebook I'd bought for the purpose.

'Jules wouldn't make a rubbish argument; he wouldn't make a really bad technical argument. When Jules argued a point, and you were his junior backing him up, wanting him to win the argument, it would be because you knew he *believed* in that point,' he said.

He described meeting Jules, and the first case he did as his junior – a case that involved the conscientious objector, David Hartman. Edwin spoke of Jules's warmth, of his generosity of spirit.

I couldn't have been more proud: sitting in this historic building, listening to one of South Africa's most respected public figures speak with such admiration for my grandfather (and my subject). Whether it was from this that I drew sustenance, or from the image I had of myself walking out through the sun-enchanted foyer, moleskine in hand, I can't be sure. But I drove home that day feeling fortified, charged up. I couldn't wait to get home to type up my notes.

After that I tracked down more of the important characters from my grandfather's world. In the Metropolitan Council building in Braamfontein I met Aubrey Ncongwane, assistant to the integrity commissioner. Aubrey took me to Diepsloot to look at the site of a case they were investigating, in which a city councillor was accused of selling a building that wasn't his to sell.

In Orange Road I spoke to Brian Currin, the director of Lawyers for Human Rights in the early eighties, when my grandfather was its chairman. According to my grandfather, Brian took Lawyers for Human Rights from being a small organisation with only a 'rather desultory' local office to being an influential national organisation. When I met him, Brian was on his way home to Pretoria from Madagascar, where he was doing government-level mediation in the wake of a coup.

On the phone I chatted to the advocate Denzil Potgieter about the work he did as a junior in the Trojan Horse trial. I exchanged emails with Leon Schubart, the Port Elizabeth attorney who briefed my grandfather in the case of the Watson brothers. Sometimes I recorded these interviews on Thenji's iPhone; sometimes I scribbled notes.

The advocate Denise Fischer told me about Group 14, the maverick group that Jules formed in 1993 to provide leadership and – more importantly, she said – *mentorship* to the city's junior advocates, who at the time were floundering, excluded from established legal networks. Keith Matthee – an advocate and a lay preacher – told me how my grandfather once settled a bitter personal dispute between him and a judge by forcing the two of them to sit in a room and talk things through.

One person on the list I didn't speak to then was Arthur Chaskalson, the first president of the Constitutional Court and an old friend of my grandfather's. I kept putting this off because Arthur was someone I saw quite often – usually at Shabbat suppers at his son Matthew's house. I figured I'd get round to talking to him soon enough.

I typed up these interviews with a sense of something starting to happen. Introducing these various voices into the book was going to give it new dimensions, facets, complexity. They would also lend it an authority that had – I realised now – been sorely lacking.

This was the biography for real.

Yet one day, reading through one of these interviews, wondering how I might thread it into what I'd done so far, I had a disquieting thought, which led to a restless, uneasy feeling – an oblique hunch at first, but one that turned over the next few days into a worry. I thought about Prof. Kariithi and his rudiments of good reporting. 'Get both sides of the story,' he'd said. Adding, 'You will rarely get the full picture if you only hear one side.' If that was true for a news article, surely it was true for a biography. I knew the word for a biography that focused on only the positive side of its subject: *hagiography*. The word originally referred to a book written about the life of a saint. I did not want to write one of those.

At first I tried to ignore this concern, and for a time I succeeded in forgetting about the interviews altogether as I concentrated again on the stories. I had, by now, worked his childhood into a more-or-less cohesive opening section, and had moved on to the war stories. My plan was to isolate these into one hard-boiled section, and call it 'Wagtail' – his radio codename during the Italian campaign.

But before long the thought came back, and the worried feeling, and one morning I found myself looking through the file for self-incriminating evidence – something to prove he was no saint.

What I found was a story set in 1972, when he took a case as a prosecutor in Lesotho that some of his colleagues thought he should not have taken. I thought back to the interview and remembered it well. It had been a difficult story for him to tell. I'd felt it in his tone and in the way he looked at me as he told it: how much the criticism had stung him, how he hadn't been sure himself of what to do. But most of all I'd felt how much the support from Arthur, who defended him against his critics, had meant to him. Arthur Chaskalson knew what he was talking about, I told myself, and I dismissed the case for the prosecution.

So what kind of book was I writing here anyway? In whose interest was it? With what was it complicit? The pantheon again rose up in front of me and I saw once more the ghostly cast. This time they were all looking at me, these august figures, mockingly. They wanted to know the same thing: Who *was* he? Where *did* he stand in relation to history? How did he *compare?*

I wasn't sure I knew the answers (nor was I sure that I wanted to know them). I thought about a scene from a novel I'd read in high school. It was a scene that had stuck with me, that came to mind once in a while. But now I began to think about it almost obsessively. Two writers are sitting in a bar and one of them says to the other, 'So when did *you* realise that your father was a jackass?' (They are nursing beers. Real writers, hard-living.)

The other writer answers the first: when he was sixteen, that was when he realised his father was a complete fool …

And they go on like this, talking about what schmucks their fathers are. They seemed to take it for granted, as if realising this was a necessary moment in the life of a writer. I hadn't realised it yet, and this sometimes felt like a hurdle I would never be able jump over.

In high school I used to *wish* that I despised my parents. There was this goth kid I sometimes spoke to in the sick bay: he despised his and I envied him his freedom. His mother was a witch and his dad was a drunk, at least according to the stories he told me. (I used to go to the sick bay sometimes if I got a headache. He basically lived there in an ongoing protest against the timetable.) I imagined that if *my* mother was a witch and *my* father was a drunk I'd be able to think more clearly about them, and thus about myself and the world. But unfortunately my mother mostly tried to understand where I was coming from and my father drank only occasionally, and when he did he'd make corny puns for a while and then fall asleep on the couch.

This fine rope of affection that tied me to my parents was the same rope that tied me to my grandfather, and tied my hands behind my back to keep me from writing a proper biography.

I kept thinking too, at that time, about something that had happened the second time I lived with them – in early 2004, after I came back from Grahamstown and before I moved into the flat in Norwood. I'd gone out that night to a club on Louis Botha and when I came home I was still slightly drunk and struggled with the key in the front door. It was late – two or three in the morning. When I finally got the key to turn, and pushed open the door, there he was, standing with his hands at his sides in the half-lit hall, creased with sleep, his hair sticking out all over the place. He was already deep into his eighties then, and I'd woken him. I had nothing to say. I just stood there feeling like a dunce. But his eyes crinkled as he smiled. *'You made it,'* he whispered. Then he blinked once – still smiling – nodded sleepily, and headed back to their bedroom.

So how could I possibly measure him the way a biographer is supposed to measure his subject? Lucidly, objectively. Maybe I would never be able to see the world with the cold-hearted precision a great artist needs. Maybe I would never be able to write the biography about him that I should: a contribution to history, a catalogue of his inconsistencies. Because isn't that what every good biography amounts to? Could he have joined the underground resistance like Kasrils or Slovo? Would he have been a more worthy person if he had? If he had not lived in a house with a pool but in bush camps with a pistol at his hip? I comforted myself with the thought that if I did ever get down to writing the book properly, I would leave that for someone else to say. Lost in the crystalline mists of family and partiality, I could never really be trusted.

BOBBY LOCKE
MY FATHER'S STORY

Date recorded: 21/06/2011

My dad was always the champion of something. He was the South African snooker champion, the South African light heavyweight boxing champion and the Olympic decathlon champion. He played cricket for Transvaal and came second in the Russian chess championships.

We were very young when he told us of these marvellous achievements, and somewhere deep inside we knew they were probably just stories, just his love of keeping us entertained. But there was still always a drop of lingering doubt – and hope. Was it was *possible* it could all be true?

And then something very strange happened.

One of the things my dad had done was to beat Bobby Locke in the final of the South African Open Golf championship, which was then played in the match-play format.

And one day in about 1959 – when I was about eight years old – I was sitting with my family on the beach at Fish Hoek in the Cape, probably listening to some or other magnificent exploit of my dad's, when out of the water emerged the unmistakable figure of Bobby Locke, who was not only one of the greatest golfers ever, but the man *our* dad had beaten in the final of the SA Open. This was our chance to verify. Our chance to see if all the stories we had heard over the years were indeed true.

'Go on, Dad, go say hello,' we urged.

'Don't be silly,' he said. 'He'll think that I'm rubbing it in. Anyway, if he wants to greet me he'll come over here.'

Our disappointment was short-lived. Locke, who was heading across the sand straight for the parking lot, suddenly became aware of us, took a look, another look, made an abrupt turn and walked briskly towards us.

'Hello, ol' chap,' Locke said to my dad, extending his hand. 'How have you been? Still playing the ol' game?'

We nearly died of shock. Could the SA Open story be true? Could all the stories have been true? Was our dad indeed Superman?

'Hello, Bobby,' my dad said. 'Nice to see you again.'

'How long will you be here for, ol' chap?' Locke asked.

'About two weeks, Bobby,' he said. 'We're actually staying in Kenilworth, but we come out this way quite regularly.'

'Have you ever played at Clovelly?' Locke asked.

He said, 'Many years ago, Bobby.'

'Well then, ol' chap, it's time you played it again. Give me a call anytime and we'll have a round. Clovelly is in great nick, you know.'

'I'll certainly do that,' my dad said.

At that, Bobby Locke shook my dad's hand again, bade us all a hearty farewell, and strode off.

Shock! Astonishment! Dad was telling the truth! Man alive, he was the greatest sportsman that had ever lived! Cricket, tennis, boxing, snooker, athletics … golf!

Being a sensitive human being, my dad knew that it was risky to let the truth out too fast. To deflate our morale too quickly could do damage. So he took his time. About six months, I would say. Each time I told the story to anyone in front of him, he would water it down a drop, allowing the truth to emerge bit by bit.

Finally, when the time was right, he told us the truth. None of the stories was true. He was not the South African snooker champion, nor the South African light heavyweight boxing champion. Nor had he ever been in the Olympics, let alone won the decathlon. The gradual and empathetic manner in which he set the record straight ensured that we took it in the right spirit, and that instead of feeling humiliation or anger we were left with a warm and fuzzy feeling.

And Bobby Locke?

My dad had no idea. 'He must have mistaken me for someone else,' he said. 'I couldn't believe my luck!'

chapter twenty-one

In which three people go on an outing

There were hours, even whole days, when I felt proud of the work I'd done on the book, but that feeling was difficult to hold on to. Reading over what I'd written was like staring at one of those line drawings that change depending on how you look at them: you can see either the young woman turning her face away, or else the old woman with the headscarf and crooked nose, never both at once. Sometimes the book seemed fluid and compelling, but more often it felt disjointed, *slapgat*, embarrassing. Never anything in between.

I'd been working on it for four months, which meant I had two to go. My grandfather would often ask me how things were 'coming along'. His expectations felt uncomplicated; he was waiting, trustingly, for something good. And I always gave him the good report: 'It's going really well'; 'It's going great.' I never shared with him the doubts I was having. What could he do about those anyway? What could anybody do? The biographer's job, I suspected, was to just get on with it and not complain.

So I spent days describing episodes from his life only to find that his transcribed stories had more life than what I made of them – so I threw my versions away. I spent days pondering family and old age and throwing these musings away. I went back to the notes I'd made while reading *The Jews of Lithuania* in the Brenthurst library, but they just looked like lifeless notation, not sparks and kindling, and I threw these away too.

I'd planned for some time to go on a series of outings with him, but, bewitched by the problems of the text, I'd put this off. Now, with time running out, the idea resurfaced: a last throw of the dice.

The first outing I wanted to do was to visit the houses he'd lived in as a child. I wanted to go backwards in time: so first the house on Page Street, Yeoville, where he lived from when he was four until he was nineteen, and then, after that, the house in Bertrams, where he was born in 1919. I knew (he'd told me) that when he visited the Bertrams house a few years before he'd had an experience he didn't particularly want to remember. He'd spent only a few minutes inside before he had felt afraid and left in a hurry. I asked Thenji if she'd come with us to film some of the outing on her phone. I thought that if I chose to write about any of it later, this would help me to describe it accurately.

We fetched him from his house one morning in my Tazz, which I'd tidied before we left. I threw all the accumulated junk into the boot, and jammed the CD boxes into the cubbyhole. I didn't think it was fair to ask him to understand that I didn't intend to be like this forever, so disorganised.

'Hello, laddie,' he said as he got in, already turning to say hello to Thenji in the back.

'Hi, Jules,' she said.

'Hello, Thenj!' His face lit up to see us. 'How are you, love?'

It took me a few minutes to adjust to having my grandfather as a passenger, but after a few nervous stop streets I felt like my feet were going to do more or less what I wanted them to, and I relaxed into it.

'Do I need to tell you how to get there?' he asked.

'I don't think so,' I said.

'All right. You get us there.'

He was looking around him. Once he slapped his hands on his knees and said, 'Yes, well.'

Thenji was silent – in the rear-view mirror I could see her holding her phone a little way in front of her face and looking into the screen.

It was only when we got to Raleigh Street that I needed his help. This was as far as I knew. We were close. He told me to turn right onto Kenmere Road, and then left into Page Street.

It was a bright morning and the sun was pouring down. There were six or seven men standing inside the gate. Everything was brightly illuminated: house, leaves, faces. 'Let me go and speak to them,' he said.

Thenji and I watched from the car as he approached the gate. He was wearing dark trousers and a matching blazer over a white collared shirt. After a conversation that lasted longer than I could explain to myself, he came back and leaned one hand on the car. 'It's fine. That's Mboke. He's the fellow who owns the place now,' he said. I looked back at the gate. The shortest of the men was explaining something to the others. Some of them were nodding their heads slowly.

Thenji and I followed my grandfather and we greeted the men standing at the gate. They were friendly, deferent, watchful.

In those first minutes of our visit I learned that this short man – who I knew only as Mboke – had bought the house nine years before, and rented out its rooms. He had also built a rudimentary double-storey flat in the backyard and rented out rooms in that too.

We walked up the steps onto the covered patio outside the front door. A pulsation of tiny flies zigzagged about the light fitting.

For our eyes, accustomed to the bright day, inside was so dark that we had to wait a few seconds before we could see anything at all.

'This is where the lounge used to be,' my grandfather said, looking around him, left and right, up and down.

'That was where the dining room was,' he said, nodding towards a set of double doors on our left. The doors were locked. My grandfather kept walking. Mboke and one of the others, a tall lean man wearing trousers and a long T-shirt, followed us quietly.

In the room he shared with his brothers – at the end of the short passage that ran through the middle of the house – were three double beds and not much else. A young man with a narrow face sat on the edge of the bed under the window, studying his phone. Mboke greeted him. He looked up at us crowded into the doorway.

'My grandfather slept in this room in 1925,' I told him. He smiled and got up and squeezed past us out the room. On the far wall were two posters: one of Tupac Shakur and the other of someone who looked like Eminem, but wasn't.

He pointed at the bed along the near wall. 'That's where I slept,' he said. 'That's where I used to have the dream about floating off into space.' He looked from the bed to the window opposite, and back again.

'What dream was that?' Thenji asked me in a whisper, still pointing the phone in his direction.

I mouthed: 'I'll tell you later.'

In the kitchen, plastic tiles were peeling, lifted in places to reveal the concrete underneath. The old world was here, but you had to look hard. We stood at the window for a moment and looked down at the backyard. It was a cracking cement construction site: work on the double-storey flat was not finished. 'There were four or five fruit trees in this garden,' my grandfather said enthusiastically, as if he could still see them.

I followed him outside. Going down the steps that led from the kitchen into the yard, I remembered the game he'd told me about, one of those complicated games his brother Len had devised, which involved bouncing a golf ball off different parts of these steps.

Now there was a plastic soccer ball lying at the bottom. He sidefooted it along the concrete. This impressed Mboke's tenants, who had come round to the back and were sitting on the steps of the half-built flats, watching us. One of them complimented him on his soccer skills.

Backyard of the house on Page Street

'I used to play soccer in this garden almost ninety years ago,' my grandfather said, with a smile that rippled across his lips and disappeared.

Here was the cellar where his father and grandfather had made wine, but it was locked and Mboke didn't have the key. The other cellar, where his family had kept charcoal, was packed with sheets of corrugated metal. I observed the men on the steps, who watched with interest as the old man, whose glasses had darkened in the sunlight, looked around at a world that wasn't there any more.

He sidestepped some thick planks to get to the corner of the house. I followed and stood behind him as he peered around the corner into a concrete alley about two metres wide. This house was separated from the next one by a cracking prefab wall. 'It has all changed,' he told me. He said it softly so that only I would hear.

We walked around to the other side of the house. In the wall that ran alongside the driveway was a round stained-glass window that looked like a porthole. As we walked past it, I thought I saw someone move behind the glass.

Thenji filmed part of the goodbyes. She got my grandfather speaking to Mboke, thanking him, promising to return some day, thanking him again, shaking his hand. And then shaking hands with some of the tenants who had come back to stand at the gate, where they had been when we arrived.

I thanked Mboke and shook his hand. He had a round face and a very warm smile. Only his kind and calm manner illumined what could otherwise have been a sombre visit.

Because we had to go back in the other direction, I did a three-point turn, back and forth in the street. 'But the world has changed,' my grandfather said, letting us in mid-sentence to an argument that must have been going on in his head. 'There has been a population explosion.'

I looked around at Thenji. She was holding her phone in her lap. I tugged the indicator down.

'No. Turn left,' he said.

I explained my route plan: to get us back to Louis Botha and then make our way down to Bertrams on Joe Slovo Drive. His expression indicated that it wasn't a *bad* idea, but he said, 'Make a left. I'll show you another way.'

I saw Thenji lift her phone to film.

We drove past a low building with a red iron roof. 'This was the Yeoville Shul,' he told us. 'That's the yard where we used to play soccer. And there,' he pointed at the brick wall, 'that was where the drainpipe was. I told you the story, Dan. When I climbed up to get the globe and almost got electrocuted. Go straight.'

I thought about how I was being shown around these streets by someone who knew them before they were even tarred. It was a heavy pride I felt then, a melancholic pride. Some lives are lived in many places, most are lived in just one. His had been lived here, in this mining town. This was where he was born, grew up, went to school. His parents are both buried here. It is where he earned his keep and raised his family. It was some relief to think that whatever I wrote or didn't write, his story was already stamped into the stubborn material of the city.

He was born in Bertrams, went to Observatory Primary School, had his bar mitzvah eighty years ago in the Yeoville Shul. When I had mine, sixty years later, it was in the Sydenham Shul, and he sat in the front row with my grandmothers and my parents and beamed up at me.

He watched the city grow and change through all the decades of the twentieth century except the first: from dirt roads to global internet confusion and ragged teenage boys begging at every street corner.

'Left again,' he said. 'And then immediately right.' We were moving through the edges of Hillbrow now.

He sat at his desk in his chambers on Pritchard Street, writing the city on his lined legal pads. In its courts, he argued it into being. I thought of how he had been rewarded by a deep knowledge of its streets and shortcuts.

'Now down here.'

I pointed the car down a very steep road that, as if by magic, connected with Saratoga Avenue near the base of the Ponte Tower. Twenty seconds before, I'd had no idea where we were. I turned left before he told me to.

'Do you know where you are now, laddie?' he asked me.

As we went under the flyover I said, 'I used to live near here. The Buddhist centre is just up there.'

'Oh, that's right,' he said.

Saratoga Avenue becomes Charlton Terrace, which in turn becomes Bertrams Road on the sloping curve, and I turned left off Bertrams into Ascot Road.

Thenji watched it all on her screen.

At first he thought that maybe the house numbers had been switched around, because from the street 32 Ascot Road was unrecognisable to him. The wall and the house behind it were made out of sandy face-brick, and there were two black, solid steel gates, one for people and a wider one for cars. From the pillar between them hung a hand-painted sign: ROOMS R160.

'Maybe just drive to the other side of Liddle Street,' he said. 'Sometimes they reverse the numbers. So 32 may be down there now.'

I drove slowly. He pointed out the spot where the man had jumped onto the coach on that morning when he was four years old and the horses were running away with him.

On the other side of the intersection with Liddle Street, he became confident, for a few seconds, that his house might have been this side. 'Just a sec … Ah …' He looked back between the seats. His eyes glinted hopefully, but the excitement passed.

At the intersection of Ascot and Fuller Street I did a U-turn and I took us back to 32 Ascot, with its sign. I brought the car to a stop a little way from the house, in the shadow of one of the bulky trees that lined the road.

Just as I stopped the car, the big gate opened a little and two women came out from behind it. They were both small and in loose-fitting tracksuits, one pink and the other blue. They started to walk away from us along the pavement, and the gate closed again. When I climbed out of the car they turned to look at me. One smiled, one didn't. They had their hair tied up in ponytails. They turned around and carried on walking.

I knocked on the narrower gate and waited. A few seconds later the big gate opened again, just a crack. Another woman, kind of skinny, stood in a similar tracksuit, hers white with some silver writing on the front. She had reddish hair extensions, which she had tied up carelessly as if she'd been in a hurry.

'Hi,' I said.

She nodded.

'We're looking for the house my grandfather was born in,' I smiled, and looked back at the car to indicate the old man sitting in the front seat.

The tree above the car was reflected in the windscreen, but through the veil of leaves and sky I could see his face. Though he was look-ing right at us, his eyes seemed blank and hopeless. Thenji was leaning between the seats and watching intently.

The woman said, 'This is a guest house.' She smiled sadly, as if that news would be disappointing to us.

'Okay,' I said. The probable meaning was dawning on me; I thought of the women who had walked out as I arrived.

As I contemplated my next move, I heard the car doors opening. Thenji and my grandfather were climbing out. They started towards us along the pavement.

'Sorry, one sec,' I said to the woman.

I saw that my grandfather hadn't locked his door, and I realised that my backpack was still in the car. I walked past them and locked the door, shut it again. Three men walking on the other side of the road were watching me. I was making eye contact with one of them when I heard my grandfather say, 'No. It's no good.'

He was leaning forward slightly to take in the house over the shoulder of the woman in the white tracksuit. I could tell from his wary posture that he didn't want to cross the threshold of the gate. I went back to join them and tried to see what he was seeing. An empty beer bottle stood abandoned on the low wall of the stoep. The windows were double – even triple – barred.

'It's a completely different house,' he said.

We thanked the woman, who was still smiling her sad smile, and got back in the car. Thenji wasn't filming any more. The outing was over. As I drove us up Joe Slovo, no one spoke. But by the time we got back to Orange Road, my grandfather at least was in a happier mood. He had not been fazed – at least not as far as I could see.

'Well, thanks Dan,' he said.

'Thank *you*, Broncs.'

'I don't know if that helped you,' he said.

I said of course it had, and Thenji backed me up.

'So when am I going to see you chaps?' he asked, and we spoke about the possibilities. Then he gave us each a kiss and let himself in through the security gate. Once he'd closed the gate behind him, he smiled and waved to us one more time. Then he walked up the steps and disappeared into his house.

He felt it. I had seen it for a few seconds in his face through the windscreen in Ascot Road. I had heard it in his voice as he looked over the woman's shoulder. But whatever shadow had insinuated itself into his blood had been absorbed by a complex, century-old system of dealing with hope and disappointment, expectation and blame. It had vanished into him.

Thenji and I were stumped. Silenced. There was too much and too little to say about what had happened. When we got back to the flat I sat down at the table in the living room with my exercise book and a pen. She sat at the computer nearby and started some work of her own. I looked up now and then – at the side of her studious face, at the branches outside with their nests and the sky behind – but mostly I looked down at the lined pages. I got down as much as I could remember about the morning – where we'd gone, what we'd done. I didn't think I'd need it for the biography. It was all too obviously loaded with symbolic significance. *The old world: going … going … gone!* But still it felt good to write without paying attention to how the words sounded or fitted together. Just thinking back and writing.

MUIZENBERG

Interview 2
Date recorded: 30/04/2005

When he thought it was appropriate, my dad made my older brother take me along with him to various places and events he attended. My dad gave him money to go to the bioscope, for instance, or to sporting events, on condition that he took me with him. As a result, some of my earliest memories are of going places with Len.

One very early memory I have is of going with him to watch the All Blacks play rugby against Transvaal at Ellis Park stadium, which had just been built on the site of the old quarry near our house in Bertrams. He and I sat on what was called the 'popular side', which was the side of the ground facing the sun. I recall the roar of the crowd and my excitement at being with my brother inside the great stadium, which until then I had seen only from the outside.

The referee in that match was a man called Neser, and I'll never forget the sight of Neser, who was a small man, pointing to the pavilion and sending off the field for foul play a chap called Finlayson, one of the All Black forwards, a real giant. Finlayson walked off the field with his head bowed all the way, and it was a terrible thing to see.

But the story I want to tell you concerns something that occurred when Len took me on holiday with him to Muizenberg. It was December of 1929 and I was ten years old. Ten and a half.

Len was eighteen and had just written his matric examinations. To celebrate, he and a few of his friends wanted to go down to Muizenberg to enjoy themselves. They had all saved up some money to pay for their expenses.

At first my parents refused to let him go. They said it was extravagant for a group of youngsters to go by themselves. Len was terribly upset. He marshalled all sorts of arguments in favour of his going. And ultimately my dad gave in, but on one condition, the usual condition: 'You can go as long as you take Yoshke,' he told him. My dad used to call me Yoshke, which is a sort of Yiddish term of endearment. 'As long as you take Yoshke with you.'

This led to some more consternation, as you can imagine. Len kicked up a real fuss. But my father was adamant, and in the end Len agreed to take me along.

So I went with these four big boys to Park Station, and we boarded the train. I was so excited to be going with them. My brother's three friends were Gussie Braude, Mervyn Lazar and Tobie Greenblatt, who was actually a relation of ours, a good-looking fellow and a practical joker. I did everything I could to please them. Everything I *could* do, I did. One of the shutters in the compartment didn't work properly. It was one of those that you pulled up with a leather strap so as to keep the light out in the early morning. But this one wouldn't stay up. No matter how they all tried, it came crashing down. So I said, 'Don't worry, I'll stay awake and hold it up.' I was actually prepared to do that. They had such a laugh, man. Because imagine me lying there all night holding up the shutter.

We stayed a few hundred yards from the beach in an annex of the Seacombe Hotel. It was the first time I had been away on holiday, the first time I had been at the coast, and I thought it was marvellous. I remember distinctly the smell of the sea mixed with the smell of coal smoke from the train as we arrived, and the first time I saw the waves.

The older boys used to leave me alone a lot, but I didn't mind. My goal was not to be an encumbrance to Len. I knew he wanted to have fun and not have to bother about me, and I didn't want him to regret having to bring me along. So I learned to be responsible for myself.

And I remember exploring on my own. In those days Muizenberg wasn't built up very much. Only one street was tarred by then, as far as I can recall, and the sparse traffic presented little danger.

Between the annex where we were staying and the sea front was an open field. Here they had set up a fairground, with a merry-go-round and a coconut shy and that sort of thing. My dad had given me a bit of pocket money, and I used it at the fair. They had the most terrific mechanical games, one of which I got quite good at: you had to put a coin into a slot and this caused a little ball to drop from the top into a steep maze, and then you had to watch this ball carefully to see if you could catch it at the bottom in a sort of cone-shaped hat. I recall I also bought hot dogs from a man called Mike. A very friendly man who took quite a shine to me.

Len and his friends spent the long hot days sitting on the beach near the pavilion, with lots of other boys and girls of their age.

I used to go along, too. I'd sit a little way away from them and mind my own business. I would go into the sea by myself. I loved that. There were crowds of people in the sea. I recall women my mother's age jumping slowly with the rising and falling swells, large women in black bathing suits and white bathing caps. They spoke English with the same heavy accent as my dad, scooping up the waters and splashing themselves, and with each splash crying, *'Oy, a maichel! Oy, a maichel!'* – which in English means something like, 'Oh, such a treat!'

I used to stay in the water for ages, and when I came out I'd sit in the sand and look around at everybody coming and going.

A few years earlier, in 1926, the Johannesburg municipality had built a public swimming pool in Yeoville, on the corner of Raleigh and Kenmere roads, and I used to go there a lot with my friends. That was where I learned to swim. But for some reason Len never came to the pool, and, as a result, he had never learned to swim. He never *did* learn to swim, by the way.

In some ways, I was more intrepid than Len was.

This is something I mention because of what occurred one day when I was coming out of the sea. I had been in the water for quite some time on that particular day – longer, perhaps, than usual – and I was walking out through the shallow surf when I saw someone who appeared to be hiding behind one of the pillars of the pavilion and watching me. The pavilion was raised on several wooden pillars and behind them was a rather dark, gloomy area, hidden from the sun. I couldn't see who it was. I even thought I might have imagined it, because when I looked again there was no one there. But a moment later, the person put his head out again and looked at me, and I saw that it was my brother.

This image of Len is one that persists in my mind's eye, even these many years later. It is something I still think about occasionally, and it makes me think that Len was a very complicated person. He was keeping an eye on me after all. But he was hiding behind the pillar because he didn't want me to see.

chapter twenty-two

In which the young storyteller and the old storyteller
visit two graveyards

The doors to the administration offices were open and there were two men standing inside. Both wore slacks, collared shirts, and ties with clips. They greeted us gently, but without smiling. When my grandfather told them why we were there, the tall one told us to take a seat and his shorter colleague disappeared into the next room. After a minute, he came back into the office, straining under the weight of three enormous books. The books contained the names of all the people buried in Westpark Jewish Cemetery, and the location of their graves in terms of section and number.

Once we'd found the number of his mother's grave, the shorter colleague took out a photostat map of the cemetery and showed us how to get there by drawing lines on the map with a green ballpoint pen. He then passed the map to my grandfather, who took a long look at it.

Just before we set out, my grandfather asked them if they didn't perhaps have a hat he might borrow. He hadn't brought one himself, he said, and his doctor had told him not to go out in the sun bareheaded.

Without a word, the shorter man went into the next room again, and came back with a dusty brown fedora. 'Ah, that's very kind of you,' my grandfather said. He put it on. I could see it didn't fit him very well – it was a bit too small – but it was good enough.

We walked out of the building into the stillness of the day. All around us it was quiet. He smiled at me as he jostled the hat on his head, trying to make it fit better. 'I'll bet I don't look the part now,' he said.

We walked along the tarred road, glancing now and then at the map, until we saw a low brick wall, and then we turned left. The road went down towards a grove of trees.

'Yes, that's right, my mother is down among the trees.'

As we walked he looked at the headstones and sometimes read the names out loud. I let him get ahead of me and I took some pictures of him stepping between the graves. I was on a mission now: a recording mission. I had only a month to go and I didn't know if I was going to make it. I didn't know what I was going to tell them. Could I ask for more time?

Jules Browde at Westpark Jewish Cemetery, Randburg, Johannesburg

There was a hole in his mother's grave. Not a big hole, but big enough. The soil must have become eroded beneath the gravel chips that lay on top, because a sinkhole had appeared right in the middle. It wasn't a hollowing or a crater but a proper *hole*, and unless you went right in close it seemed to lead all the way into the other world.

'Barbara's right,' he said. 'There's a hole.'

My grandfather took off the hat they'd given him and held it with both hands in front of him. The inscription on the grave read:

IDA BROWDE

PASSED AWAY 27TH OF OCTOBER 1973

After a couple of minutes, in which neither of us breathed a word, he said, 'Well, there she is.'

And then, another short while later, 'Well she's not there, of course. It's just bones.' I had heard him use the same words at other times, at other graves.

He stood still and silent for a long while, the hat still in his hands.

Before we left the grave, he wanted me to take some pictures of him standing next to the tombstone. I tried to flatten out my angle so you couldn't see the hole. But in most of the shots you can still see it. It looks like a wound.

'I must have this hole fixed up,' he said.

'We can talk to them when we go back,' I told him. I also wanted it gone. The cemetery is supposed to smooth it all down like a sheet, help us to believe that they are resting in peace. Otherwise what's the point?

When we'd walked a little way away, up past the row of trees, he stopped and turned and looked back in the direction from which we'd come. Smiling, he said, 'She wanted to be buried out here, my mom. Out here by the trees. Because she said there was a lot of fresh air out here.'

Then he prepared to laugh, but did not. He was still looking back. It was as if he'd thought the thing about the fresh air was going to be a joke, but then it turned out not to be.

We stopped twice on the way back to the offices. The first time was at the grave of his sister. My grandfather took the hat off his head again. On the tall dark stone was carved:

LILY RABINOWITZ
PASSED AWAY 26TH OF JULY 1989

I recalled that late in her life Lily had married a man called Louis Rabinowitz. Many years after her first husband, Phil, had died.

We'd been standing there for a few minutes when my grandfather asked, 'Did I ever tell you about Phil Greenberg?'

'Yes, you did.'

'A nicer chap you could never meet,' he said. 'A really lovely man.'

He stood at his sister's grave for about ten more minutes while I cleaned bits of grass and leaves and twigs off it, placing them carefully to one side.

The grave of his brother Len was back near where we'd started. It was in a special section of the cemetery, in the shade of some tall trees.

Graves and trees were surrounded by a white picket fence that was less than knee-high. An age-dulled bronze plaque just inside the fence informed us that this section was for people who had 'contributed in a special way to the community'. And there it was, about three rows in:

LEONARD BROWDE

PASSED AWAY 24TH OF JULY 1971

We didn't stay long here. My grandfather took off his hat again, and seemed uncomfortable. I asked him why Len was buried in this section. As we walked away he explained to me that it was because Len had helped to start the Oxford Shul in North Road. The Oxford Shul was a large synagogue down the road from where I lived. I found it surprising that nobody had ever mentioned this to me.

When we were back in the cool of the office, Frank – the tall one's name was Frank – explained the maintenance options to us. I remember the 'Eternal Care' package because that was the one my grandfather chose for his mother's grave. He put his brother and sister on it as well.

After that we looked up the location of his father's grave. This information was right at the end of one of the books, because his father was buried at another cemetery, in Brixton – an older cemetery, closer to town.

The shorter one, whose name was Bram, said he would come with us. 'Brixton is no longer a good neighbourhood,' he explained.

My grandfather picked up the hat, which he had put down on the counter. 'I'm still going to need this,' he said. 'If you don't mind.'

Frank, who was staying behind, told us to prepare ourselves for a shock because part of the cemetery had been vandalised.

My grandfather looked thoughtful. 'An anti-Semitic thing?' he asked.

'No, just vagrants,' Frank said.

I sat in the back seat because Bram was sitting up front. I took out my exercise book and a pencil. I wrote down that Bram had brought with him the rusk he'd been dunking in his coffee back at the office, and that on the seat next to me was an old copy of *The New York Review of Books*.

We passed the botanical gardens. Bram was explaining the

predicament. The vandalised shrine at the Brixton Jewish Cemetery had been designed by the famous architect Herbert Baker, and since all Baker buildings had been declared national monuments, technically it was the city's responsibility to fix it up. I thought that was interesting.

I stopped taking notes and looked out the window. We were driving through Melville with its bottle store, its pool bar, garage, pharmacy. Then we were out of Melville and ascending the steep hill with the SABC offices on our left. At the top we passed the enormous base of the Brixton tower, and then descended the hill on the other side, entering the suburb of Brixton itself.

'Why has this become a bad neighbourhood?' my grandfather asked.

'Like everywhere else in this country,' Bram replied.

My grandfather said, 'No. Not every neighbourhood in this country is bad.'

There followed a long pause, in which I could almost hear the cogs turning in Bram's brain. At the end of the pause, he said, 'I suppose what I mean is that you get bad neighbourhoods all over the country, and this is one of them.'

At a traffic circle, at the bottom of the long curving road, Bram told my grandfather to turn left. He took the turn, and we headed east now, towards town. Through a high fence on the right I started to see gravestones, many of them obscured by long grass.

On Bram's instruction, my grandfather stopped the car on a short steep driveway, in front of a great, black, wrought-iron gate in which some long-ago ironmonger had fashioned two *Magen Davids*. I had been to Brixton hundreds of times and had never noticed this place.

The gate was not for opening. Bram led us some way along the pavement – back up the hill – until we came to a section in the fence that had clearly been trampled down. We took it in turns to step over the muddy threshold. Bram offered to help my grandfather, but he refused his hand. One by one we stepped over broken glass and beer bottles, mattress springs, chip packets, sections of trodden newspaper half submerged in the mud.

Ahead of us the shrine, the *ohel*, looked like a building after a bombing raid. There was no glass in any of the windows, and bricks around the edges of the square cavities were missing. The ceiling, whatever it had been made out of, had been completely taken out, and some of the rafters had obviously snapped during its removal and were dangling haphazardly in the gloom. There was broken glass on the concrete floor. The only thing left intact was the roof.

I hung behind and took a photograph of my grandfather and Bram heading out of the structure into the bright sunlight on the other side. Bram was shorter than my grandfather, and wider. On my way through, I saw that in the side rooms were several sodden mattresses, and in the room on the right there was a washing line with a few items of clothing hanging on it. I didn't want to think about this too much, so I caught up with the other two, who were pulling away from me. They had separated: my grandfather, shaking his head slowly, was drifting off down a row of graves in the sunshine.

Brixton Jewish Cemetery, Vrededorp, Johannesburg

My grandfather – who had been here ten years before – had told me it was a lovely cemetery with lots of room between the graves, but these graves were packed even closer together than at Westpark and it was quite brambly and overgrown. Also, the ground was uneven underfoot. You could step onto what you thought was solid ground and sink into a deep, soft hollow in the long grass. When I caught up with him, he was breathing audibly. 'You know, this is bloody difficult,' he said.

He thought he had an idea where the grave was, but for the longest time we couldn't find it. I had to hold his arm and help him over and between graves. We were looking for 1938, but there seemed to be no stones from that year. We moved from the graves of people buried in 1940 to the graves of people buried in 1939. *Gordon; Lurie; Abrahamson.*

At last, to help the search, we split up. I went this way, towards the fence, and he went that way, towards the middle of the cemetery.

After about ten minutes, I started to despair of ever finding it. *Solomon; Ginsberg; Skudowitz; Tobiansky.* Also I couldn't see Bram any more. I looked over at my grandfather, stooped in his religious man's hat and battling in the long grass, holding on to tombstones to prop himself up.

At last I spotted a grave from the year 1938, and after that it wasn't long before I found the one we were looking for. It was almost at the end of the row, a few steps from a wire fence covered in dark foliage. It was a black obelisk, about five feet high. There was a lot of Hebrew writing on it – and then underneath, in English, it said:

ISAAC BROWDE
DIED 10TH OF OCT. 1938 AGED 59 YEARS

The grave was in pretty good nick, considering how some of the others looked. I called out into the quiet day.

My grandfather came stepping slowly towards me. And I saw Bram now; he appeared as if from thin air, far away, lumbering towards us. Behind him, further in the distance, I noticed the Brixton tower, and for a second it looked like a tall solitary tombstone against the blue of the sky.

My grandfather took off the hat again. Then he stood close to the headstone and read the Hebrew, trying to translate it for me. He pointed out our surname formed by the ancient characters.

After reading the Hebrew out loud, he fell silent. He came to stand next to me at the foot of the grave. It was a Sunday, and except for the occasional hollow swoosh of a car there was only silence.

My grandfather asked Bram if he could put this grave under the Eternal Care package as well.

Bram said, 'Of course.'

'I really think I should, you know,' my grandfather said to me.

We stood there a few more minutes, and no one said anything further. It was hotter now than it had been earlier at Westpark.

On our way out I hung behind again, reading the names on some of the stones. I saw the grave of Annie Slovo, Joe's mother; she had also died in 1938. Back near the gutted *ohel* I saw an image that has stayed in my mind: a beer bottle standing upright in the middle of a grave. I don't remember the name of the person whose grave it was. I thought of taking a picture, but I'm glad I didn't. Sometimes it's better not to take a picture of something just because you can.

Once we'd dropped Bram and the helpful hat back off at Westpark, I got back into the front seat. Bronco was looking very tired and worn out. The colour was gone from his face and his cheeks looked sunken. I thought I could see his lips trembling slightly.

'I'm absolutely parched,' he said.

So on the way home we stopped at a restaurant in Greenside to have a drink and something to eat, an Italian-themed place called Doppio Zero. On the mustard-yellow wall outside were the words NOTHING ADDED BUT TRADITION.

He asked for the homemade lemonade and an egg salad; I ordered a quiche and an Appletiser. While we ate, I asked him a few questions about his parents (dates and things like that) – trying to fill in some stubborn gaps – but he answered in the most perfunctory way, hardly even looking at me. He used his knife and fork carefully, working the bits of salad onto pieces of rye bread with meditative determination.

When his lemonade was finished, he asked the waitress if she wouldn't fill up his glass with some cold water. He handed it to her.

'I'll bring you a new glass,' she said.

'Don't worry,' he said. 'The same glass will be fine.'

She took it away and brought him his water in a new glass.

When we got back in the car I turned around and reached out my hand to pick up the copy of *The New York Review of Books* that was on the back seat. But I changed my mind and left it where it was. What I hoped to achieve by reading a few paragraphs on the way home, I don't know. Instead I just sat there in the front seat and zoned out as he took me back to my flat.

Thenji had left a message on my phone to say that she'd gone to her studio to paint. I lay down on the couch in the empty flat. I usually avoid napping during the day, but almost as soon as I lay down I succumbed to a deep and dreamless sleep. When I woke, whole sections of the room were dark. The sky beyond the black branches was a pale violet. Thenji was home: I could hear the muted gush of falling water coming from the bathroom. I lay still in the deepening shadows and listened. The sound of her shower was the reassuring sound of companionship, but in it I could also make out the sound of my own time passing away. The burden of proof falls on the old, and they cannot provide it, and then we too are old.

chapter twenty-three

*In which the young storyteller and the old storyteller
don't see eye to eye*

My grandparents were the first people we told. Of all the reasons we
were going to do this, the most important was to make others happy;
and of all those we wanted to make happy, my grandfather was top of
the list. Thenji's father – who was approaching eighty – was a close
second. These two had leaned on us the most consistently. Neither of us
had really wanted to get married. In fact, since she was a little girl Thenji
had been dead against the whole idea of it. I was ambivalent: marriage
seemed unnecessary, a bit ridiculous, but not really *offensive*. On that
balance it had seemed like something that probably wouldn't happen.

But our own feelings and fantasies were not the only ones that had
to be taken into consideration. There were others who really *did* want us
to get married, people we loved and whose needs and wishes we cared
about. Over time, certain loving pressures were brought to bear. On two
separate occasions my grandfather asked us why we *wouldn't* get married
'if, as you say, you love each other'. I assured him we loved each other
without a marriage certificate. 'Yes,' he said. 'But how do *I* know that?'

Once, in a moment of love or weakness, I told him that if we
ever did go through with it we would do so only if he could officiate.
This was an idea Thenji and I had thrown around, probably on little sleep. That same day he phoned Edwin Cameron and asked how
he would go about obtaining temporary powers as a marriage officer.
Edwin emailed the deputy minister of justice, who promptly wrote
back to say he would be happy to grant this long-time public servant a

temporary licence to preside over the marriage of his grandson.

When he told me this, I was upset with myself for speaking reck-lessly. I reminded him that it was just an idea we were experimenting with, and that we probably weren't going to do it. Privately, I also felt angry with him. Was he trying in this way to pressure us into getting married? Whether he was or not, he didn't hide his disappointment that the answer was still no.

For his part, Thenji's father told us several times how important it was to Jules that we got married. He said it so often that one day Thenji said, 'Baba, why don't you just admit that it's important to *you* too?'

By this time we were starting to feel as if it might just be simpler to do it and carry on with our lives. One night in the middle of winter – dodging cold drafts in our room, because the windows didn't shut properly – we said what the hell, let's get married. And the following morning I phoned my grandparents to ask if Thenji and I could pop in for a visit to talk to them about something.

When we got to their house the next evening, we all sat down on the couches in the entrance room, the two of them side by side on the long one, and Thenji and I on the shorter one. I remember their faces, solemn and radiant before I'd said a word. And the couches, the cushions, the light in the room – silvery, mother of pearl – I remember it all clearly. I remember saying the words and what happened next. My grandfather bowed his head, and with thumb and forefinger pinching the bridge of his nose, entered the long deep pause of someone trying not to cry – and then sobbed. My grandmother leaned towards us, her eyes flecked with saltwater and flame. 'A few years ago, he wouldn't have cried,' she whispered. 'It's his age. He has become *emotionally labile.*'

'No, it's … not that,' my grandfather managed to get out, holding his body unnaturally still, his face still in his hand.

A few days later, after we'd told everybody else – endless days of emails and phone conversations, and long weird looks at each other like, 'What the hell have we done?' – we told our families about our plan for the actual wedding. We would have a ceremony in my grandfather's study, we said, with the legally necessary two witnesses (one from each of our clans). And afterwards we'd have a tea at the house for close family members.

This information didn't fall too well into the swirling currents of joy. Now that we were going to marry, the common sentiment appeared to be that we should make it a celebration. Champagne and crowds of well-wishers. Sunsets and streamers and cows at the gate. Even my father, who until then hadn't leaned on us at all, said he thought a tea sounded 'depressing'. 'A *tea?*' he said, looking at me and cocking his head. He wanted me to listen to how it sounded.

In the end, we gave over on this too, and discussions began for our really ordinary, big middle-class wedding, with a venue and catering and invitations – all that Father of the Bride stuff that teenage Thenji had sworn, at midnight in a thunderstorm, to fight against until the last drop of her blood was spent. There were still pockets of resistance in my own mind (I didn't want a seating plan, for some reason) but even that I could already see vanishing in a moment. It was all very surreal now, and not a little confusing, but the family was happy – my grandfather and Thenji's father especially – and that, we reminded ourselves, was the reason we were doing this.

The last thing we had that was really *ours*, and that we wanted to keep ours, was the ceremony. We had a few ideas. One was that we wanted my grandfather to officiate. At the age of ninety-three he was many years older than anybody else in either of our families. To have someone of that age officiate – a real *elder*, and one so beloved to both of us – felt semi-mystical. It also meant we didn't have to have a rabbi or a priest or some other stranger do it. That was the other thing we were most sure of. We knew we didn't want to cloud the issue with traditional religious or cultural observances that meant nothing to us. And that's what I was trying to explain to my grandfather in his study one evening a few weeks later.

Edwin Cameron had phoned him that afternoon to explain what we would need to do to make the wedding official, and he wanted to tell us in person what he'd learned from Edwin. He also said he wanted to start discussing the ceremony. He knew we planned to develop the ceremony with my uncle Paul, but he wanted to start the conversation tonight anyway.

We were still months away – four or five at least – but he was already obviously thinking a lot about it. A mixture, I think, of excitement and something that had started to creep in to his life in small and big ways: a desire to know what was going to happen.

The study had changed in recent months. He'd given his desk to my parents to use as a dining-room table, and replaced it with a small writing desk. That was on the side of the room near the main bookshelf. On the other side of the room there was now a low rectangular coffee table flanked by two small brown couches.

Thenji and I were sitting on one of those couches; he was on the other, facing us. On the table between us was a tray with a decanter of port and some glasses on it, as well as a few big books.

After he'd recounted his conversation with Edwin (what papers he needed to get, from where, and so on) he told us the story of a wedding he'd been to five or so years before, at which the son of a friend of his, who is Jewish, had married a woman whose one parent was Hindu and the other Muslim. 'They had all three religions represented in the ceremony,' he said.

His friend, the groom's dad, did the Jewish parts, and – he said laughing – it was simply wonderful. At the end of the ceremony, when his friend's son broke the glass, 'all these Muslim chaps from Durban wore yarmulkes and shouted *mazel tov!*'

With tears coming into his eyes, he said he imagined us doing something similar. 'So you, Thenji, can have traditional Greek and Zulu observances, and you, Dan, can have traditional Jewish observances.'

Thenji and I looked at one another. As I faced my grandfather again, I was trying to think of what to say to him. His eyes were still joyful, but his expression was now touched with concern. We weren't reacting to this story in the way he'd expected.

I thought I'd try to explain it straight off the bat. I said, 'You know, that wedding sounds really beautiful. It really does. For *them*. But I don't know if it makes sense to us. Not the way that we're thinking about it. We don't want to have any of that cultural stuff.' I was fighting a compulsion to swallow. That his face had now contracted into an expression of confusion didn't help. 'Like, I don't know if either of us knows what that word *culture* even means,' I said. 'We both sort of feel like people, like, first and foremost, you know. Before we feel Jewish. Or Greek or Zulu. And we kind of, like, want this ceremony … you know … *(gulp)* … to sort of represent that.'

I think that, despite my swallowing, I managed to communicate more or less what we felt. I ended my little speech by trying to make it clear, again, that we weren't judging any of that traditional stuff that his friend's son had done. I looked at Thenji; she was holding her face, her emotions, in check. But I was clearly, he must have known, speaking for both of us. If she had anything different to say, she would have said it.

'That was right for them,' I said. 'It's just not right for us.'

He no longer looked confused. He looked distraught.

He said to Thenji, 'Do you also feel this way?'

I saw her nod reflected in his face. His eyes had taken on a desperate, watery aspect, as if he was out of his depth, unused to feeling like this. His thin hair suddenly looked dishevelled. He fixed his eyes on me again, and in that moment he seemed wild and unfamiliar and *old*.

Bronco was smaller these days, his face thinner, its hollows deeper. The sockets of his eyes seemed to have grown, the bags under his eyes bulged and protruded, his skin everywhere was brittle and marked – but in his eyes themselves I had, until then, seen only a hopeful light. The usual metaphors of aging – winter, twilight – had seemed not to apply to him. Yet as he looked across the low table at me now I did see winter in his eyes; I saw the electric storm of ego flickering in the evening of his body; and as in one of those accelerated nature films, I saw this winter spread through the whole person. I saw, as he set cold eyes upon me for the first time, an old man approaching the end of his life.

'But it's such a lovely thing to do,' he insisted. 'Thenji, your brother can come and hold a pole, and your parents can come and stand under the canopy.'

I said, 'You mean a *chuppah*?'

I said it because I wanted everything to be on the table, and because I wanted him to know that I knew what a chuppah was. (Which, just then, I wasn't sure he did know.)

'A chuppah, a canopy,' he said, as if what the hell's the difference, as if calling it a canopy was the most natural thing in the world.

This was the last, the very last, thing I felt like doing: arguing with him about this.

I said, 'I don't think we *do* want to get married under a chuppah.' (Don't *think* we do? I knew we didn't. We had discussed it, agreed on it. I also knew Thenji had registered my tentative phrasing.)

His response was to tilt his head to one side, and open his eyes wide, as if fighting some physical pain. Then, taking a long look at me, and for a moment – I could see – not quite sure who he was looking at, he said, '*Surely* you'll break a glass?'

Gathering strength from some obscure place of pain inside of me, I said 'No'. I said it politely, but point-blank, looking him in the eye.

'Why not?' he asked, matching my gaze.

He was angry now. Properly angry, and not hiding it.

I suddenly felt totally exhausted. I wanted to be somewhere far away and by myself. But I tried again. Summary, recapitulation. Culture: a foreign word to both of us. Same for religion. New kind of people, new kind of wedding. Et cetera, et cetera.

While I was talking he stared at me defiantly, screwing up his eyes as if I were speaking a terrible language that consisted not of words but of sharp points of light and glare.

And when I finished, he simply shrugged. He looked down and he looked up again, making it clear that what little he'd been able to decipher from my laboured babble, he didn't think much of.

'You break a glass and everyone says *mazel tov*,' he said quietly, to himself as much as to us. And then he shrugged again. A big shrug this time: he lifted his shoulders and dropped them heavily. *Gadonk*.

Houses creak in such silence as overtook us then. Houses fall down completely. He had nothing else to say. Thenji wasn't about to wade into this minefield. I could feel my back to the wall. I could feel all our backs to the wall. I had to say something to get us out of that corner. So I did that thing where you pretend you are going to think about something more than you intend to. Shuddering inside, I said, 'Look, we haven't made any final decisions. So. We'll think about it.'

He said, 'All right,' but he said it half-heartedly. I could hear he only half-believed me.

I wasn't about to try again to convince him of our cause, but I also wasn't about to back down either and agree to anything. So I left it there, open as a wound. Thenji was quiet. I could feel her concern like a subtle atmospheric front.

After a few more minutes of sparse, superficial conversation in the study, we got up and walked into the main part of the house. My grandmother stood in the middle of the entrance room and stared at the three of us, her confusion obvious. It was supposed to have been a joyful discussion, the start of a beautiful journey, but I think we all looked how we felt: like people who'd just been in a car accident and were still not sure if they were completely okay. Both my grandparents saw us to the door. The tips of my fingers were trembling. When we said goodbye, Bronco was friendly, but that is all he was. He didn't even ask me how the book was coming along.

The Secret
My Uncle Paul's Story

Date recorded: 14/03/2014

My mother and I rarely spoke of the secret we shared. She suggested that we not tell my father; she said, 'You may never get sick, so he may never need to know.'

What she told me only recently was that the real reason she didn't want to tell him was that she knew I was going to die, and did not feel it necessary for him to suffer prematurely. I now believe that she and I kept this secret from my father as a way of protecting ourselves from having to face the horror of what was happening.

Sure that life would be short, I gave up medicine and pursued my dream of being an actor. So a year after finishing my internship, I found myself at drama school in London.

While I was at drama school, my mother came to London to see me in the end-of-year production. She recalls a drive we took together to visit friends of hers who lived in the countryside near Bath. 'When we were driving in the country,' she remembers, 'you started talking about dying. We both knew you were going to die, because everybody was dying. It was just a matter of how long it would take.'

She tells me that I said, 'You know, I'm not afraid of dying. I've had a good life and I'm prepared to go.'

She says, 'I nearly died to hear you say that, but I didn't say anything. I don't know how I carried it all inside me. It was really a most terrible, terrible time.'

But a year later, I was still alive. Several of the people I knew in San

Francisco had died. A friend of mine from Johannesburg went from being infected to dying in six months.

Drama school was over and I was visiting my brother, Ian, in California. I had by this time told my two brothers, and a few close friends. My father was there too. He was visiting, for some reason, without my mother. I still had not told him.

We were in a house on a beach. I don't remember exactly whose house it was. What I do remember is that it was an overcast, cool day and that the room was dark. I had made a decision. I had come to realise that not telling my dad about my being HIV-positive was interfering with my life. It was creating distance between us and was depriving him of truly knowing me, and depriving me of the support I knew I could get from him.

I have an abiding memory of sitting at the piano in my father's study in Johannesburg. It's after the work day and my dad is reclining in the brown leather chair, his feet up on the piano stool, as I practise scales, over and over again. Every time I pause he says, '*Hell*, you play well. One of my biggest regrets is not learning the piano.'

Saturday mornings my dad takes me into town, to Diagonal Street, to the magic shop owned by Mr Kardani. We watch a magic show and then my dad buys me a trick and I spend the afternoon practising my magic with him as my audience.

Many years later I found myself at the top of a dingy staircase in a hotel in Toronto. I had travelled there to live with my boyfriend, Simon, but my timing was off, and he told me he was not ready for me to join him. I called my dad from a payphone, unable to breathe I was crying so hard. 'Give him space,' my dad said. 'If you are meant to be together, you will be. Now put down the phone and call me back in five minutes.'

I did that, and when he answered he said, 'I've called a friend of ours, Zoe Girling. She lives in Toronto, and is expecting you. Get in a taxi and go to this address.'

So on that cloudy afternoon, I told him. My heart was pounding in my chest; my head was swimming. I felt the fear of his reaction. I imagined his sadness and it felt unbearable, especially as I was having such a hard time feeling my own.

I came out with it. I explained that it had been two years that my mother and I had kept the secret from him. I said that we had not wanted him to worry, and that so far I was okay.

He stood up. He raised his voice and spoke stridently and forcefully as if he was angry. 'How could you not have told me?' he said. His voice cracked and his face was red; he was visibly upset. 'For God's sake, I've lived through a war, through a son almost dying in an accident – how could you think I wouldn't be able to deal with this?'

Those were very powerful words. I felt a tremendous and instant relief. He was not angry with me, but was upset that I had not trusted our relationship sufficiently. I don't think I regretted not telling him before, but I certainly knew it was right that I now had. 'I want you to promise me now,' he said, 'that you will *never* hide something so important from me ever again.'

I don't know if I said it out loud, but I made that promise to him inside my own mind. It has been twenty-six years since that conversation and I talk to my dad about many things and certainly do not feel like I keep any secrets from him.

Later, towards evening, he went for a walk on the beach with Ian. Many months later my brother told me that the walk on the beach had been a harrowing and highly emotional experience. I am grateful that my dad was able to feel what he did, and also grateful that he spared me witnessing it.

chapter twenty-four

*In which the young storyteller remembers
different shapes of disappointment*

I turned on the hot water and went to sit on the end of our bed. Thenji
was at the computer in the other room. We weren't ready yet to talk
about what had happened in the study. To the sound of the water I
followed my thoughts to a table in the shade of a tall grey-barked tree.
I recognised it as the tree in front of our old house on Shipston Lane.
On this low wooden table was a large brown plastic bowl filled with
Smarties, and clustered around the bowl were five or six tiny children,
their faces expectant, sugar-dazed. This was Emma's second birthday
party. I would turn five the next day, and I was giving these toddlers a lot
less attention than I was giving the grown-ups, silhouetted, from where
I stood, against a tree-crossed sky.

Nana and Bronco were there that afternoon. They stood talking with
my parents' friends. I didn't know either of them very well yet. Bronco's
outline was sharper: trousers; loose-fitting collared shirt, tucked in; confident moustache. Nana's form was more ill-defined, and I didn't know
what to make of her grave and curious gaze.

With an eye on my swashbuckling grandpa, I came up with a plan.
As a child I was always devising schemes with the same intention:
to win acclaim from a chosen adult. Mostly my tactic was to impress
them with my proficiency in what I took to be their natural tongue, the
language of intrigue. Adult life seemed to me to be an intricate game of
feelings, in which strategies had to be mapped out secretly and executed
with perfect timing.

So I went over to Bronco, who was talking to another man, and patted him on his knee. When he looked down I gestured for him to follow me. I knew I was being mysterious; this was part of my plan. He excused himself from the man by smiling and raising his eyebrows, and followed me to where the slasto ended and the sloping lawn started. With a curled index finger I called him down to my mouth level – which was then about three feet off the ground. He bent forward, placing his hands on his knees, and inclined his ear. With one hand cupped to the side of my mouth I whispered, 'I love you more than I love Nana.'

It was as if I'd poured ice water and not words in. Straightening up to his full height and shaking his head firmly, he said, 'No, I don't want to hear that. I don't like to hear that.'

I remembered feeling bewildered, shocked because I thought he was going to rub my head and love me more than he already did, but instead he walked back to the grown-ups without even once turning back to look at me.

I went into the bathroom to check on the water. The bath was about a quarter full. I stood in the middle of the bright room and stared at the fine wobbling patterns that the light made on the bottom of the tub, and I thought about the time I told him I wanted to be a criminal.

We were on the way down to the coast in our annual two-car convoy, and I was sharing the back seat of his car with Emma. I must have been about ten, so my sister must have been about seven. The kombi was a few hundred metres ahead or behind.

We were riding through a flat, dusty part of the country and talking about what we wanted to be when we grew up. My grandmother was taking part in the discussion, while as usual Bronco seemed to have his whole mind on the road. Emma was at the stage where she couldn't decide whether she wanted to be a dancer or a hairdresser. I remember announcing emphatically that I wanted to be a criminal. This must have penetrated my grandfather's concentration, because he turned his head briefly and said something like, '*Oh, go on,*' before looking back at the road. Somehow I'd said it for him to hear – assuming he'd find it unusual or interesting – but just like at the birthday party those years before, things were not turning out as I'd expected them to. 'You're not being serious,' he said.

I said that, yes, I really wanted to be a criminal. At that time, in any movie I watched or book I read, I usually found the villains more ingenious and appealing than the so-called heroes.

'So you're telling me,' he said, 'that if you owned a house that had a big crack in one of the walls, and you decided to sell that house, you would just put wallpaper over the crack and not tell the next person, because that way you'd be able to get more money for the house?'

Jules Browde with Daniel Browde,
Knysna forest, circa 1986

That didn't sound right, but I felt like I had to stand my ground. So I said yes, that was what I'd do. I'd put wallpaper over the crack and fool the next person. (A criminal is a criminal, I figured.) But I felt out of my depth now and there were butterflies in my stomach. My grandfather, who was visibly upset, told me he was 'very disappointed' to hear this, and then we all sat in silence for a long time. I felt like crying, but I didn't. I just stared straight ahead into the back of the seat in front of me.

The bath was almost half full now. I closed the hot tap and started to run the cold. I thought about the way Emma had turned to look at me in the car. Curious and consoling. I also remembered that a little while later we stopped and went into some gloomy roadside restaurant. I recalled my mother asking me if I wanted a milkshake, and me choosing not to have one because I was so upset, or else having a milkshake and not enjoying it – something like that.

Sitting on the hard white rim of the bath, still in my clothes, I tested the temperature of the water now and then by dragging my fingertips through the steaming surface.

The only other time I could remember him being cross with me was one Friday night at the Shabbat table. I was older now, in my early twenties, going to university, and I was advancing a theory (if you can call it that) about books and reading. Still trying to win the approval of the adults in terms I guessed were their own. I was telling them why I couldn't enjoy a book if someone had recommended it to me. With my whole family listening, I explained that if someone recommended a book, it meant they had already discovered it and there was nothing left for me to discover.

My grandfather was not impressed. 'Oh, *go* on,' he said, furrowing his brow.

I didn't back off. I'd had that thought in high school and had stuck with it since. It seemed like a good dissident opinion. I decided it was worth defending. This one I was going to go down with: no recommended books, not for *this* guy.

Bronco developed a pained expression, the unmistakable shapes of disappointment, and he looked at me with eyes that were clearly pleading. 'So you're saying that if I tell you about a book I've enjoyed, you won't want to read it? Because I have read it and enjoyed it?' Putting me on the spot, bringing himself into it like that.

By now I was giving my theory some serious second thoughts, but for some reason it felt important to stick to my guns – and that's what I did.

'Yup,' I said, looking right at him. I felt light-headed but defiant.

He gazed at me for a moment longer and then looked down at his food, as if he couldn't bring himself to look at *me* any more, and said quietly, 'Well I must say I find that absurd.'

He was upset. I had made him upset with my crackpot theory, which still I was determined to stick to. I looked at the top of his head for a second, and then had a mouthful of something I couldn't taste.

The conversation turned to other things, but a few minutes later he had something else to say about the matter. He spoke out of the blue, interrupting somebody else; he spoke reluctantly, but urgently, as if he was compelled. 'But that's how one *finds out* about books,' he said. 'By speaking to people one loves and respects. Like for me, speaking to you, Dan. Or speaking to your mother. That's precisely how I find out about books.'

I just sat there, looking at him and not saying anything, and he shook his head, confounded.

The water was the right temperature now, but I didn't get in. I thought of the story he'd told me about his own wedding at the old synagogue in the Company Gardens in Cape Town. How my grandmother's father, though still a young man, was so frail that he couldn't stand under the chuppah. *They had to have a chair for him so he could sit down nearby.* I also thought about his bar mitzvah and how instead of having a fancy party, his father had invited to the house on Page Street the boys from the Jewish orphanage – *boys who could really do with a party* – and how, after being shy of one another at first, he and his friends and the kids from the orphanage had had *a great game of soccer* in the backyard. I thought about the dining-room table in that house, extended to its full length every Friday night. How his grandmother cooked *wonderful Jewish recipes* and always sent him home with food. I wondered what I owed the tradition carried in these stories, and where my duties lay. I also knew it wasn't just about the glass. His frustration had boiled over that evening but it had been there under the surface all this time.

It was a year and a half since the lunch with Allan Greyling and his offer to support me for six months while I worked on the book. The six months we'd agreed to had turned into nine, and still, after nine, the pieces had refused to come together.

I'd emailed Allan to tell him I was close to the end, and would finish the book very soon on my own steam. And with the book still shapeless, malformed – a monstrous unborn marshmallow – I got a job. Because I had to.

For years I'd known that my father needed help writing his press releases. He'd hired one writer after the next and each had let him down in ways more spectacular than the last. I knew I could help him, but I'd never thought of leaving my subbing job to do that – and he had never seriously asked me to consider it. It occurred to me now that working for him might be a way to help both of us, and I met with him to talk about the idea.

My parents had sold the office in Norwood and set up shop at home in Sandringham, converting one side of the house into offices. We sat in my father's new office, which was Kate's old room. Before we spoke about what I might do to help him, we discussed the difficulties I was having with the biography. He asked me a series of questions and I tried as best as I could to answer them. I found it difficult to explain why I was having so much trouble moving things along.

His proposal was this: I'd work for him in the mornings and in the afternoons I'd carry on working on the book, trying some new things. He suggested I adopt a different strategy as a way to break the deadlock. It was the same advice he'd given me when I was at school: get everything out first and go back and fix it up later.

When it comes to writing – writing *anything* – my father is a big believer in not trying to get it right the first time, not trying to think of the perfect words. He told me I should just sit and write. I said I would try. I recognised it as the same advice Prof. Kariithi had given us during the training programme.

I was going to share an office with my mother. She was working in the outside room attached to the garage, which had been my bedroom when I was at university. The three of us carried a second desk into that room and pushed it up against the wall under the window. This was my desk and I set up my laptop on it. The first time my mother offered to make me Provitas with Marmite I folded up inside. I felt useless and taken care of. Things had calmed down in the months since, though, and I'd found my feet in the new job, just like any other.

I climbed into the bath. The hot water was enveloping and soothing. I listened to the gentle tapping of Thenji at the computer and felt the last bits of the horrible mood lift. I looked down the length of my body, most of it below the water's surface. I was thirty-five, no spring chicken myself any more. I could already feel it in me, too: age. There were things I couldn't do any more. Like handstands. If I did a handstand my back hurt. So I hadn't done a handstand in a year. My body was reluctant now. Sometimes I woke in the night from pain in my right shoulder. I shifted that shoulder in its socket, then I lifted my arm out of the water to give it a closer inspection. I studied my forearm, dripping, water-glossed. I could see on the skin the same pale spots I'd seen on my mother's arm when I was a child. And high up on my ribs, just below my chest on the left side, a little raised dot, ruby red. *Age spots* is what I called them when I saw them on my grandfather's torso when he swam or changed his shirt in front of me. I had an age spot too. I also had more grey hair than I had the year before. I wondered if one day all my hair would be grey, like his. Grey hair: the living body turning to ash.

THE BUILDERS

Interview 5
Date recorded: 02/07/2005

During the first quarter of the twentieth century, the Jewish community of Johannesburg was largely centred in Doornfontein. The houses in Doornfontein were comparatively small (my family's home was on a stand of fifty by fifty feet) and, generally speaking, the amenities were rather basic. It isn't surprising, therefore, that once people had saved up a bit of money, they started a search for a more desirable area that would bring them closer to the better secular schools, for example; to houses that stood on more ground and had sewerage, not to mention garages for cars (which were beginning to be seen on the roads); and *tarred* roads, if possible. All that brought a slow but general exodus from Doornfontein up Harrow Road to the north, and the occupation of a new suburb where Jews once again formed a close community – that was Yeoville.

I was born in 1919 in Doornfontein and when my brother Bernard was born, in 1923, my parents started making plans to move with their children to find what was referred to as 'the better life'.

So in 1925 we moved to 45 Page Street in Yeoville. A street where, as I think I've told you, one side was largely Jewish and the other side almost all Christian.

I remember my dad, shortly after we moved to Page Street, standing on the bottom of the steps into the back garden, where a few fruit trees grew, standing in the presence of my mother, my brothers and Lily, my sister – the whole family was standing there looking at the house from that perspective. And my dad put up his right hand, pointed at the house and said, '*This* is a *balabatische* house.' (*Balabatische* is a difficult word to translate; I think the closest you get to it in English would probably be 'of some consequence'.)

The centre of the community was the synagogue, and by the time I approached the age of bar mitzvah, I had made a large coterie of friends who had, like I had, started school in the nearby suburb of Observatory, and then received their primary education at the Yeoville Intermediate School on Bedford Road. We spent a lot of time in and around the shul – mainly *around*, playing soccer in the open ground behind the shul building and attending the Talmud Torah, where Hebrew classes were carried on.

And, well now, this is what I wanted to tell you.

One Sunday afternoon my friends and I were playing soccer there – this was January of 1932 – when two men came through the gate, and walked over to stand on the wide steps leading up to the entrance to the shul. They both were in their early twenties, no older than that, but to us, who were all around bar mitzvah age, they were grown men. They both were rather well dressed, too: one wearing a suit and the other a university blazer.

When one of them called to us, we picked up the ball and went over to see what they wanted. The first fellow said his name was Colin, and the other introduced himself as Louis. Then, taking turns to speak, they told us a story, and that story is partly what I wanted to relate to you today, because it had a most profound influence on my life.

They started by asking us if we had ever heard of Norman Lourie. We shook our heads 'no', and stood silently, waiting for more. The name meant nothing to us.

Norman Lourie, they told us, came from a well-established family in Johannesburg, and after he finished high school, they said, he'd been sent to England to attend the London School of Economics. There he met two young Englishmen – David Goitein and Wellesley Aron, two young English Jews – and the three of them became fast friends.

When Lourie finished at the School of Economics – at the end of 1931, they told us – he decided not to come home directly, but to do a short tour of continental Europe first. And it was during this short trip that he witnessed the rise of anti-Semitism there. Did we know what Fascism was, they asked us.

When we said we didn't, they explained it to us. And they told us how it struck Norman that this was going to lead to a lot of problems

– and not least for the Jews of Europe. So instead of coming back to Johannesburg, as he'd planned, he decided to go back to London to discuss the position with Aron and Goitein. And that, they said, was what he did.

None of us had had much to do with politics. Nor, frankly, had we heard about the problems they spoke about, so we waited with bated breath to hear more.

The three of them – Lourie, Goitein and Aron – had then gone around the streets of London, talking to young people, and they had found that there was a lot of anti-Semitism in London, too. Jewish youth were being unfairly singled out in schools. Jewish boys were not made to feel welcome in the Scout Movement. Things of that nature.

So these three fellows decided to start a youth movement for young Jews, a sort of equivalent of the Scouts, but for boys and girls. They called the movement Habonim, which in Hebrew means The Builders. They envisioned that Habonim would include a number of different aspects. It would teach young people to value their history, the history of the Jewish people; it would also have a physical element, camping and athletics and that sort of thing. And it would focus on the idea of the state in Palestine – an idea that was gaining traction with Jews around the world at that time as a place that would provide refuge from the anti-Semitic threat that was evidently growing in Europe.

A short while later – they continued – Norman Lourie returned to South Africa with the intention of starting Habonim here, forgetting all about his promising university studies. Naturally, the first place he went to was Doornfontein, and there he'd walked the streets, just as he and his friends had done in London, talking to young people. And it wasn't long before he had started a chapter of Habonim, a *gedud*, with young people from the neighbourhood. Colin and Louis were two of them.

And on the steps of the shul that afternoon, these two fellows – who had both started practising as young advocates at the Johannesburg Bar – painted a picture of what Habonim could do for us. I remember it vividly, though it is nearly eighty years ago. Standing there with all my friends, listening to these two young guys speak about the importance of 'building', what it meant; and about the bricks, the *levenim*, to be built out of cardboard and suitably decorated, that would symbolise the building up of the Jewish homeland. They were very talented storytellers.

When they'd finished, they asked if any of us would like to come to a meeting the following Sunday to hear more. We all looked at each other and agreed unanimously that yes, we would all like to do that.

So our first meeting was held the following Sunday evening, at seven o'clock, in a classroom on the ground floor of the building behind the shul. Colin came alone to the meeting and told us that Louis had taken over the leadership of the Doornfontein *gedud*, and that he, Colin, would be the leader of ours, if we wanted to start one. If any listener had heard the way he spoke to us – with affection, respect and love for his subject – it would not come as any surprise that soon we started attending regular meetings on Sunday evenings. Nor would it come as a surprise that he had an influence on us that would remain throughout our lives.

On that first Sunday night he showed us the Habonim handbook, which Lourie, Goitein and Aron had devised. Using this manual, he described how the movement would involve different elements of scouting – cooking over fires in the open, living in tents, as well as swimming and matters of athleticism, for which we would receive recognition by the award of badges we could sew onto our shirts. He told us how we would also learn songs originating from the early Jewish settlers in Palestine and compete with other *gedudim*, each of which, he said, would adopt the name of what the handbook referred to as the 'master builders'. Our *gedud*, by the way, we decided would be known as Gedud Maccabee, after Judas Maccabeus.

And that is how began perhaps the most significant experience of the first twenty years of my life. Because although I continued to apply myself diligently in the classroom, my high school could not compete with my interest in Habonim, in which I became more and more involved. I found in Habonim something I did not find at King Edward school. We had discussions about *ideas* – ideas about the world and the future. And while I found school interesting, particularly the masters, I was never inspired by what we were learning there in the same way as I was by the comparatively young people who were running Habonim.

Colin's amazing versatility included a rare ability to write lyrics based on the popular music of the day, as well as plays, which he produced with us as the actors, before large audiences at various venues in Johannesburg. He was a superb writer and I had the great fortune to act in many of his creations. I remember many of the wonderful lines he wrote to this day.

Soon a girls' *gedud* was formed in Yeoville, Gedud Devorah, which was our sister *gedud*, and then there was Gedud Esther in Doornfontein and Gedud Israel in Berea.

The movement spread like wild fire. Norman Lourie was a wonderful speaker; he had the fire of a missionary. Soon there were *gedudim* all over the place. Practically every town in South Africa had its *gedud*. Towns like Benoni, Krugersdorp, Bloemfontein, Oudtshoorn and Heilbron – not to mention the larger cities like Cape Town, Port Elizabeth and Durban, in all of which there were several *gedudim*. Right up into Rhodesia, as it was then called.

And this indeed led to exciting rivalries, in scouting and sporting events, culminating in the year-end camps, which were held at camp-sites at Nahoon or Lakeside, or other parts of the southern coast of South Africa. Camps that were reputed to be among the largest youth camps in the world. We made friendships on these camps that endured all our lives. Many years later, meetings between people in different parts of South Africa and the world would commence with the words, 'I remember you from Habonim camp ...'

The fact that after the war I became the national leader of the movement is another story for another time, but of course it shows the depth to which Colin nurtured my interest in the subjects I've mentioned.

I have told you that Colin Gluckman and Louis Pincus both qualified as lawyers. And both went to Palestine and became very involved with the young state of Israel. Louis Pincus became the chairman of the Jewish Agency, which is the highest position ever held by a South African in Israel. Colin Gluckman also went to live there. He changed his name to Gillon, and as Colin Gillon he served from 1952 until 1961 as the Attorney-General of Jerusalem.

Jules Browde at Habonim camp, Somerset West, 1936
'Perhaps the most significant experience
of the first twenty years of my life.'

chapter twenty-five

In which the young storyteller considers the
nature of the problem

Working for my father was not as much of a drag as I thought it would
be. In fact, there were parts I found I enjoyed – like learning how hi-
tech machines worked so I could write about them, visiting clients in
sections of the city I'd never been to, or simply getting 500 words to do
what I wanted them to do. My father expected me to work hard, but
never as hard as he did, and he also made sure that, whatever I was busy
with, I always left at lunchtime and went home to give attention to the
biography.

The piles of printed pages (what I thought of as the 'book in
progress') lay around our flat like a series of monuments to hopeless
ambition. The higher they piled, the more it all felt like a fool's errand.
I was at that time, I remember, frequently overcome with the feeling
that I had willingly become swept up in a delusion, although I couldn't
tell whose delusion it was: mine or my grandfather's. Perhaps it was
the fantasy of the whole family that I was lost in, the strange organism
dreaming itself a role and a significance. Is that not what all families are
guilty of? Is that not their whole point? To provide a sustaining myth
for its members to hold on to? During those afternoons, lengthening
with the spring, these questions felt increasingly urgent.

They also led, inevitably, to this thought: that by failing to finish the
book, I would be disappointing not only my grandfather (near the end
of his life!) but I would, in fact, be letting down the whole family, and
breaking the unspoken pact that our entire self-concept be solidified

through this lionisation of our patriarch. And what would I be then if I failed to deliver? A lazy David, a wicked son?

At the same time, the glass he wanted me to break lay in a corner of my mind, glinting ambiguously now and then through a fine layer of dust. Though I waited for it to roll to one side or the other – to break, or not – it stayed, improbably, where it was, and I didn't know what I was going to do about it. So I did nothing, and nothing was what Thenji did, and we buried our heads in questions of venue costs and which of our friends would DJ. The wedding was in January, which was still four months away – more than enough time, I told myself, for things to work themselves out of their own accord.

So it was that the question of the glass and the question of the book combined to put what felt like tectonic pressure on the relationship between grandfather and grandson. I was trying to separate out how I was feeling and how he was feeling, to find the elusive boundary between his expectations and mine. If it came to that, could I disappoint him totally? And what would be left of our relationship then?

I began to think – sometimes hopefully, sometimes wistfully – about how much our relationship had withstood over the years. I thought for the first time in years about how it was just before I went to live at the Buddhist centre. Something that had concerned me then, I remembered, was what he thought about me moving in there. I even planned to write him a letter, something along the lines of 'What Buddhism is to me', something to reassure him that I wasn't joining some cult – although I never did. He seemed fine about it though. Maybe he took his cue from my parents, who both supported the move. Everyone had been desperately worried about me because of my depression, and my decision to move to the centre after months insensible on the couch must have seemed a welcome sign of life and movement. So they got behind it. (Although once, when I'd already been living there six months or so, my father did ask me why I called it the Buddhist *centre*, as if he was worried I thought it was the actual centre of the universe.)

My grandfather never said anything about it at all. I think that had he seen me turning into some sort of glassy-eyed devotee he would have worried, a lot, but as it was, I carried on much as before – just a bit happier – and I suppose he took that as a decent argument not to be too concerned.

He came there three times in the three years I lived there. The first was soon after I moved in, to have a look at my 'new place'. The second time was the day he fetched me to take me to the hospital when I had an infected sinus and couldn't see to drive. But the visit I thought about most was the third one – on a Saturday morning in the last year I was there.

Akong Rinpoche, the Tibetan meditation teacher who'd started the place, had come to stay at the centre for a week or so. Akong's visit was a big deal for all of us in the house, and in the Buddhist community of Johannesburg in general. Scores of people started arriving at the quiet house on the hill to listen to him lead meditations and give talks on a variety of subjects. Some of those who came were people who had once lived at the house, people I'd heard about, and I was happy to put faces to these names; happy, too, to learn that these people had left the centre and had gone on (most of them) to become normal adjusted people in the world.

On the final Saturday morning of his visit, Akong gave what were called 'personal sittings'. Anybody could go into the room where he was sitting (which was actually the administration office, right across the courtyard from my room) and you could ask him a question, any question you liked, and he would answer it as best he could.

My father was away that weekend, but I remember that my mother and my grandparents came to the centre that morning. I remember that soon after they arrived, my grandmother joined the long queue that had formed outside the room.

My grandfather had no interest in asking Akong a question. The picture I have of him in my mind from that morning is of him standing around the front of the house, arms folded, his back to the stone wall, looking around the garden and out across it to Bez Valley below.

'It's actually jolly nice here,' he said, when I went to stand next to him. I pressed my own back to the big cool oval stones. We stood there like that without saying anything, and it occurred to me that he was looking down into the valley where he was born.

My grandmother came straight from her personal sitting to find me, standing with Bronco around the front.

'Very interesting,' she said, nodding. She looked impressed, but also puzzled.

'So, *nu*? Did you ask him a question?' my grandfather asked her with a playful challenge.

'Of course,' she said. 'Of course I did. What I asked him was this. I said, "How can I stop worrying about all the bad things going on in the world?" Because *you know me.*'

My grandfather smiled and turned to me. He was amused, proud, still in love.

My grandmother was thinking back to those moments in the room. 'He said I should *train my mind*.' She spoke the last three words slowly, and then looked at me. 'But I'm sure he means something more than that,' she said.

I didn't realise, when I scribbled this story down one afternoon, how much it would come to illuminate for me. But after I went back to it, it seemed relevant to the corner we'd painted ourselves into. It seemed to say something about my grandfather's ability to let me go my own way, to trust, maybe, that I knew what I was doing.

I left the story like that, open-ended. My grandmother looking at me, a question in her eyes.

It wasn't the kind of story I'd thought could be part of the book. It was not so much about him as it was about *them*, and about me too, in a way; it was about all of us. But there it was now, and I thought *why not?* I regarded it with the patience of someone whose best-laid plans have long gone seriously awry.

I was ready to try anything now. It had become clear to me that the standard biography was not going to work. My attempts at that – I'd completed three huge chapters detailing his childhood and adolescence – were both dense and thin, a dull mishmash of generic history and fine personal detail.

Stories I Told When I Told Stories About Him. That felt like a worthwhile new front. At the same time I resolved to continue with the ordinary biography I was writing, and now revisit the war. The third front was the law stories and what they said about the country, but I wasn't sure how to do that one. There were still people I wanted to talk to, books I needed to read. I still hadn't interviewed Arthur Chaskalson, for example, even though I'd had a million opportunities, and I couldn't say why I hadn't.

I think I was procrastinating because a part of me didn't believe any more that the book could amount to anything. It was as if the once-bright machine of the idea had sprung an oil leak – a serious, persistent leaking; a stubborn dripping; a perpetual misgiving.

Even if I did finish it, I thought at the time, it would be a failed thing – important only because it would put an end forever to my quixotic vision of myself as a writer, and I could then start to apply myself to something more useful to myself and the world.

Another part of me, though, was gaining strength from this sustained close fight with my oldest fears. And I started to take more pleasure in working on the different fronts than I had before.

Another one of the *Stories About Him* I wrote down at that time seemed – like the story of his visit to the Buddhist centre – to hold a relevance beyond any value it might have for the biography. It had always struck me as meaningful, but I'd never tried to say why. Now I thought that I might have some idea. It seemed to capture something important about his relationship to his Jewishness, to the world and to me.

It took place on an afternoon during those few months I lived with them after I came back from Grahamstown. I know the exact date – 12 February 2005 – for reasons that will become clear.

We were sitting opposite each other at the wooden table in the corner of the kitchen. On the wall behind him the faded Monet print; to his right (my left) the courtyard, the tree, the feeder. I was reading a novel and he was busy with a crossword. We also had a couple of conversations going on the outskirts of our attention.

One thing he was telling me about, in fits and starts, was the lunch they'd been to earlier that day at the home of their friend Jane. It was a lunch she apparently hosted every year on the same day to celebrate the birthday of Charles Darwin, who was, as he put it, her hero. 'She knows everything there is to know about Darwin,' he told me. 'Really an absolute expert on the whole business.'

She had explained – he told me – to all assembled, as she did every year, how fantastically ahead of his time Darwin had been. Somehow in the 1860s, he told me, Darwin had hit upon these ideas that would only be verified by scientists seventy years later. Some minutes after that he told me how she had become 'quite animated' as she railed against the grip Creationists still had on the world, and on the minds of children especially.

I remember telling him about a film I'd seen once on TV, in which an American high-school teacher, accused of 'teaching evolution' in the 1960s, had laughed when the court asked her to swear on the Bible. 'She said that if they wanted her to take a solemn oath, they should rather make her swear on *Origin of Species*.'

'That's actually jolly good,' he said. 'Quite right.'

Then we went back to our other business – him to his crossword and me to my novel. The kitchen was still and quiet.

Then a minute later I heard him chuckle, and looked up to see him taking a sip of coffee and smiling to himself as he did so. Then he set his mug down on the table, looked at me and said, lecturing in a Lithuanian accent, *'Darwin Schmarwin! As long as you've got your healt'!'* When I laughed, he raised his snowy eyebrows and went back to his clues.

My theory was this: just before that line came to him, some unconscious force opened the door to his mind, and while this force may not have been his Jewishness, the light that came in through the aperture had come in at a peculiarly Jewish angle. He wasn't mocking his friend the Darwin expert, nor was he mocking the old Jewish man who might have said those words for real; no, in that heart-lifting, mind-blinding moment there was no mockery or rancour – although neither of them was being let off the hook entirely, either. Both were being warmly teased and simultaneously forgiven. But for what? For existing at all in this imperfect world.

Even now this seems to be the closest I can get to any essential description of his Jewishness (or mine): this teasing, innately contradictory thing that can only be hinted at, brushed up against in a story, and which nonetheless binds him to his parents and grandparents, and to some of his friends, just as it binds me to some of my friends, and to my parents, to my grandmother and to him. What it meant to me then was that always I would be held accountable *and* forgiven; that no matter how I failed him – in writing his biography or at the wedding – we would be able to dust ourselves off and carry on; that always there would be a better option than this doubt and fear. I understood (or hoped I understood) all this only after I'd written down the story, late in the afternoon, at our dining-room table, Thenji still at her studio and the leafy branches of early summer cross-hatching the sky.

Still, I was wary of feeling like I'd made any kind of breakthrough. So many times I'd felt like this – like I'd penetrated as far as some insight – only to hit my head the very next moment against something hard and, sitting back, find myself even more confused and lost than I'd been before. But the biography did feel alive again, and I allowed myself to think that I might complete it.

THE WINTER LINE

Interview 13
Date recorded: 25/01/2006

I was told at the time that we were doing something Napoleon had thought impossible – leading an army up the Apennines against an enemy, and successfully negotiating what he called the spine of Italy.

The Germans had formed certain defensive lines east to west across Italy. One was known as the Gothic Line. This had been a very strong line for them, north of Rome. But we got through that. Now we were just south of Bologna, where we were held up for about five months. This was known as the Winter Line. It was the European winter of 1944.

By this stage I had been selected to be the forward observation officer, the officer who works in close cooperation with the infantry. So when the infantry was pushing on ahead and artillery assistance was needed, I did what the name suggests: I established a post in the very front of the front line from where I could see the enemy and direct fire from the guns, which could be up to five miles behind. I had a tank at my disposal but I used it only on occasion. When I was with the infantry, and they were on the walk, then I was in my jeep and I travelled behind them.

But now just let me tell you ...

South of Bologna there is a mountainous area, and we were up in those mountains. I was holed up with two assistants in a farmhouse high on a ridge on Mount Silvaro. The guns were back in Grizzana, a couple of miles south. We called this point on the ridge Eight Two Six, because it was 826 metres above sea level. It was also the highest point in the area, and this house – an old farm house – afforded whoever occupied it not only a perfect view of the Vergato valley below, which the Germans occupied, but also the protection of the walls. Which is why the Germans had commandeered it, and why we had decided to take the house from the Germans.

There had been heavy fighting during our assault. They called up their artillery, as we did ours, and shelled us as we advanced. But ultimately we pushed them back along the ridge. They abandoned the house and formed a line less than half a mile north of the house. And that was where the matter rested when we occupied it.

The house was painted a bright pink, and it came to be known as the Pink House. And thereby hangs a tale ...

The side walls of this house had both been damaged. One of our shells had hit the southern wall and there was a very large hole in it. So what we did soon after we occupied the house was that we found, down below in the cellar, a heavy velvet curtain that must have belonged to the Italian farmer whose house this was. (This was all farmland.) In order to make sure we could light a candle at night without showing our presence, we hung up this curtain with nails. So if you approached from the southern side of the house all you saw was this dark reddish-brown curtain.

The northern side also had a hole in it. It was quite a big opening; it must have been a very large window in its day. From up there we could look out down into the valley, which the Germans occupied. It also offered a view along the ridge, to where this battalion of German infantry had dug in.

Our own infantry had a detachment of about eight to ten men on the upper floor. They came up at dusk. It was their job, among other things, to watch out to the north – to see if there was any activity from the German position. They would also sometimes leave the house and go on night patrols. On occasion I went with them. The object was to take a prisoner in order to establish the strength and identity of the German presence in the vicinity.

I call them men, by the way, only from force of habit. These were boys of seventeen, eighteen, nineteen. From Natal, most of them; they were members of the Natal Carbineers, an infantry brigade based – when in South Africa – in Pietermaritzburg.

We had some very frightened people in the Pink House, I can tell you. We were so close to the German position that we conversed only in whispers. We never spoke in a normal voice, since we feared that this would be heard by the enemy. We spoke only in whispers to the infantrymen on the second floor, who spoke in whispers among themselves. We spoke in whispers to each other. Can you imagine? All day, all night, only whispers.

So you will appreciate that being in the Pink House was no bed of roses. And no one was expected to stay there for any real length of time. The longest I stayed there unrelieved was about ten days. After ten days I would go back to the gun position in Grizzana, and another officer would take over from me there. And we did that in rotation. We would stay there for a week, ten days at a time, and then go back to the guns.

Between Grizzana and the foot of Mount Silvaro was a road called the Mad Mile. One of my assistants would drive us in the jeep to Grizzana, and then back again to the foot of the mountain. To get from there back up to Eight Two Six was a very cold, steep and rough climb, so we went by mule.

We'd been in the Pink House about a month when there took place an episode I'd like to relate to you now. It had been snowing heavily. The whole of the Winter Line was covered in snow. The Pink House and all the surroundings were covered in snow. I was the only officer in that house that night. And these two fellows were with me – my assistants. We were down on the ground floor.

I was fast asleep when I was woken by one of the infantrymen. They had seen something and he wanted me to come and have a look.

He said, 'Sir, please come up. We need you.'

(At twenty-five, I was the oldest in the house by several years.)

I got out of my sleeping bag and climbed the ladder that went up through the hole that these chaps had cleverly cut in the ceiling. These infantry fellows were gathered on either side of the hole in the wall. I crept over to them and crouched beside the boy who lay at the Bren gun, staring tensely out into the darkness. A light snow was sifting down.

The boy on the gun was a particularly young member of the detachment. Keane, his name was. I crouched beside him.

Speaking in a whisper, he said, 'Look out there, sir. Look what's happening out there.'

At first, I couldn't see anything unusual. A carpet of snow lay over the mountainside; a few trees, also dusted with snow, along the ridge. Nothing looked different from how it always did at night.

'No, sir. Up *there*.'

I looked to where he was pointing, and there I saw them. Tiny white figures on the ridge, moving very slowly towards us. At least, it *looked* as if they were making their way towards us. They were still a few hundred metres away, and they were moving so slowly that it was impossible to tell exactly what was going on.

'Should I fire, sir?' this boy Keane asked me.

I told him no, not yet. I said, 'They're still too far. Let's wait and see what happens.'

So we waited as these ghost-like figures continued their painstaking procession along the ridge.

A few minutes later it became obvious that these people were moving in the direction of the house. They were now about 300 metres away. And we could see that there were about ten of them, maybe a few more or a few less, walking in single file. Terribly slowly, man. And each was wearing long white pants, a white long-sleeved shirt, white shoes, white gloves and a white snow cap. The snow was coming down in drifts. These guys were waiting for me to tell them what to do. I didn't know what to do.

This fellow Keane was shaking. He had his finger on the trigger of the Bren gun, trembling, waiting for my order. The other boys squatted on either side of us. No one moving, virtually. Holding their breaths.

When these white figures were about a hundred metres away, and we could just about see their faces, I whispered, 'Okay, get ready to fire.'

He nodded. I heard him swallow.

'All right,' I said. *'Fire.'*

Then there was a series of incredibly loud explosions and I watched – *oh, man* – as this boy's head snapped backwards and his body folded to the floor. I tell you – I looked down to see blood spreading in a pool around his head.

The firing of the Bren gun, the spurt of flame, must have been seen by someone posted for that very purpose, and so as he fired there came this awful reply. And he was killed on the spot. Shot right through the forehead. A youngster, a real youngster ...

Well, we sprung away from the hole. I told them to come down the ladder. There was nothing else we could do but descend – and wait. I thought the rest of us were done for too. We left his body up there and went down and waited: waited to be taken prisoner, waited to be killed. We sat in darkness in the most dreadful atmosphere imaginable. There was little we could do to stop them if they wanted to come into the

house, except protect ourselves with the rifles carried by the infantrymen and revolvers with which gunners, including me, were equipped.
But they didn't try to do that. All they did was they skirted the house
and set alight a hayrick on the southern side. And then they ran away.
I think they were just as frightened as we were. Darkness was soon re-
stored when the hayrick burned out. We stayed there like that the whole
night. Huddled together. With the body upstairs. Oh, to think of it now
restores the unbearable picture of that night.

The next morning, as soon as it was light, the infantrymen took his
body back to infantry headquarters – which was also near Grizzana, not
far from ours.

And I reported this by field telephone to my battery commander,
Major Petersen. Black Pete. What had happened in the night. He
sounded unmoved. He said, 'Well, you haven't got much longer to stay
there. Stay there another week or so and everything will be all right.'

Now Dan, there is just one more thing I'd like to tell you, one other
story: something that happened, also at night, a week or so later. Which
explains why they had set fire to the hayrick.

I was on the ground floor again, with my assistants, sleeping on and
off. Those nights up there were awful, the sense that anything could
suddenly happen. Some of us slept while others kept an eye on what
was going on.

So, as I say, I was downstairs asleep, when I was woken by the noise
of an ear-shattering explosion. It was very nearby. The chaps rushed
down from the second level, everyone wide-eyed with fear. The radio
had been knocked around to such an extent that it couldn't be used. It
was almost morning. We all simply sat there close together, waiting for
the next explosion. But it never came. When it was light, some of us
gingerly ventured outside. And we found – about ten yards from the
house, on the southern side – an enormous crater, which had obviously
been caused by a very large rocket. The curtain we'd hung up (which, I
told you, was a very large heavy curtain) had disappeared.

A short while later we found it, rolled up perfectly and deposited, undamaged, on a shelf at the end of the ground floor, which was
perhaps six or seven metres away. There was a shelf where the farmer
used to keep great tins of this and that. The curtain was on that shelf. It
had been rolled up by the blast, carried, and deposited on that shelf. The
curtain had saved our lives.

The following night the colonel came up from the guns. Colonel

Fraser. He brought with him a bottle of gin. He knew I would share it with the others, but anyway, he gave it to me and asked me to walk with him outside.

I trudged with him through the snow and he said to me, 'You know the problem with you people? The reason everybody is so nervous up here is that you're all talking in whispers.'

He said this in an ordinary speaking voice. I was very nervous for everyone there, because at night – it was the evening now, the sun was already going down – at night *especially* your voice carried for miles in those mountains.

He said, 'I see that things are difficult up here, but anyway, we haven't had any casualties here apart from that infantryman. From now on you talk in your normal voices. You'll find that you won't be nearly as nervous.'

And then he went off. He went back down to the guns. And within an hour of Colonel Fraser's departure, the Germans opened fire on the house again.

This was a dilemma that was really insoluble. Because we couldn't give up our position there. The house was in a very important strategic position; we had to occupy it. So that night we put the curtain back up. We worked most of the night, but we got it back up.

chapter twenty-six

*In which the young storyteller and the old storyteller
talk about the book, among other things*

Caught up in the details of organising the wedding (which Thenji and I were determined to do ourselves), and confused about the book I was supposed to be writing, I was battling to make progress on any of the fronts I'd settled on. The most industrious thing I'd done recently was to string together a series of stories, written in the third-person, covering my grandfather's involvement in the Italian campaign in 1944 and 1945. Even this had turned out badly. All I'd managed to do was to cleverly strangle out whatever life there'd been in the original stories. It was demoralising to think that I'd spent all this time (at least two months) going backwards.

I had also recently written a series of long emails to my friend Daniel in New York, complaining about how badly things were going. Glancing over one of these emails I realised that in it I had expressed myself with an urgency and clarity I'd never achieved when I was writing about my grandfather. So that was when I had the idea of rewriting the book as a letter. The idea had a built-in name – *Letter to My Grandfather* – that I liked.

My first experiments had *something*: I discovered that if I could con myself for long enough into believing that I was writing to him, I could recreate the lucidity of the emails to Daniel and at the same time access a sensitivity of feeling I hadn't yet brought to the project. It was a blade of light in the dark clouds, and it stopped me from becoming completely despondent.

When I saw Bronco on Friday nights (or whenever else it was that I saw him) he would ask me about the book. He had started to phrase his inquiries as joking accusations; he'd point his finger at me as if he'd caught me red-handed. 'Why aren't you working on the book?' he'd say, and smile. But what seemed clear to me was that he was only half-joking, he was using humour to say something he really wanted to say: that he was getting frustrated. I'd smile along but I'd feel awkward, at a loss for how to act my part in the scene.

'It isn't coming along at all, Broncs. Not at all. The pages are piling up in every corner of the flat but they're full of unreadable nonsense and worse. Now I'm pretending to write you a stupid letter.' Maybe I could have said that – but I didn't.

Instead, what I would do is I would lie. I would say it was coming along well, only slowly. But I am not a good liar. When I lie my voice comes out at a seventy-degree angle and the colour of an under-ripe banana, with another little squealing voice in the middle of it that says, 'This is bullshit.' As a result I don't like lying. And I would feel resentful towards him because I'd had to lie to him. (Why was the truth not good enough for him, I thought, petulantly, without once trying to *tell* him the truth.)

And so the worst – the *worst* – thing happened. I started to dread seeing him and, when I could, I dodged him. On Friday nights, when total avoidance was impossible, I would avoid sitting next him. I'd even try to avoid making eye contact with him across the table. And if I did look up at him I was always sure that I saw him looking at me with suspicion.

The wedding offered some distraction from all this – but it was a distraction fraught with its own confusions. Though Thenji and I had had two long discussions about the glass, we hadn't come to an agreement, let alone made any decision. In my head and my heart I was confused, and all the time I was trying to reason it out alone. I could see how beautiful that vision was to my grandfather: Thenji's brother, Mandla, holding one pole of the chuppah, and her parents standing under it next to mine. It was beautiful to me too. (How *could* it be anything but beautiful?) And I could see how very beautiful the vision of me breaking a glass was to him. Like my dad had, and like he had, and like his father and grandfather had before him. Sitting there, on my own, I could imagine breaking a glass. Easily. But I knew there was another vision to consider, and that was the vision Thenji and I had for this together. And that vision specifically didn't include any traditional religious or cultural observance: Greek, Zulu or Jewish.

This was the reason, after all, that we had asked my grandfather to officiate in the first place. Because we didn't want a rabbi or a priest or anyone like that. That was the whole point. Giving my grandfather what he wanted, breaking the glass – even though I'd be giving it to him out of love – would mean taking something fundamental away from a sacred agreement I had made with Thenji. The unavoidable symbolic meaning of breaking the glass would be choosing what he wanted over what she and I had agreed we wanted. It was a harsh situation. I would, I knew, be making either choice out of love, and to honour someone I loved, but either action – breaking or not breaking – seemed as if it would echo ambivalently in my mind for the rest of my life.

My most trusted source of support and sanity wasn't any help here either. My father was struggling to see things from my point of view, struggling to see why we would not simply relent for Bronco's sake. *You break the glass and everybody says mazel tov.* Was that such a big deal? On the other hand, he seemed to be saying, breaking Bronco's heart *would* be a big deal. Though I tried to describe to him the complexity of my predicament, he could not see it. To him a straight refusal seemed cold and unnecessarily severe. He was pinned. We were all pinned.

One night, around that time – mid-November of 2012 – I woke out of no dream and, even with my eyes still closed, knew it was not yet morning. I opened them cautiously, and saw what I knew I'd see: the side of Thenji's sleeping face, moonlit, her hair across the pillow. I didn't want this to be happening any more, not with her. I slid out of bed and crept into the other room to sit on the couch. I sat there a long time in the dark, watching as the sky turned from blue-black to purple, and then to lavender. I knew what was out there, too, beyond the branches, nearer than the sky. It was the precipice: my thoughts were summoning it.

So many years had passed since I'd been really *ill* with depression – but what I realised in that cool dawn was that it would always be with me as the most terrible escape. Over the side of that precipice there were no glasses that wanted breaking, no books that needed figuring out, no decisions at all – only an inexpressible pain that would buy me time and win me sympathy, even if it killed me off in the process.

On a Saturday morning, a week or so later – late November now, the wedding six weeks away – Thenji and I pulled two chairs up to the computer to chat with my uncle Paul on Skype.

I had told Paul in an email about the disagreement over the glass, but I hadn't let on to just how tense it had been, nor had I told him (or Thenji, really) what had happened to my relationship with my grandfather: that I was avoiding him and registering distrustful looks from him in my direction.

Paul – a narrative therapist, among other things – has an abiding personal and professional interest in the power of storytelling and ritual. Thenji and I both thought he might be able to help us to shape a ceremony that worked for us. I had long looked forward to this conversation and what it might yield. But now, even as he greeted us, his voice sounded dim to me – dim and flat and useless. I knew I was sliding over the edge. Sitting in the chair beside Thenji, visible to my uncle, but beyond reach.

Thenji and Paul exchanged scraps of news while I sat staring at the screen, suspended, teetering, between worlds. I saw myself in the little box in the bottom corner, dull-eyed, slumped. Why was I acting like this? My early-morning thoughts from the week before rushed back to me: I was *choosing* this, and I could choose something else.

So I balled my fists and without any introduction I spoke out loud the things that, until then, I hadn't even allowed myself to think: I said I felt like my relationship with my grandfather was broken. And as soon as I'd said that I started to cry. Speaking loudly, around and through thick sobs, I said I'd given up on ever fixing it. I heard myself say, 'And I don't think it will be so hard when he dies, because in a way he has already died.'

Paul's husband, Simon, heard me sobbing and came to sit down beside him. They looked stunned and sad. Thenji put her hand on my knee and then took it away. In the little square on the screen I saw myself shaking and sobbing and I looked away.

Now I was crying for a hundred different reasons. I was crying because of how far we manage to get from each other, how even in love there are gaps. I didn't try to say anything else for a while; I just sat there crying.

When I stopped, Thenji brought me a tissue and I blew my nose in it. Still teary, I said, 'I suppose I've had a great relationship with him and I'll always remember that. I suppose relationships don't have to make it all the way to the end.'

There followed a long silence in which, it seemed to me, each of the others – Paul, Simon, Thenji – withdrew into themselves to look for something to offer me. I saw Paul close his eyes a couple of times.

It was he who spoke next: 'You need to go and talk to him,' he said. I watched his eyebrows knit thoughtfully. 'Because it's *not* over. He is still alive, and these are all things that can be spoken about. When he does die you are going to *wish* that you had done it. And I bet you,' he said (Paul is always betting you), 'that the conversation you have with him will make it into the book.' Through a film of tears I saw Simon nodding. Thenji had turned her head and was looking at me and not at the screen. Paul spoke with an enthusiastic certainty he gets sometimes, often in the darkest times. I don't know if he really is certain in these moments or if he believes in some things so deeply that it carries through into his voice, with great beauty. 'This book is stuck,' he said, 'because your relationship with him is stuck.'

Thenji made sure I called my grandfather that same afternoon.

I steadied my voice and asked him if I could come and talk to him. 'How is tomorrow afternoon?'

He said, 'Come on over, laddie.'

I was hearing so many things in every nuance of every word that I couldn't describe how he said that; I didn't know.

That night, I was in the shower and Thenji was doing something else in the bathroom. I think she was flossing her teeth. It was late; the light in the room was bright; the water was falling on my neck and shoulders. Having made the arrangement to go to see my grandfather, I already felt a degree of relief. Thenji said something. It sounded as if she wasn't even concentrating on what she was saying, like it was a half-thought that had occurred to her just then. And maybe it was. She doesn't remember saying it, but I remember it clearly: 'Dan, no matter how well you write this book, it isn't ever going to be enough to stop him dying.'

I pressed the intercom and waited for him to buzz me in. He welcomed me in the hall and we went straight through to the lounge, the room where we sat when we did the interviews. Except, that afternoon we sat on the opposite side of the room.

Past his profile, in the garden, I could see the lamb. Out there in the small square garden, a lamb made from wire and beads stands with its feet hidden in a dark tangle of ivy-green ground cover. This, combined with the fact that it is life-sized and skilfully made, gives the lamb a realistic look.

'Yes, laddie?' he said. As if to say, I'm all ears.

I could feel my heart beating, so I said it straight out. I said, 'Broncs, I'm worried. I'm worried that the book is having a bad effect on our relationship.'

He looked surprised, maybe even relieved. I realised that he'd probably been thinking I was going to tell him I had decided not to break the glass.

Then he looked puzzled. I saw him thinking. He shook his head. 'Look,' he said. 'Dan. The book is the book, but really nothing could come in the way of our relationship.'

'I just sometimes get the feeling that, you know, you're ... frustrated with my lack of progress,' I said.

He was tilting his head, just listening to me.

'And I can understand that ... I can understand that. I have been stuck.'

He nodded to show me that he was listening.

'I've been going about it in the wrong way. I've been going round in circles. Vicious circles. Round and round. But I feel like I've actually found some better ideas for getting it going.'

I told him about my idea of writing the book in the form of a letter to him, and I took out the copy of *Bright Lights, Big City* I'd brought with me. 'This is by an American writer called Jay McInerney,' I said. 'The whole thing is written in the second person. It's amazing.' I handed it to him. He flipped it over, read the back cover slowly, and gave it back to me.

He nodded. He was thinking of something he wanted to express.

Not upset, just sort of matter-of-fact, he said, 'Look, boy. All I've felt, really, is that you haven't been working on the book with the discipline that a book demands. To really write a book,' he said, 'you need to give it a lot of time, every day, and I feel like you have been letting all sorts of other things distract you.'

He thought about whether he wanted to say anything more. He didn't.

'I think to a degree that's true,' I said. I was light-headed with relief. We were having a conversation. With blood now rushing to my brain, I said that one reason for it – especially lately – was that there were all these other things I had to do. I mentioned the wedding, and working for my father. And I said I hadn't found a way to balance it all yet, but that this was changing. (I was defending myself, like a normal person!)

'But you're right,' I said. 'You are right.'

I looked down at the floor and nodded, to myself as much as to him. It was true. To write a book, you really did need to work with discipline over a sustained period. And my attention had been in different places.

Still, defending myself was addictive. I told him that when I did have all day to work on it – during those six months that Allan Greyling paid me a salary – I didn't know what I was doing. I compared it to fumbling around blindly in a dark room. I told him how I'd spent two weeks reading about the Rand Revolt, because bullets falling on their roof was his first memory.

He gave me all the time I needed to say these things. I could see he was trying to believe me, rather than just believing me. But it didn't matter. The main thing was that I felt the mist clearing, the book growing distinct from our relationship.

I told him some other ideas I had for the book in case the letter didn't pan out. Like splitting it up into different sections, each section representing an element – Wood, Air, Fire, Water – and organising episodes from his life under their appropriate elements.

I said, 'In a way, all the things I've done haven't been wasted.' I told him something Thenji had said: that I had been learning on the job, learning how to be a writer. And that though I had made mistakes, that was part of the learning. I was arguing my case, marshalling my witnesses. And all the while, through all this nonsense, he was trying to keep an open mind.

It wasn't the scene of catharsis I thought it might be, that maybe I wanted it to be, but it was even better. We were talking to each other! I was looking him in the eye! And even if I had given him a heap of excuses, I hadn't felt as if I was lying.

I told him that, working in this way, I thought I could finish the book in about three more months.

He said, 'Well, let's see,' and the line of his mouth crinkled into a smile that was both sceptical and, I hoped, forgiving. 'You know, I thought you were going to tell me about the glass,' he said.

I smiled. 'No.'

'Oh well,' he said.

Before I left him there, I hugged him. He was still sitting down, so I knelt alongside the chair and put my arms around him. He hugged me back, wrapping his right arm around my shoulders and using his left hand to clasp my right forearm.

When I got back to my feet, I said something I don't often say to him. 'I love you, Broncs,' I told him, looking down at him.

He looked up at me – surprised, then not. He said, 'My dear boy. Everything pales next to that.'

That evening in my inbox I found an email from Paul. 'I have wondered if I should send this letter,' he had written, 'not wanting to intrude on your process, and then thinking that you know how I support and love you no matter what.' He was worried. He asked if I'd had the conversation with Bronco. At the end of the email he'd pasted some alternative meanings that the breaking of the glass can have. 'I have found some explanations for the breaking of the glass, in case you decide that it's an action you want to take.' He was afraid that the glass was going to end up breaking the relationship between me and his dad.

The fragility of the glass suggests the frailty of human relationships. The glass is broken with the implied prayer: 'As this glass shatters, so may your marriage never shatter.'

We break the glass to remember during a time of personal joy that there is endless suffering in the world and that we have a responsibility to help relieve some of that suffering.

The broken glass reminds us at a time of celebration that pain is an inevitable part of life and so we waste our time trying to avoid it.

A FINE SENSE OF HUMOUR

Interview 27
Date recorded: 11/04/2008

My brother Len was very ill and I made a decision I have often thought about. Talking to you now makes me wonder about it again.

Selma and I had arranged to meet friends of ours overseas. And we went. To this day I'm not sure if we did the right thing or not, but we went. It was 1971. I remember we travelled to Israel first, and we phoned from Jerusalem to find out how he was, and he seemed to be not too bad. Then we went to Corfu, and when we were in Corfu I got a telephone call from your father to say that Len was very bad and I should come home. I didn't know that he'd already died.

Selma and I left our friends in Corfu and hurried to Athens, where we caught the first plane home. And we arrived at the airport – Jan Smuts it was in those days – and your father was there. Alan. He was nineteen years old. Waiting for us.

And he said, 'Dad, it's all over.'

And I knew. And I … I was so upset.

Alan said, 'Thank God you're here. Rose was so upset with you for not being here that she wanted to have the funeral without you.'

Rose was my brother's wife. Things between us had not always been easy. I was very distressed to hear this – and how your father bore the brunt of it. Because he'd had to fight when she wanted to have the funeral without me. He fought a lone battle, and in the end he prevailed, and I was at the funeral.

I remain eternally grateful to Alan for his sensitivity – even at that young age – for his sensitivity for me and for my feeling towards my brother, Len.

On balance ours was a good relationship, and I have realised what an important role Len played in my life. So many years have passed since he died – it is almost forty years now – but I still miss him. Because although there was a disparity in our ages, which prevented us from becoming real friends, we had the same background. He was also in Bertrams; he was also in Yeoville. He and I played games in Page Street – wonderful games that he and his friends invented. He was there at all the Seders. We had all that in common. We knew the same things.

He was a very unusual older brother to have. I think I've told you the story of how, when my dad said to him, 'You can go to Muizenberg on condition that you take Yoshke along with you,' he didn't say, as many young people might have, 'Well then I'm not going. He will spoil our holiday. I want to go with my friends.' He could easily have said that, but he didn't. He took me with him and he watched over me. My dad said, 'You must take him to the rugby.' He took me. My dad said, 'You must take him to the cinema.' He did. And he put up with me, even though I was so much younger than he was.

He was also a very amusing man; he had a fine sense of humour. I've told you already that being a lawyer was a very bad choice for my brother. He should have been an engineer.

The only joy he got out of his practice was speaking to his clients. He had a family practice that gave birth to many amusing stories. Stories Len couldn't wait to tell me. For a few years, we worked in the same building – Innes Chambers, on Pritchard Street. The Bar had moved there from His Majesty's Building in 1961, and he and Isaac Mendelow came there from Winchester House a year or so later. And Len often used to come up to my chambers, breathless with laughter, to tell me about something that had just happened. Have I ever told you, for instance, the story of Turffontein Wholesale? Let me just tell you.

A man called Sacks, a Yiddish-speaking immigrant from Lithuania, had made a great deal of money out of his store in Turffontein, in the south of Johannesburg – Turffontein Wholesale, he called it – and had decided to move the store to the popular market area in Central Johannesburg. And he enlisted Len to do all the conveyancing required.

Len related to me how he'd tried to persuade Mr Sacks to change the name of his store. Even if Sacks wanted to retain the word Turffontein, Len told him, Turffontein Wholesale had no meaning in English. In the new spot, Len told him, it should be called Turffontein Wholesalers, or Turffontein Supply Company, or something of that nature. Sacks said he'd think about it.

A day or so later, Sacks came back to Len and told him, excitedly, 'Mr Browde, I have a new name!' But because he spoke only Yiddish, what he actually said was, *Ich hob a nya nomen!*

Len spoke Yiddish, by the way. My dad had spoken to him in Yiddish and he had absorbed the language pretty well.

So Len said, *'Verre hed aich der nomen gegebben?'* Who gave you the name? (He knew Sacks didn't know enough English to come up with a name on his own.)

Sacks said, *'A frainte fun mir hot dos fir mir gegebben.'* A friend gave it to me.

'Nu?' asked Len. *'Vos gate zine der nya nommen?'* So, what's the new name going to be?

At which point, Sacks put his hand into his shirt pocket and pulled out a little piece of paper and a pair of spectacles. He put on the spectacles and read out the following, which Len, to his unceasing delight, saw had been written in Hebrew letters: *Formerly Turffontein Wholesale.*

Oh man, my brother loved telling that story.

But then, in about 1969, he got ill. He was diagnosed as having a malignant melanoma on his back. He was in his late fifties, the age my father was when he died. The age your father is now. And when he became ill, I often went to see him, to sit with him, and we spoke about a number of things. He expressed pride in me. He said he was proud of what I'd achieved at the Bar. He also mentioned the fact that I'd gone to war at the time. I think I'd always known he was proud of me, but these were not things he had said before, and it meant a great deal to me to hear him say it. He was my older brother after all.

Something interesting was the way my mother responded to his death. Because the natural order had been disturbed; she should have died before him. But my mother – who was of a ripe old age by then – accepted my brother's death with a sort of equanimity that I can explain only by thinking that, with her own death approaching, she did not find his as unacceptable as otherwise she might have. She was quiet at his graveside, even distant, and appeared to have accepted what had happened. She died two years later. My brother died in 1971 and my mother died in 1973, of complications arising from the swallowing of a fishbone.

chapter twenty-seven

In which a good friend dies

The wedding was set for mid-January, so in early December Thenji and I flew to Cape Town to spend a week at my grandparents' house in Fish Hoek. This trip was instead of a honeymoon: an attempt to steal some calm before the storm. I also thought that without the ordinary distractions and obligations of home I might be able to get some work done on the book. So I took the file and my laptop and set them up, full of hope, on the dining-room table upstairs.

The wide upstairs living room, which stretches almost all the way across the second storey, has enormous windows from which you can see the full sweep of False Bay. On a clear day you can see right across the bay to the mountains of the Kogelberg Nature Reserve. When my grandfather spends any time in this house he spends most of it here, at this window. He takes one particular chair, a cane armchair with blue-upholstered cushions, and he sets it up by the window and sits there for hours, alternately reading and looking out at the bay.

From where I sat at the dining-room table, I could see the empty chair. The last people to use the house had left it facing the window. I imagined my grandfather sitting in it. The older he got, the more time he spent sitting there; less and less of it reading and longer and longer stretches looking out at the changeable vastness of the bay. What did he think about when he sat there ignoring his book? I wondered if he ever thought about his own death as he sat there meditatively gazing. Or perhaps, stirred to dreaming by the swell and heave of the ocean, the coursing of the invisible wind, the cry of the gull, did he ...

On the laptop screen it all looked pretentious, groping. I thought I might make more sense if I wrote with a pen on paper. So I took the exercise book out of my bag and found an empty page. Two minutes later, I wrote: *An old man sits by a window and stares out at the sea.*

This looked clear and good. I liked it. But nothing else sprung to mind. For a minute, another minute, I looked across at the empty chair, the blue cushion. I thought: what more is there to say?

An old man sits by a window. Tall trees on a slope. A red hat on the sand. Elemental images, the building blocks of memory. Anything after that is conjecture, supposition, the intoxication of stories. The ocean heaves, waves pound or thud, the mountains across the bay glisten in a cleaning light. The lies begin.

I walked across the room and sat down in his chair. Thenji looked up from her book and looked down again. I stared out across the dark water and thought about the sentence again, about its lack of specificity: *An old man sits by a window and stares out at the sea.* Something else came: a newspaper. *A newspaper neatly folded to reveal a half-completed crossword.* Then: *age-speckled scalp; tall ears; spider-silk-thin white hair.* I thought again of the words 'an old man sits by a window'. If I could find him – Bronco – in that elemental image, I could go back to the table and write the book in one go. All I would need to do would be to communicate it clearly to a reader. Even one sentence might be enough.

We walked down to the beach most mornings and stayed until it got too hot or too windy. We bought soft serves and sat on the low wall near the outside showers and watched people coming and going along the walkway.

One day we came back from the beach around noon and I saw on my phone that I'd missed a call from my mother. When I phoned her back she asked me if I'd seen the papers. I told her I hadn't looked at a newspaper for days.

She said, 'Arthur Chaskalson has died. Maybe you should give Broncs a call.'

Even though I knew he was ill, the news came as a surprise. I thought about the last time I saw him (a Friday night supper at his son Matthew's house only a few months before), about how vital and *keen* he'd seemed. My next thought was of my grandfather. How this would affect him. One drawback of living into your nineties is that you out-live everybody, and not just people your own age. Arthur was ten years younger than Bronco.

It happened relatively often these days – that someone he knew died – and I'd noticed that instead of getting used to these deaths he was more and more affected by them. For days after such tidings he would become quiet and ruminative. And Arthur was more than just someone he knew: Arthur was his friend.

My grandfather doesn't have many friends. I mean friends who weren't my grandmother's friends too, or *their* friends as a couple. I mean pals. He does not seem to see the need for these sorts of friendships.

I do remember a few, though, from when I was a child: a few men who seemed to be mainly, if not exclusively, *his* friends. One was a man named Frank, who would arrive outside their house in Houghton in an old-fashioned Land Rover. Frank looked like Captain Haddock from the Tintin comics, except without the beard (if you can picture that), and he spoke in a strange way – which, I realised as I thought about him again, was probably just an English accent. Frank, I knew (strange that I knew), was unmarried. He was an attorney and wore a perpetual expression of mild surprise.

There was also the kind man with a patch over one eye and squiggly blue marks on the side of his face. I knew him by his two names: Geoff Kark. Geoff Kark spoke to me in a warm, serious manner, which meant that I always enjoyed talking to him. I would try hard not to stare at his eyepatch or the markings on his face. The patch and markings – my grandfather explained to me – were the results of an enemy grenade that had blown up in his face during the war. It was for the same reason that Geoff Kark was deaf in one ear. I liked seeing him but I didn't seem him often. And then, of course, I didn't see him at all.

Arthur and his wife Lorraine, a poet and scholar, were friends with my grandparents as a couple, but Arthur and Jules were unmistakably pals in their own dimension too. Arthur had the reputation of being uncomfortable in a crowd, but it was always clear to me that, if this were true, it was only because he was, for all his brilliance, a shy person. I always found something especially warm and welcoming in his face, especially in his eyes, something bright and embracing and kind.

In this way, he and my grandfather were cut from the same cloth. They may have had different personalities (my grandfather is more gre-garious) but both were kind-spirited, large-hearted, thoughtful – and wanted to be so, almost as a matter of principle. Their politics (neither were politicians) were predicated on this thought-through tolerance, and it was something they shared with other South Africans of their generation. Theirs was an outlook shot through with heart and humour, a commitment to peaceful engagement, an unshakeable belief in the possibility of coexistence. And a belief that the law could help us; that, as a guide to what is fair and just, the law needed to be at the heart of social life.

There were other links too. They both had grandparents in Yeoville (though Arthur grew up over the ridge in Houghton). They were both great readers. Lovers of games in general, and cricket in particular. Fathers of boys. And they followed a similar path in the law, doing their LLBs at Wits before joining the Bar. Both were regarded as outstanding legal minds, and founded organisations intended to improve the practice of law. Yet this too: both shunned the spotlight many others in the profession sought out.

I wanted to phone Bronco to tell him I was sorry his friend had died, but at first I couldn't do it. I was scared to tell him that the book was going nowhere. I didn't want to let him know that I was sitting here night after night, reworking the same passages, over and over again, about him staring out of a window. Summarising the same stories I'd summarised in Joburg. Filling in the details of a story before supper, and taking them out again after supper. Waxing lyrical about the ocean. Groping for poetry because everything else was in short supply.

I was scared, too, that he would ask me about the breaking of the glass. I still didn't know what to do about that. Which was more and more of a problem every day. The wedding was less than a month off. Thenji wasn't trying to force me one way or the other, but I knew what she wanted. Which was what we had agreed on. Conversations about it went nowhere, ended in painful silences, with me answering questions she hadn't asked, defending myself against charges she hadn't made.

When at last I forced myself to phone him, it was in the early evening. I realised that though it was still light where we were, it would already be dark up in Joburg.

I took my phone out onto the balcony, but it was too windy so I came back in, shutting the double doors and leaning my forehead against one of the long panes of glass.

'Mm ... hello?'

'Hi, Broncs.'

'Oh hello, laddie.'

'How you doing?' I asked. 'I heard about Arthur.'

'Yes. I'm all right, I think.'

I told him I'd been reading the obituaries in the papers. All the papers were full of tributes to his friend.

He said, 'Ja, man. They've been bloody good.'

He told me that he'd gone to the funeral at Westpark. He told me how Thabo Mbeki had come up to him afterwards and had said, 'Jules, hello.'

'He seemed surprised that I was still alive.

'"Hello, Thabo," I said.

'He said, "How old are you now?"

'I said to him, I said, "Thabo, at my age, you have to count in months. I am ninety-three years and seven months." We both laughed like hell.'

'That's great,' I said, feeling the cool glass against my forehead and the cooling sensation of relief as he told me a little more about the funeral. Who was there; the order in which things had happened.

Then he said, 'You know, I was speaking to Yvonne Makgoro, and she summed it up in a few words. She said, "Arthur was a good man."'

The silence that followed this, though deep, felt natural, warm, shared. I looked out at the sea. I couldn't believe I'd been so scared to phone him.

After the silence he said it again: 'He was a good man.'

Neither of us spoke. We let this sink in. I watched the sea. The sea was doing what it was always doing: it was moving on. After about ten seconds he said, 'Ja well, laddie. How are things with *you*?'

On her phone, a few months earlier, Thenji had made a short video recording of Jules and Arthur at a bat mitzvah reception. The bat mitzvah girl was the daughter of close family friends, and our whole clan had been invited. Paul is godfather to the child's older brother, so he and Simon had arrived from New York a few days before. My sister Kate had flown up from Cape Town. So of my siblings only Emma was missing.

The function took place at a soundstage at the bottom of Braamfontein. It was a cavernous steel-and-concrete structure softened for the evening by a thin layer of tiny white feathers that blanketed the screed floor. Teenagers stood around in anxious pockets while younger children chased hula hoops between the tables, sending clouds of feathers dancing into the air. On the balcony outside, grown-ups smoked and regarded the changing colours of the Nelson Mandela Bridge.

It was after the speeches, during the dancing part of the programme, that Thenji noticed Jules and Arthur sitting together at the end of a table. They were always seated at the same table on these occasions: two elders, respected and adored. They made a beautiful pair: tall, lean Arthur with his tight grey curls; Jules with his wide scalp and a garland of delicate white hair. She decided to film them.

The video shows my grandfather sitting in front of a bowl of soup at the end of a long trestle table. His arms are crossed and he leans forward on them, his shoulders hunched. Arthur sits next to him, at the corner of the table. He is also leaning forward, dipping his head low and to the right to hear a story my grandfather is trying to tell him over the thumping music. My grandfather wears a dark-blue jacket and Arthur wears a brown one with beige patches on the elbows. Towards the end of the video, Arthur sits up abruptly and leans back into his chair. Either the story is finished or else he has simply given up trying to hear it. Bronco, still doubled over his folded arms, lifts his eyes.

Even before Thenji showed me the video, I had started to see their interactions during these celebrations as a kind of living installation: a performance piece about the difficulty and importance of listening to one another. The minute-long recording gave me something to hold on to.

the dream

If the boy closes his eyes, he might sleep. If he sleeps, he might dream. So he keeps his eyes open. The room is not so dark any more: the moon's light slips in through the gap between the curtains and paints everything with a cool, silvery radiance. His older brother's bed, for one thing, which is close enough that if he reached across he could almost touch it, and his brother too, asleep, tangled in his blankets. At the other end of the room, his younger brother lies curled, facing the wall. Is he also sleeping? The boy props himself up on his elbows and shifts around to get a better view. The curled shape is motionless.

The boy lets his head collapse back onto his pillow, and he stares up at the hazy expanse of the ceiling. He tells himself that in her room at the other end of the passage his sister is sleeping too. So are his mother and father. And so is Bessie sleeping in her room at the back of the house. And so is Solomon in his room outside. They are all asleep.

Next door, Old Man Creewel is sleeping. And in his house up the road, Dov, his best friend, is sleeping. Mrs Mendelowitz is asleep in her house on the corner. Mr Lipiansky is asleep, Mr Luckin is asleep, and Sharpie Shapiro, the shammas. All the members of the shul committee are sleeping. Poor old Mr Friedlander with his hump is, too. And Jake and Lolly and Sam and the rest of his friends are all asleep.

Everyone in the world is sleeping, except him.

The boy lies a long time listening to the sounds of his brothers breathing. Once or twice he forgets, and feels his eyes closing. Sleep is calling him. He must not listen. He turns on his side and feels the pillow settle smoothly against his cheek. The material is soft and cool on his skin.

Maybe he will rest his eyes for just a few seconds. He allows them to close, and when they do, he thinks of something strange: his face with its eyes closed. His thoughts feel thick and joined together. With all his will he brings his heavy eyelids back open, but his thoughts are sliding now. His eyelids are closing again; his thoughts are switching places.

The boy's eyes snap open. He realises that his head is no longer touching the pillow. He sees that his shoulders and his legs have left the bed, too. From a high part of the room, he looks down and recognises the unmade bed below him.

Then through the ceiling he rises, blindly breaking its surface, and out into the night's wilderness of air and stars. The air is cool and at first it tickles his nostrils, as still he rises. Beneath him he can see the sloping roofs of the houses on either side of Page Street and the darker shapes of the peppercorn trees, kneaded by the wind. Mysterious and beautiful. Gentle currents glide over his skin.

The boy is high above the tallest trees when he feels the twinge in his chest, that cold tightening that tells him he is afraid. Pretending he hasn't felt it he turns his head to look out across the patchwork earth. The vision sends an icy jolt through his whole body and he clamps his eyes shut as if he could hide from his fear, but in the darkness inside he only feels more boundlessly afraid.

So he looks down again. The earth is now a copper coin surrounded on all sides by smooth black space. The higher and higher he goes, the smaller and smaller the coin becomes. Soon it is just a speck in the starstrewn blackness; and then even the speck is gone, lost amid the stars. Now all is lost. The boy wants to scream but no sound comes. He presses his fingernails into his palms and turns, slowly, drifting end over end through vast silent dimensions.

Some of the stars are brighter than others, but none holds any promise. The boy knows only one thing: that he is still moving away; away from everything he understands. And just beneath the surface of his fear, he discovers an enormous sadness: the idea that he will never see any of it again is too painful to hold inside him. Desperate, fighting back tears, he starts to sip at the air, forcing it into his lungs; he sips and sips and when he has enough in him he summons his breath and he uses it to cry out in a great voice – and like this, body taut and a frozen shout on his lips, he wakes again into the arms of his brother.'

'Shhh,' the older boy says. 'Everything's all right.'

The boy looks up into his brother's moonlit face, recognising it and all that it means. He is on earth. He is home.

He folds the fingers of his right hand around his brother's forearm and lets out a barely audible gasp of relief. His heart is pounding double-time, but he can also feel the terror steadily leaving his body, as his brother says, 'You had the dream again. That's all.'

He nods. The dream.

At the foot of the bed he sees his younger brother standing nervous-ly, clasping his pillow in front of him, his face puckered with concern.

The boy closes his eyes and presses the side of his face into his older brother's chest. Soon he becomes aware that the sound he is hearing is his brother's heart, pulsing behind his breastbone. As he concentrates on that simple, repeating sound, he can feel his own heartbeat slow and the remains of his fear turning into something else. The boy doesn't want his brother to go back to his own bed. He doesn't say this out loud but his brother understands. He stays with him, continues to hold him.

'It's all right, now,' the older boy says. And again, 'It's all right.'

acknowledgements

Firstly, my thanks to Allan Greyling, without whose generous support I would not have been able to start working on a book at all.

Then, my thanks to Carlos Amato, Lavendhri Arumugam, Gwydion Beynon, Simon Chislett, Rangoato Hlasane, Anthony Klein, Richard Penn, Monica Seeber, Amichai Tahor and Motlalepula Twala, who all gave me important feedback on early thoughts and drafts.

Particular thanks to Patrick Bulger, Sarah Flemmer and Digby Ricci for their help, guidance and encouragement.

A big thank you to Jeremy Boraine, for giving this book a chance. And to this book's two editors: Ann Donald, who showed me where the right track was; and Sophy Kohler, who experimented fearlessly. Thank you Sophy for all the smart, sensitive work you did on this book. To the rest of the team at Jonathan Ball: the whole experience of publishing this book has been a pleasure.

Thanks too to James Bourhill, author of *Come Back to Portofino*, a comprehensive and moving account of the Sixth South African Armoured Division's journey through Italy in the Second World War. Thanks for meeting with me and my grandfather, and for sending us the picture of Jules in 'Flippy'.

And big thanks to my cousins Barbara Sacks and Diane Fleishman for sending me pictures from Australia.

And to Sue-Ann Bright.

And to my uncles Paul Browde and Simon Fortin (CFA), for

reading drafts and for helping me think clearly about the book and the project. Thank you Paul for sharing your story 'The Secret'.

Thank you to Ian Browde and Melissa Berrengé-Browde, my uncle and aunt, for reading parts of the book in Cape Town. And to my Californian cousins, Tristan and Carrie.

Thank you to my parents-in-law, Morley and Joanna Nkosi, and my brother-in-law, Mandla Nkosi, for your consistent love and support.

Special thanks to Ivan Vladislavić for his incredible generosity: reading an earlier draft of this book, in full, and being so careful to help me find a more certain shape inside the rock.

And special thanks too to Daniel Klawansky, a great listener. Your ear helped shape this book in so many ways.

Then thank you to my parents, Alan and Suzie Browde, for giving me life and helping me to deal with it. Thanks Mom for (among other things) sharing with me your love of books and for encouraging me to get Bronco's stories down in the first place. Thanks Al for being an ally through the toughest times, and also for contributing the story of Bobby Locke.

To my remarkable sisters Emma Browde, Kate Browde, Cara Browde and Micaela Browde, who lived, and live, this all with me – with huge love.

A particular thank you to Cara, who gave me the idea for the book's structure and then lent me her brilliant, uncanny mind in thinking about what I was doing, from the beginning to the end.

To my grandmother, Selma Browde. A short acknowledgement cannot do justice to your influence. An 'ethical inspiration' not only to Bronco, but to me and to all of us. With love and deepest admiration.

And finally, to Thenjiwe Nkosi. I could not have written this book without you. Thank you not only for your unceasing encouragement, for our conversations about the book and the subject matter, and for all your editing help over years. More than that: I learn and am strengthened every day because of the way you see the world and the world that could be.

Jules Browde died in his home in Orchards on 31 May 2016,
ten days after his 97th birthday and less than a month
before this book was printed.

CPSIA information can be obtained
at www.ICGtesting.com
Printed in the USA
LVOW13s2153250117
522207LV00013B/1061/P